NIGHT
SKY
IDENTIFIER

NIGHT SKY IDENTIFIER

AN OCEANA BOOK

Published by Grange Books
an imprint of Grange Books Plc
The Grange
Kingsnorth Industrial Estate
Hoo, nr, Rochester
Kent ME3 9ND
www.grangebooks.co.uk

ISBN-10: 1-84013-937-4
ISBN-13: 978-1-84013-937-2

This book is produced by
Quantum Publishing Ltd.
6 Blundell Street
London N7 9BH

QUMPGTN

Manufactured in Singapore by
Universal Graphics Pte. Ltd.
Printed in China by
L. Rex Printing Co. Ltd.

CONTENTS

INTRODUCTION

The night sky has fascinated people since the dawn of civilization. The first recorded writings in the Middle East, in cunieform and hieroglyphics some 5,000 years ago, bear witness to a thorough knowledge of the stars and constellations. But, by and large, the heavens remained mysterious and awesome.

It was not until the early seventeenth century that the night sky started to give up some of its well-kept secrets. That was when Galileo trained his telescopes on the heavens, and spied moons circling Jupiter and phases of Venus. It was the beginning of an age of astronomical enlightenment that in turn saw Kepler explain the motion of the planets, Newton elaborate the phenomenon of gravity, and Herschel discover Uranus.

However, it was not until Bessel determined the distance to a nearby star, 61 Cygni, that the enormity of the stellar universe became apparent. Then, early in the twentieth century, Hubble, using the newly completed 254-centimetre (100-inch) Hooker telescope, proved that spiral nebulae are separate island galaxies millions of light years away. The Universe began to assume dimensions beyond the grasp of the human mind.

In recent years, radio astronomy and space astronomy by satellites and probes have brought to light an array of enigmatic

The Hubble Telescope

bodies such as quasars and pulsars, bursters and blazars. It seems that the deeper we probe into the make-up of the universe, the more complex it becomes, confirming J. B. S. Haldane's remark:

> *The Universe is not only queerer than we imagine, it is queerer than we can imagine.*

The star-studded firmament has lost some of its former mystery and, because of increasing light pollution, some of its former brilliance. But, when you are away from city lights, look up and enjoy the night sky with eyes, binoculars and telescope. Nighttime images of the Earth have been obtained from the Defense Metereological Satellite Program (DMSP) of the US Air Force since early 1970. The first global image was obtained by Woodruff Sullivan in late 1980.

RIGHT: A view of Earth from space.

THE UNIVERSE

Anyone who has ever looked up at the clear night sky from a dark location will have experienced the sense of awe and mystery that comes from considering our place in the vastness of the Universe. The Universe is enormous and includes Earth and the remainder of space – the Sun, the Moon, other planets, stars and galaxies. Astronomy is about exploring and understanding more thoroughly the wonders of our Universe.

LOOKING INTO SPACE

On a clear, dark night, the sky invites you to the greatest show on Earth and you do not need a telescope to actually get started. Your eyes are actually good enough to allow you to look billions of miles into space, and although humans have travelled no further than the Moon, we already know a lot about what goes on in the night sky. Provided the sky is clear you will see hundreds of stars, the Moon and possibly some other planets. Our planet Earth, the Moon and eight other planets and their moons belong to the Sun's family, or the solar system. The solar system and all the stars that you can see belong to the Milky Way Galaxy, which is our home galaxy. By using telescopes, astronomers can see much more than we can with the naked eye. They can see millions of faint stars belonging to our galaxy, and the stars of other galaxies that lie beyond.

The shape or geometry of the Universe is determined by its density. If the density of the Universe exceeds the so-called 'critical density', then the shape of space is curved just like the surface of a huge sphere. However, if the density of the Universe is less than the 'critical density', then the shape is flat like a sheet of paper. For many years astronomers have been trying to accurately measure the shape of the Universe and the most widely accepted theory is that it is flat.

Although it is possible to have thousands of solar systems, there is no way to observe whether there is any other Universe other than our own. Our Universe is unique and totally self-contained.

The Universe

WHAT IS OUT THERE?

The nearest objects to Earth are the Sun and the planets, moons and comets of the solar system. The solar system belongs to a galaxy which contains literally billions of stars and enormous clouds of gas and dust. Our galaxy shows in the night sky as the Milky Way, which is just one of the countless galaxies in the Universe. The Universe is so vast and the distances so great that accidental collisions very rarely occur and this is why the Sun, along with its family of planets can run like a perfect clock, and has done for billions of years.

Earth's nearest neighbour in space is the Moon – a planet which has no atmosphere or liquid water and cannot therefore sustain life.

The nine major planets in the solar system have at least 63 moons among them, while other stars in our galaxy might have planets and moons, as well. On a clear night you can see hundreds of stars in the sky, the nearest of which are thousands of times further away than any other planet in the solar system. Beyond the Milky Way Galaxy, millions of other galaxies populate the Universe, and each galaxy is a family of billions of stars similar to our own galaxy.

Over the last 70 years, since the discovery that the Universe is constantly expanding, astronomers have made some significant steps in understanding how the Universe began and how it must have evolved into what it is today. Through the use of powerful telescopes we are learning more and more about our Universe daily, such as the exciting discoveries of new stars being born, of new solar systems, and the mysterious black holes.

Diffuse Nebulae

Diffuse nebulae are clouds of interstellar matter, namely gas and dust. If they are large enough they are often places of star formation, thus generating big clusters of stars.

The Universe

PLANETS, STARS AND GALAXIES

Our galaxy is only one of billions of other galaxies in the Universe, but it is special to us, because it is home to Earth and our solar system. The Sun, the planets and their moons are the main things in the solar system, but there are asteroids, comets and lots of dust as well.

The closest star to Earth is the Sun. The stars of the night sky are all similar to the Sun but, because they are so much further away, we see them only as little points of light. Stars are in fact extremely hot balls of glowing gas, which give out large amounts of energy and shine using their own light. Generally speaking stars are much larger than planets.

Over 100 planets are known to orbit the stars, but these extrasolar planets cannot yet be seen. Instead, they are being detected by the effect of their gravity on their parent stars, and many of these stars are visible to the naked eye. Unlike stars, planets and moons do not produce their own light but shine in the sky because they reflect the light from the Sun. The stars are separated by distances which are much greater than the size of the solar system, the next nearest star after the Sun being nearly 300,000 times further away.

On a very dark, cloudless night you can sometimes see the light coming from billions of distant stars in our galaxy – and this is known as the Milky Way. As a galaxy, the Milky Way is actually a giant, as its mass is probably between 750 billion and 1 trillion solar masses, and its

The Universe

diameter is about 100,000 light years. The Milky Way viewed through binoculars is a magnificent sight, with thousands of stars in each field of view.

UNDERSTANDING THE CONSTELLATIONS

Our modern constellation system comes to us from the ancient Greeks. The real purpose of the constellations is to help us tell exactly which stars are which. On a very dark night you can look up and see around 1,000 to 1,500 stars and trying to tell which one is which is very hard. The constellations simply help us by breaking up the sky into more manageable pieces. The constellation charts have been formed by astronomers to act as mnemonics, or memory aids. For example, if you noticed three very bright stars in a row one winter night, you might know that this is part of Orion, and then suddenly the rest of the constellation will fall into place. Once you can recognize Orion, you can then remember that Orion's Hunting Dogs are always nearby.

Apart from the obvious interest of the astronomers, do the constellations have any other uses? The answer here is yes. Around the world, farmers know that most crops need to be sown in the spring and harvested in the autumn, but in some regions there is very little difference between the seasons. As different con-stellations are visible at different times of the year, the farmers can use them to tell them what month it is. As an example,

Scorpius is only visible in the Northern hemisphere's evening sky in the summer.

Astronomers officially recognize 88 constellations. They are currently, 14 men and women, 9 birds, 2 insects, 19 land animals, 10 water creatures, 2 centaurs, 1 head of hair, a serpent, a dragon, a flying horse, a river and 29 inanimate objects are represented in the night sky (the total comes to more than 88 because some constellations include more than one creature.)

Fixed stars

Astronomers in the past used to speak of the 'fixed stars', which they said maintained permanent positions in the sky. Indeed, the stars do seem to be almost fixed in one place, especially as the patterns they form appear the same today as they did when the constellations were first named over 3,000 years ago. But, in truth, the stars are all moving relative to the Sun, and most have speeds of many kilometres per second. However, because they are so very far away, it will take thousands of lifetimes to see any significant changes in the star patterns – but over time they *will* change.

The Universe

TELESCOPES

Men and women have looked up into the sky and wondered about the things they see for as long as man has lived on Earth. Unlike the objects we see on Earth that we can study by touching, seeing, listening, smelling and tasting, the only way ancient watchers could study the sky was with their eyes and their imaginations.

Man decided that he would like to take a closer look at these magnificent, but very distant objects, and the first man to make this possible was Galileo Galilei. Galileo pioneered modern exploration in the early 1600s by using a device that was originally intended for naval operations to explore the heavens. He called this device, the telescope, and it was an instrument used to gather and focus light. His first telescope was made from lenses that were available at the time, and gave a magnification of around four times. To improve on this Galileo learned how to grind and polish his own lenses and by

August 1609 had produced an instrument with a magnification of around eight or nine. By the end of 1609 Galileo had turned his telescope up to the night sky and he started to make some remarkable discoveries. He was the first person to actually write and record what he saw. For example, in 1610 he discovered four moons going around Jupiter. He also found that the hazy light of the Milky Way comes from many faint stars.

Over the next several decades, lens-grinding and polishing techniques improved gradually, and a specialized craft of telescope makers slowly developed.

MMT
An important innovation in telescope design is the multiple-mirror telescope (or MMT), the first of which was completed in 1979 on Mount Hopkins in Tucson, Arizona. It has an amazing 6.5 m (256 in) mirror.

RIGHT: Galileo and one of the 60 telescopes he designed.

The Universe

THE KECK TELESCOPES

The world's two largest optical and infrared telescopes are situated at a remote outpost on the summit of Hawaii's dormant Mauna Kea volcano. These twin telescopes are called the Keck Telescopes and astronomers at the Keck Observatory are able to probe into the deepest regions of our Universe.

Each telescope stands at eight storeys tall and weighs around 300 tons, and yet it can operate with unprecedented precision. At the heart of each Keck telescope is a revolutionary mirror measuring 10 metres (33 feet). This mirror is composed of 36 hexagonal segments that work in unison as one piece of reflective glass. The Keck Telescopes track objects across the sky, sometimes for hours on end, as the Earth revolves. This constant, although subtle, movement results in a very slight distortion of the images, and without a computer to correct the primary mirror, scientific observations would not be possible.

Astronomers use the telescopes in shifts of one to four nights. Observing assistants operate the telescopes while astronomers gather data from the science instruments.

The Keck I Telescope began its observations in May 1993, while Keck II came into operation in October 1996.

Keck is positioned in a perfect place right on the summit of the volcano and Keck's capabilities make full use of this summit site. It is surrounded by thousands of miles of relatively thermally-stable ocean, and has no nearby mountain ranges to pollute the upper atmosphere or throw light-reflecting dust into the air. There are few city lights to taint the viewing, and for most of the year, the atmosphere above Mauna Kea is clear, calm and dry.

The Keck Telescopes are used by astrophysicists to seek answers to some very large questions. For example: How did the Universe evolve? How were solar systems formed? How many planets orbit nearby stars? In just the past few years tremendous progress has been made in the search to find answers to these and many other questions.

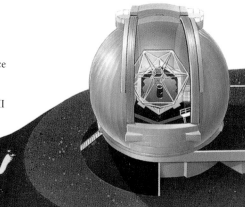

The Universe

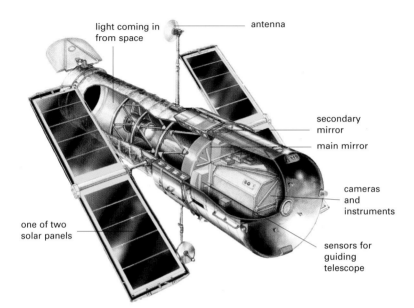

light coming in from space

antenna

secondary mirror

main mirror

cameras and instruments

one of two solar panels

sensors for guiding telescope

THE HUBBLE SPACE TELESCOPE

The Hubble Space Telescope was launched in April 1990. It orbits above Earth's turbulent atmosphere and has a much clearer view of the Universe than any telescope positioned on the ground. The Hubble Space Telescope has a main mirror which measures 2.4 metres (94 inches) across and it has taken images of every kind of object from planets to the furthest galaxy. It circles the Earth every 90 minutes and is positioned 610 km (380 miles) above the Earth. Its power comes from the telescope's two solar panels, which turn the sunlight into electricity.

At the end of this decade the Hubble Space Telescope will be replaced by the James Webb Space Telescope which is an orbiting infrared observatory.

Hubble's Job Description
- To explore the solar system.
- To measure the age and size of the Universe.
- To search for our cosmic roots.
- To chart the evolution of the Universe.
- To unlock the mysteries of galaxies, stars, planets and life itself.

The Universe

Buying a telescope

There are good telescopes and there are cheap telescopes, but there are few, if any, good cheap telescopes. The cheaper the telescope the poorer its optics and consequently the poorer the image. Before you buy your own telescope it is advisable to seek advice from an experienced

reflecting telescope

refracting telescope

stargazer in one of the many astronomy groups or clubs found across the country.

There are two basic types of telescope: refractors, which use lenses to collect light, and reflectors, which use mirrors. Most small telescopes are refracting ones, which are relatively easy to use. About

the smallest useful size for an astronomical refractor is about 60–75 mm (2–3 in) aperture, or about double this for a reflector. Refractors are in general more robust than reflectors and need less attention, but they are comparatively expensive.

The Universe

Refracting telescope

Here are a list of points to consider when you are making your first purchase:

- The diameter of its lens (usually given in millimetres). A 50 or 60 mm (2 or 2.4 in) lens is typical
- Make sure the lens is corrected for false colour. It should be an 'achromatic' lens
- The maximum magnification a telescope can give is twice the lens size in millimetres. Separate eyepieces are usually better than a 'zoom'
- Your telescope should show the Moon with a sharp, hard edge, free from colour.

Remember

NEVER use a telescope when the Sun is in the sky – you could very seriously damage your eyes.

NEVER observe through glass, or through an open window. Defects in the glass and air currents through the window can spoil the view.

Refracting telescopes use a lens to gather light and bring the image to the eyepiece. These are the type of instruments that most people think of when they think of a telescope. They are fairly maintenance-free and generally provide superb images of the Moon, planets, star clusters and general sky-gazing. They tend to be smaller in aperture than other types so they are not as good for viewing fainter sky objects such as galaxies and nebulae. Good quality refractors tend to be expensive but ensure that you get one with good optics and reasonable aperture. Beware of cheap refractors!

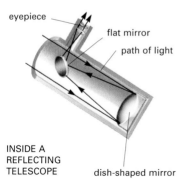

eyepiece
flat mirror
path of light

INSIDE A REFLECTING TELESCOPE

dish-shaped mirror

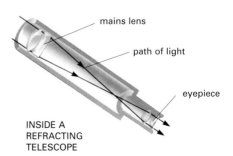

mains lens
path of light
eyepiece

INSIDE A REFRACTING TELESCOPE

The Universe

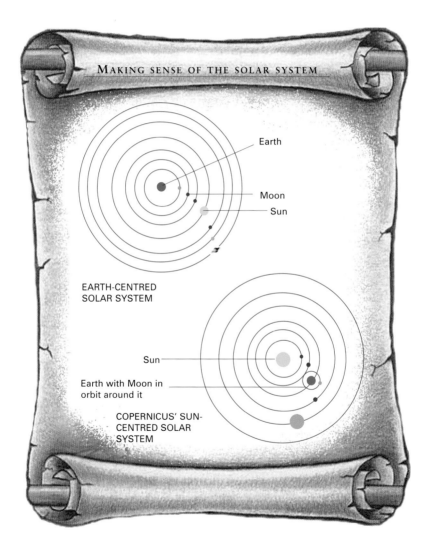

MAKING SENSE OF THE SOLAR SYSTEM

Earth

Moon

Sun

EARTH-CENTRED
SOLAR SYSTEM

Sun

Earth with Moon in
orbit around it

COPERNICUS' SUN-
CENTRED SOLAR
SYSTEM

The Universe

THE SOLAR SYSTEM ACCORDING TO NICOLAS COPERNICUS

Although Chinese astronomers had come up with the same conclusions centuries before, it was the great astronomer Nicolas Copernicus (1473–1543) who, in the early 1500s, determined that the Sun was the centre of our solar system. Before this radical new idea was proposed, it was believed that all the planets, stars and other heavenly bodies circled around the Earth.

In the second century AD Claudius Ptolemy, an astronomer who lived in Egypt, claimed that the Sun, stars and other planets orbited the Earth at varying speeds, but that Earth was completely motionless. Ptolemy had believed in his geocentric or Earth-centred view for several reasons. First, due to gravity, all objects were attracted to the Earth, which suggested to him that the Earth must be in the centre. Second, he thought that the Earth did not move. He showed how an object is thrown in the air and falls in practically the same place. He theorized that if the Earth moved, the object should fall into a different place. Even today, these arguments would be difficult to disprove just by observation, and his views remained undisputed for centuries.

Copernicus, however, had his own ideas. Through his studies and observations, he became convinced that the Sun was stationary, with all the bodies in the solar system circling it. Aware that his theories would probably be seen as heresy, Copernicus decided to share his ideas with only his most trusted colleagues. At first Copernicus' theories went practically unnoticed. However, in the 1600s a German astronomer, Johannes Kepler, supported his beliefs with mathematics. Both Copernicus' and Kepler's breakthroughs laid the foundation of modern day knowledge of the solar system. After 30 years of secrecy, Copernicus finally published *Six Books Concerning the Revolutions of the Heavenly Spheres* in 1543. Copernicus died at the age of 70, only hours after receiving the first printed copy of his theories.

The Seven Axioms

Around 1514 Copernicus wrote a little book called *The Little Commentary*, in which he stated seven axioms:

1 There is no one centre in the Universe

2 The Earth's centre is not the centre of the Universe

3 The centre of the Universe is near the Sun

4 The distance from the Earth to the Sun is imperceptible compared with the distance to the stars

5 The rotation of the Earth accounts for the apparent daily rotation of the stars

6 The apparent annual cycle of movements of the Sun is caused by the Earth revolving round it

7 The apparent retrograde motion of the planets is caused by the motion of the Earth from which one observes.

The Universe

TIME IN SPACE

Distances between stars and galaxies in space are enormous. Astronomers often describe such large distances by giving the time it takes for light to travel that far. In the same way that we might say a journey is a three-hour drive in a car, astronomers might say that the distance of a star is a 100-year journey for light. Because light takes so long to reach us from galaxies beyond our own, we see these galaxies as they were a long time ago. Looking deep into space with a powerful telescope is the same as looking back in time.

LOOKING BACK

The further away an object is, the longer its light takes to reach Earth. This means that astronomers can look back in time. For example, light from Neptune takes four hours to reach Earth, so astronomers see Neptune as it looked four hours ago. By comparing galaxies billions of light years away with ones a lot nearer, they can see how the galaxies have changed over time. The most distant galaxies we see today came into existence long before the Sun and its planets formed in our galaxy. They show us what galaxies were like soon after they were created.

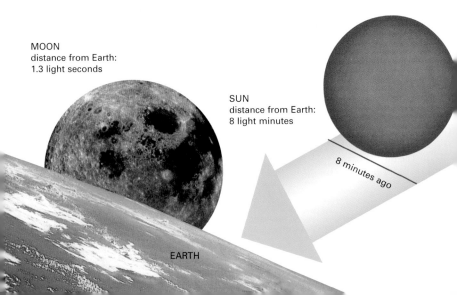

MOON
distance from Earth:
1.3 light seconds

SUN
distance from Earth:
8 light minutes

8 minutes ago

EARTH

The Universe

TIME

We measure the hours of the day by the turning of the Earth as it travels around the Sun. As the Earth spins the Sun appears to move around the sky, and the time it takes for the Earth to spin once – and for the Sun to return to the same position in the sky – is one day.

It takes a complete year for the Earth to orbit round the Sun – or 365.25 days. Because there is not a complete number of days in a year, we

ANDROMEDA GALAXY (the nearest large galaxy). Distance from Earth: about 2 million light years

2 million years ago

4.3 years ago

NEPTUNE distance from Earth: 4 light hours

PROXIMA CENTAURI (our nearest star after the Sun). Distance from Earth: 4.3 light years

4 hours ago

make our year 365 days long and add one day to make it 366 days long every four years – a Leap Year.

The time of day at any particular moment depends on where you are. When it is noon in Greenwich, England, it is midnight along the International Date Line. Time changes as you move east or west, so the Earth is divided into 24 time zones, one for each hour of the day.

Aristotle

Aristotle lived in Greece more than 300 years before Jesus. Most people in Aristotle's time believed that the Earth was flat, but he decided he could understand the world by using logic and reason. Aristotle concluded that the Earth was not flat, but in fact a round sphere. Because of his philosophies Aristotle is remembered as the Father of Natural Science.

The Universe

THE SPEED OF LIGHT

Hundreds of years ago people thought light travelled instantaneously. They thought so because after a military artillery fired at a large distance, they saw the flash immediately, but sound took a noticeable delay before you heard it.

Even in 1600 AD the famous Johannes Kepler believed that the speed of light was instantaneous and, according to him, the vacuum of space did not slow the speed of light down. However, Galileo was correct in saying that all this proved was that light moved faster than sound – not necessarily instantaneously. Galileo carried out experiments in 1667 to try and measure the speed of light. Two people had to stand at least a mile apart, while both holding covered lanterns. When one person uncovered his lantern, the other person had to uncover his own when he saw the other's light. A third person measured the time between when the first and second lanterns were uncovered. However, repeated experiments failed to accurately measure any time interval between when the first and second lanterns were uncovered. They could only say that light travelled at least ten times faster than sound.

More recently, we have been able to essentially conduct Galileo's experiment in two different ways: using high speed electronics and long lengths of optical fibre in a laboratory, or by timing laser light reflected off mirrors placed on the Moon by the Apollo astronauts.

THE FACTS

Light travels over 300,000 km (almost 186,000 miles) in one second and nothing can travel faster than light. The Sun is 150 million km (93 million miles) away from us. A spaceship flying from the Earth to the Sun would take about a year, and yet light takes just eight minutes to cross the same enormous distance. In one complete year light travels 9,500,000,000,000 km (5,900,000,000,000 miles) and this distance is called a light year.

The further away a star or galaxy is from Earth, the longer its light takes to reach us. The nearest star after the Sun is more than four light years away, and this means that it takes four years for light from that star to reach us and we see it as it was four years ago. One of the nearest galaxies to our own is at a distance of 2 million light years. The light we see today from this galaxy started its journey 2 million years ago, before humans even existed on Earth. It is not possible to know what this galaxy actually looks like now; we can only know what it looked like 2 million years ago.

Large telescopes can show us galaxies billions of light years away. But when we are looking at these galaxies, we are seeing them back in time by billions of years, to when the galaxies were first forming.

The first real measurement of the speed of light came in 1676, from a Danish astronomer, Ole Römer, who was working at the Paris Observatory. He had made a

The Universe

systematic study of Io, one of the moons of Jupiter, which was eclipsed by Jupiter at regular intervals, as Io went around Jupiter in a circular orbit at a steady rate. Römer actually discovered that for several months the eclipses lagged more and more behind the expected time, but then they began to pick up again. In September 1676, Römer actually predicted that an eclipse on November 10, would be ten minutes behind schedule.

His previously sceptical colleagues at the Paris Observatory were taken aback and two weeks later they avidly listened while he explained exactly what was happening. As the Earth and Jupiter moved in their orbits, the distance between them varied. The light from Io (which was actually reflected sunlight), took time to reach Earth, and took the longest time when the Earth was furthest away. When the Earth was furthest from Jupiter, there was an extra distance for light to travel, and this distance was equal to the diameter of the Earth's orbit compared with the point of closest approach. So when the Earth was furthest away from Jupiter, the eclipses were furthest behind the predicted times.

The speed of light depends on the material that the light moves through. For example, light moves slower in water, glass and through the atmosphere than in a vacuum. The speed of light in a vacuum moves at exactly 299,792,458 metres per second.

The speed of light through the Universe

LIGHT FROM THE	TRAVEL TIME
Earth to the Moon	1.28 seconds
Sun to Earth	8.5 minutes
Sun to Mercury	3 minutes
Sun to Venus	6 minutes
Sun to Mars	12.5 minutes
Sun to Jupiter	43 minutes
Sun to Saturn	1 hour
Sun to Uranus	2.6 hours
Sun to Neptune	4 hours
Sun to Pluto	5.4 hours
Sun to the nearest star	4.3 years
Sun to the furthest star	18 billion years

The distance that light travels in a year is so large that it is a useful unit of distance in astronomy:

- Light year: the distance that light travels (through a vacuum) in one year (9.46×10^{17} cm)
- The nearest star (other than the Sun) is 4.3 light years away
- Our galaxy (the Milky Way) is about 100,000 light years in diameter
- The distance to the galaxy M87 in the Virgo cluster is 50 million light years
- The distance to most distant objects seen in the Universe is about 18 billion light years (18×10^9 light years).

The Universe

CELESTIAL TIME

Celestial time is the original rhythm of time on Earth. It is the root of all time systems and existed even before life. The spinning of Earth on its axis provides the basis for measuring time. Our day of 24 hours is the time it takes the Earth to spin around once and return to the same position in the sky relative to the Sun. We call this, our ordinary time, or solar time.

At first sight we might also expect the celestial sphere to rotate around us in 24 hours, but this is not the case. If you note the time when a certain star rises above the horizon on successive days, you will find that on the second day the star rises four minutes earlier than on the first, and that on the third day it rises four minutes earlier still, and so on.

In other words, the celestial sphere rotates once around the Earth in 23 hours 56 minutes. Or, put the other way, the Earth rotates once relative to the stars in 23 hours 56 minutes. This is the Earth's true period of rotation and forms the basis of what we call 'sidereal time', or time relative to the stars.

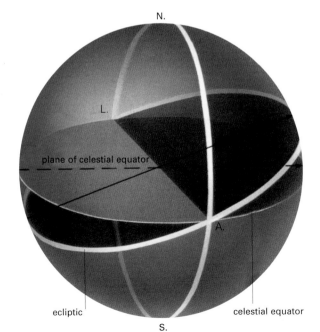

N.

L.

plane of celestial equator

A.

ecliptic

celestial equator

S.

The Sun crosses the celestial equator at two points on its annual path (ecliptic) around the celestial sphere. It crosses at the vernal equinox (March 21) at a point called the First Point in Aries, and at the autumnal equinox (September 23) at the First Point in Libra.

The Universe

When they are observing, astronomers use sidereal time. Then the stars rise, culminate and set at exactly the same time. In other words, they are in the same position in the sky at the same time.

CELESTIAL NAVIGATION

Christopher Columbus experimented with celestial navigation techniques, from time to time, but his experiments were usually unsuccessful. The most important tool used by Columbus in his celestial attempts was an instrument called the quadrant. This was a metal plate in the shape of a quarter-circle, from the centre of which hung a weight on a string that crossed the opposite edge of the circle. The navigator would sight the North Star along one edge, and the point that the string crossed the edge would show the star's altitude, or angle above the horizon.

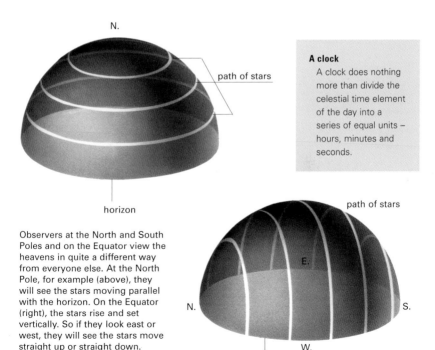

N.

path of stars

horizon

A clock
A clock does nothing more than divide the celestial time element of the day into a series of equal units – hours, minutes and seconds.

path of stars

E.

N.

S.

W.

horizon

Observers at the North and South Poles and on the Equator view the heavens in quite a different way from everyone else. At the North Pole, for example (above), they will see the stars moving parallel with the horizon. On the Equator (right), the stars rise and set vertically. So if they look east or west, they will see the stars move straight up or straight down.

The Universe

THE BIG BANG

One of the most persistently asked questions is: How did the Universe begin? Our Universe was formed about 15 billion years ago in a massive explosion known as the Big Bang, and the origin of the Big Bang can be credited to an astronomer named Edwin Hubble. Many people once believed that the Universe had no beginning and no end, and was truly infinite, however, through the Big Bang theory this was proved to be wrong. Following his discovery the Universe was forced to take on the properties of a finite phenomenon, something which possesses a history and a beginning.

At the point when the explosion occurred, all the matter and energy of space was contained at one point. What existed before this event is completely unknown and is purely a matter for

300,000 years after the Big Bang swirling clouds of gas are formed

after 1 billion years first galaxies with stars and spiral arms appear

after several million years protogalaxies and quasars begin to form

Immediately after the Big Bang everything is incredibly hot and expanding rapidly

singularity

the Big Bang

The Atom
The Atom was the first building block of the Universe. With just one proton at its centre and one electron, it is the simplest atom.

The Universe

speculation. The explosion could not be described as a regular one, rather an event that filled all of space with all of the particles of the embryonic universe rushing away from one another. The Big Bang actually consisted of an explosion of space within itself, not like a bomb explosion where the fragments would be thrown outwards. So the galaxies were not all formed into a big clump, but rather the Big Bang lay the foundations for the Universe.

The origin of the Big Bang theory can be credited to Edwin Hubble. Hubble discovered that the speed of the galaxies is relative to its distance. This means that galaxies that are twice as far from us move twice as fast. Another consequence of his studies is that the Universe is expanding in every direction and, since the Big Bang, it has been expanding continuously. This means that there is more and more distance between the clusters of galaxies. This phenomenon of galaxies moving further away from each other is known as the 'redshift'. As the light from distant galaxies approaches Earth there is an increase of space between Earth and that galaxy, which leads to wavelengths being stretched.

There is further evidence for the Big Bang theory. In 1964, two astronomers, Arno Penzias and Robert Wilson, in an attempt to detect microwaves from outer space, inadvertently discovered a noise of extraterrestrial origin. The noise did not seem to come from just one location but instead, it came from all directions at the same time. It became obvious that what they heard was radiation from the furthest reaches of the Universe which had been left over from the Big Bang.

A Black Cloud (below)
Found in southern Ophiucus, a black cloud named Barnard 68 blocks the light of thousands of stars.

The Universe

Protogalaxies
form, containing
the first stars

Large galaxies form –
some become spirals

LEFT: These galaxies are the most
distant ever seen by the Hubble Space
Telescope. Some may have formed
less than a billion years after the Big
Bang, and this picture shows them
early in their life.

The Universe

AFTER THE BIG BANG

Immediately after the Big Bang the Universe was tremendously hot as a result of particles of both matter and antimatter rushing around in all directions. As the Universe began to cool down, gravity started to play its part.

Gravity rules the Universe and it is a force that pulls every object towards every other object. All material has the pulling power that we call gravity and the larger the object the more pulling power it has. The force of gravity makes all matter want to collect together, just like the pull of a magnet. So, when the Universe was only a million years old, matter in the form of the gases – hydrogen and helium – was already beginning to draw together and settle into slowly spinning clumps called protogalaxies. These were the very beginnings of the galaxies and the small clumps of gas inside the protogalaxies became stars.

Protogalaxies were like huge star clusters or dwarf galaxies. They mostly formed in groups and were the building blocks for galaxies. Drawn together by gravity, protogalaxies began to collide and merge, at first forming very odd shapes. Eventually, enough protogalaxies merged to create the larger spiral and elliptical galaxies we can see today.

But that is not the end because in many galaxies, new stars keep on forming. Galaxies are still changing and merging, and even today new stars are being born within the Milky Way Galaxy and a dwarf galaxy is in the process of merging with it.

As the Universe ages we are able to become increasingly confident in our knowledge of its history. By studying the way in which the Universe exists today, it is possible to learn a great deal about its past. Only through further research and discovery will it be possible to completely understand the creation of the Universe and its first atomic structures.

Since its conception, the theory of the Big Bang has been constantly challenged. These challenges have led those who believe in the theory to search for more and more evidence in an effort to paint a more complete picture of the creation of the Universe.

UNIVERSE FACT FILE

The study of the Universe is called Cosmology.

Age of the Universe:
about 15 billion years

Number of galaxies in the Universe:
about 100 billion

Number of stars:
about 1,000 billion billion

Distance of furthest galaxies from Milky Way Galaxy:
about 14 billion light years

Current temperature of the Universe:
−270°C (−454°F)

The Universe

COSMIC RIPPLES

The Cosmic
Background Explorer

Everywhere in the Universe there is a faint glow, which is the remains of the energy from the Big Bang itself. In 1992, small differences were found in the temperature across the glow – the hotter areas where the gas started to form into what would become clusters of galaxies.

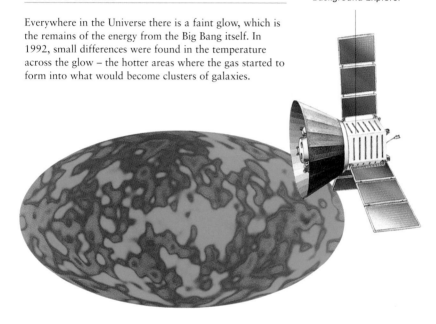

The glow reaches Earth in the form of microwaves – similar to those that cook food, but much less powerful. The microwaves are picked up by special equipment, such as the Cosmic Background Explorer (COBE).

The COBE satellite was launched in 1989 and its main job was to detect the warmth left over from the Big Bang, which is called cosmic background radiation. COBE made a map of the temperature of the whole sky and found

small differences, rather like ripples. In the map, the blue regions are cooler than average by a tiny amount, and the red regions are warmer. The background radiation COBE measured dates back to half a million years after the Big Bang. The tiny variations over the sky show that the Universe had stopped being the same throughout by the time it was only half a million years old. Once the Universe had stopped being smooth and uniform, matter began to gather into clumps.

The Universe

WALLS AND VOIDS

So far about 100,000 galaxies have been mapped from both the Northern and Southern hemispheres, to distances greater than 500 million light years. Astronomers already knew of two of the galaxy's coordinates just by locating them in the sky with their telescopes.

The first maps, published in 1986, were a great surprise to the astrophysicists, who expected to find relative uniformity within the already familiar galaxies. But this was not the case, instead the maps showed that great clusters of galaxies were arranged in thin sheets or long filaments. The longest sheet detected, called the 'Great Wall', extends hundreds of millions of light years across the maps. Interspersed among the sheets are also great holes, ranging in size from 100 million to 400 million light years in diameter, and these are almost all devoid of galaxies. These holes are known as 'voids'. Voids are like bubbles in a foam, with galaxies and clusters of galaxies forming the walls around the bubbles. Most of our Universe is composed of lightless voids, inside which stars and galaxies cannot form. Further studies, however, have proved that these voids may not be completely empty after all. Using the Hubble Space Telescope, researchers have detected clouds of hydrogen gas in nearby voids. Astronomers have detected hydrogen gas clouds before, but they've been in such remote parts of the Universe it was difficult to tell whether they lay in voids.

Sloan Digital Sky Survey

The Sloan Digital Sky Survey is to undertake the most ambitious astronomical survey ever. They plan to make the largest map in human history. It will give us a three-dimensional picture of the Universe through a volume one hundred times larger than that explored to date.

The Universe

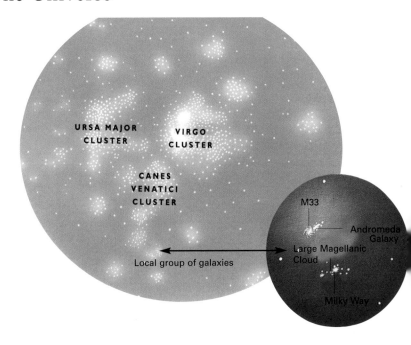

URSA MAJOR CLUSTER

VIRGO CLUSTER

CANES VENATICI CLUSTER

M33

Andromeda Galaxy

Large Magellanic Cloud

Milky Way

Local group of galaxies

GALAXIES

A galaxy is a family of billions of stars that are held together in space by the pull of gravity. Galaxies are not spread evenly throughout the Universe, they are mainly arranged in great sheets, strings or groups. Some are in large families called clusters, and these clusters can have thousands of members all held together by gravity. Many clusters of galaxies are grouped into even bigger families, which

are called superclusters. A typical supercluster can contain as many as 12 galaxy clusters and is hundreds of millions of light years across.

The Milky Way – our home galaxy – is part of a gathering of about 25 galaxies known as the Local Group. Members include the Great Andromeda Galaxy (M31), M32, M33, the Large Magellanic Clouds, the Small Magellanic Clouds, Dwingeloo 1, several small irregular galaxies and many dwarf elliptical

The Universe

galaxies. The Local Group occupies a region of space about 5 million light years across and is a relatively small cluster. The next cluster to us contains up to 3,000 galaxies and it is called the Coma-Virgo Cluster, named after the constellations in which it is found (Coma Berenices and Virgo). It is centred on the bright active galaxy M87.

But, of course, clustering does not stop here. Our Local Group and the Coma-Virgo Cluster are just part of a huge supercluster of galaxies – and of course there are many such superclusters in the Universe.

This Virgo Cluster of galaxies is the nearest big cluster of galaxies and the largest proven structure in our inter-galactic neighbourhood. The Virgo Cluster with its some 2000 member galaxies dominates our intergalactic neighbourhood, as it represents the physical centre of our Local Supercluster and influences all the galaxies and galaxy groups by the gravitational attraction of its enormous mass.

EDWIN HUBBLE (1889–1953)

One of the greatest astronomers of the twentieth century, Edwin Hubble (*bottom left*), identified individual stars in the nearby galaxy M33 and showed that it is a family of stars beyond our Milky Way Galaxy. Having proved that there are galaxies beyond our own, he went on to show that these galaxies are in fact moving away.

When a galaxy is moving towards or away from us, the light we receive from it looks a different colour from when it is still. A galaxy moving away appears redder. It is said to have a redshift. A galaxy coming nearer looks bluer and is said to have a blueshift. This change in colour is called the Doppler effect.

Using the Doppler effect, Hubble measured the speeds of galaxies and made the astonishing discovery that the further away a galaxy is, the faster it is moving. He found that the speed of a galaxy is directly linked to its distance. Today the relationship between the speed of a galaxy and its distance is called Hubble's Law. It shows that the whole Universe is getting bigger.

The Universe

MOVING GALAXIES

Measuring how far galaxies are from us tells us about the layout of the Universe today. However, to be able to predict the layout of the Universe in the future, we need to know how galaxies are moving.

Collecting information on the distances and speeds of many clusters of galaxies reveals that the more distant a cluster of galaxies, the faster it is racing away from the Milky Way. One reason why astronomers know the Universe began with a Big Bang is the way galaxies are rushing apart as if from a massive explosion. However, if we take a closer look we will see that it is not the galaxies that are moving through space. Instead, it is space itself that is stretching as the Universe expands from its tiny beginnings.

The pull of gravity between all the galaxies is slowing the expansion of the Universe. For a long time, astronomers have wondered whether gravity will eventually stop the expansion and pull all the galaxies back together again so the Universe ends in a 'big crunch'. But after peering far into the Universe with the most powerful telescopes, astronomers now think it likely that the Universe will expand forever.

Edwin Hubble was the first person to figure out how to tell the distance of a galaxy. He used a type of pulsating star known as a Cepheid variable as a kind of galactic yardstick. Hubble noticed a correlation between the period required to complete one pulsation brightness and the amount of energy the star gives off. This was the first major breakthrough in galactic research. Hubble also discovered that there was a correlation between the redshift of a galaxy and its distance, and this is known today as the Hubble constant. Today astronomers are able to measure the speed and distance of a galaxy by measuring the amount of redshift in its spectrum.

Galaxies were originally seen as isolated, mostly unevolving island structures, but it is now known that most galaxies are strongly, if not violently, affected by their environment. Most galaxies will experience several collisions or tidal interactions over the course of their lifetime, which are powerful enough to profoundly alter their structure. Consequently, it is now believed that these collisions and interactions are one of the primary causes of galaxy evolution. Also, with further study it has been revealed that what once appeared to be a random distribution of galaxies is in fact quite a complex design. They are grouped together in a very complicated sponge-like arrangement.

Sir Isaac Newton (1642–1727)
Sir Isaac Newton discovered that a force is required to change the speed or direction of movement of an object and this force became known as 'gravity'.

The Universe

BRIGHT AND DARK NEBULAE

Nebulae make some of the most spectacular pictures in any book of astronomy and some people buy telescopes especially to see these dark swirls and colourful clouds for themselves. Nebulae are clouds of gas and dust and it is these properties that give them their unusual shapes and glowing colours. They are made up mostly of hydrogen gas, with some other gases such as oxygen, nitrogen and sulphur mixed in. It is combinations of these, together with dust and the light from nearby stars, that makes the appearance of nebulae so spectacular.

BRIGHT NEBULAE

Unlike the stars, nebulae have no light of their own. But, if there is a hot star within a few light years, the gas in a nebula will probably shine brightly. Hot stars give out lots of ultraviolet light, which is absorbed by the gas and is given out again as particular colours. Nebulae that glow like this are known as *emission nebulae*. Hydrogen gas glows red, while oxygen and helium are green.

DARK NEBULAE

Besides the various types of luminous bright nebulae, consisting of light emitting gas or illuminated dust masses, there are dark nebulae which can be seen because they obscure, or absorb, the light coming from stars or bright nebulae behind them. Therefore, dark Nebulae are sometimes called *Absorption Nebulae*. A famous example is the 'Horsehead Nebula'.

DUST AMONG THE STARS

There is a lot of dust in space which comes from the stars, and it is most probably blown off as they shine or are in a supernova explosion. The dust is possibly made up of particles of carbon or iron with a coating of ice or frozen gas. The particles are about the size of those in wood smoke and, just like smoke, the dust appears bluish when light shines on it and consequently the dust clouds will appear blue if there are hot stars nearby.

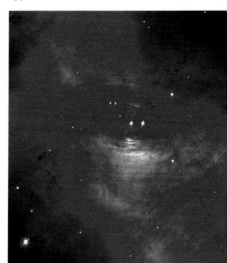

RIGHT: The Crab Nebula, M1.

The Universe

SHAPES OF GALAXIES

Galaxies come in many varieties, with different shapes, sizes and masses. While some are fairly faint, others pour out immense amounts of light and heat. All galaxies are families of stars and the tiniest ones have just a few million stars and are only a thousand light years in size. The largest galaxies have millions and millions of stars and are hundreds of thousands of light years across. There are only three galaxies that are visible to the naked eye from Earth and these are seen as faint, misty patches of light. However, if you have access to a large telescope you could see billions and billions of galaxies, thousands of which lie in a patch of sky which is the size of the Full Moon.

Most galaxies are elliptical, shaped like an American football. Giant ellipticals have ten times as many stars as the Milky Way Galaxy, but these are quite rare. Most ellipticals are dwarfs and are made up of just a few million stars.

Spiral galaxies are bigger and brighter than dwarf elliptical galaxies, and contain between a billion and trillion stars. They usually have two main spiral arms curling out of a bulging centre. These arms may be anything from tightly wound to loose and open, and as a spiral galaxy turns slowly around its centre, its arms seem to trail along. The appearance of a spiral galaxy depends on our angle of view, because it is a flattish object. If we look at it from above, we can see the spiral pattern of the arms, while from the side, we can see the central bulge and often a dark streak due to a layer of dust.

There are also a group of spiral galaxies called barred spirals and they differ from regular spirals in that they have a bar across their central region. The SBa (*see opposite page*) spirals have a prominent bar which is smooth in texture. As in the Sa spirals, the arms are smooth and not distinct. However, in the SBc spiral the bar and the spiral arms break up into knots and luminous lumps and the arms are very open. The SBb spirals are somewhere in between the two and have a smooth, but well-defined, bar and the spiral arms are quite distinct.

More than a third of all galaxies do not have a regular shape, and these are called irregular galaxies. Irregular galaxies are in a 'miscellaneous' category of galaxy morphologies. They are neither elliptical nor spiral in nature. Telescopic observations deep into the Universe show that distant galaxies are more likely to be irregular in shape than those nearby. They are usually smaller than the spiral galaxies and contain a lot of gas. Some of these galaxies are irregular because they have been distorted by the pull of gravity of another galaxy nearby.

Some galaxies do not fit into any group, but have clear shapes of their own. There are ring galaxies, such as the Cartwheel, and galaxies that seem to have horns, such as a pair of galaxies called the Antennae.

The Universe

CLASSIFYING GALAXIES

A simple code is used to describe the basic shape of a galaxy. 'E' means an elliptical galaxy. 'S' means a spiral. An elliptical is also given a number according to how flattened it looks. For example, 'E0' is like a sphere, 'E2' is lemon-shaped and 'E7' is like a short but fat cigar. The codes for spiral galaxies are 'Sa' for tightly wound arms, and 'Sb' and 'Sc' for more open arms. The arms of some spirals seem to wind from the end of a bar at the centre of the galaxy. Their code is 'SB'.

Sa   Sc   SBa

SBc   E0   E3

E7   Irregular galaxy

The Universe

COLLIDING GALAXIES

In the crowded regions of large galaxy clusters, large galaxies like our own Milky Way often collide with neighbouring galaxies. Most of the time the collision is with a smaller 'dwarf' galaxy, resulting in the smaller galaxy being eaten or cannibalized by the larger galaxy. However, once in a while, a large galaxy may encounter another large galaxy, and the result may be the merger of these galaxies, forming a single elliptical galaxy.

Galaxy collisions take a long time and a merger of two large galaxies can take as long as a billion years to occur. The pull of gravity of each galaxy distorts the discs and spiral arms, and can cause long spindly streamers of stars to fly off into deep space. It is unlikely that any stars actually have a head-on collision, because the stars are tiny compared to the wide spaces that separate them. Gas clouds crashing into each other do get squeezed, and this may cause new stars to form rapidly.

One of the most fascinating aspects of galaxy collisions is the fact that most of the matter involved doesn't actually collide with anything. This is due to the fact that most of the mass in a typical galaxy consists of collisionless dark matter, meaning that the dark matter from the companion galaxy merely passes through that of the target with no effects except for those due to their collective gravitational forces.

When galaxies collide
From top left (anticlockwise), this series of pictures shows how streamers of stars might form when two galaxies collide. Because galaxies are not solid objects, they are easily warped and twisted by the pull of each other's gravity. The stars in each galaxy are tossed on to new paths.

The Universe

CLUSTERS OF GALAXIES

Beyond our Local Group lie other clusters of galaxies, and some of these are enormous, with thousands of members. The clusters themselves are in groups, called superclusters, which are the largest known structures in the Universe.

Close to the Local Group lies the Virgo Cluster, but none of its members are bright enough for us to see with the naked eye. However, the Virgo Cluster covers a large area of our sky even though it is 50 million light years away. Near the centre of the Virgo Cluster lies a giant elliptical galaxy, called M87, and this is the largest galaxy ever recorded.

Astronomers have discovered something very strange about the Virgo Cluster. They have found that there is more material in it than we can actually see. In the same way that the orbits of double stars can tell us about their masses, the movements of galaxies inside a cluster can also be used to work out the cluster's total mass. The brightness of the galaxy also tells us how many stars there are contained in each one. However, the Virgo Cluster itself is around 200 times larger than would be expected from the amount of stars and other material that has been observed inside it.

This problem also applies to almost every cluster of galaxies, and no one is certain why there is this 'missing mass'. Some people believe that there are objects that are yet to be discovered, and this is an important task for the astronomers today to find out exactly what they are.

The Virgo Cluster, the Local Group and other galaxy clusters, make up the Local Supercluster, which is about 100 million light years across. Beyond the Local Supercluster is the Coma Supercluster, which is about 300 million light years away.

With the aid of the Hubble Space Telescope we have been able to learn a lot more about galaxy clusters. One rich cluster called 'Abell 2218' is so massive and compact that light rays passing through it are deflected by its enormous gravitational field, much in the same way as a camera lens bends light to form an image.

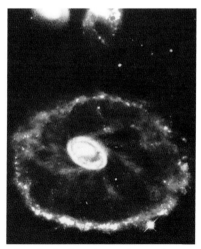

A Cartwheel galaxy shows what can happen when two galaxies collide.

The Universe

ACTIVE GALAXIES

The majority of galaxies seem to be 'normal', giving off the light and energy we would expect for a grouping of billions of stars. But some galaxies have an extraordinary energy output resulting from some extraordinary process going on inside. These are called active galaxies.

There are several types of active galaxies – seyferts, quasars and blazars. Quasars are active galaxies which are all a very long way from our planet, as many as 15 billion light years away. Blazars are very bright, while seyferts are much closer to us than any of the other active galaxies.

Astronomers are interested in these strange galaxies because, by discovering what is going on there, they can learn more about what happens inside ordinary galaxies. Active galaxies are intensely studied at all wavelengths, by using both X-ray and gamma-ray technology.

RADIO GALAXIES

Many of the active galaxies send out most of their energy as radio wavelengths. An example is NGC5128, or Centaurus A (*below*), one of the first radio galaxies to be discovered.

Astronomers first found active galaxies about 50 years ago, when they had started looking for different types of energy coming from objects in space. They got a big shock when they discovered that some far-off galaxies give off powerful radio waves, sending out far more energy as radio waves than as visible light.

A typical radio galaxy has two giant clouds of matter that lie far outside the main galaxy. The clouds look as if they have been blasted out to either side of the galaxy. Most of the radio waves come from the clouds, not from the galaxy itself.

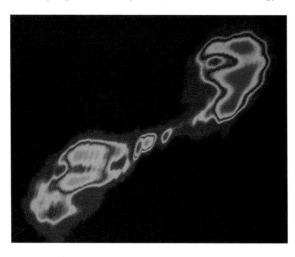

LEFT: Centaurus A.

The Universe

QUASARS

In the early 1960s quasars were known as 'radio stars' because the method used to discover the first quasars was based on coincidences between a strong radio source and a point-like optical source. Since each radio source was associated with a star it was originally thought that quasars were objects within the galaxy hence the term radio stars. The word quasar is short for 'quasi-stellar radio source'. This name, which means star-like emitters of radio waves, was given in the 1960s when quasars were first detected. In addition to radio waves and visible light, quasars also emit ultraviolet rays, infrared waves, X-rays and gamma-rays.

Many quasars, although not all of them, give off radio waves. Further away than most of the galaxies we can see are objects that look like stars, but whose spectra show them to be very distant. Quasars must be amazingly bright for us to be able to see them with the naked eye and it is this visible light that is most important. In a telescope, a quasar appears like a brilliant star, but it is actually the core of a galaxy at least 100 times brighter than a normal galaxy. The galaxy around the quasar is usually too faint to be seen, in fact all of the extra light is pouring out of the quasar at its centre.

Images of quasars and radio galaxies sometimes show two bright, narrow jets of light and energy shooting out from either side of the central region.

A quasar is probably a distant active galaxy with a black hole at its heart. Stars, gas and dust spiral in a disc around it, heating up as they get close to the centre. The hot material escapes in a jet along the axis of the disc, and we see the brilliant quasar if the jet points towards the Earth.

Light from a quasar can be bent by the gravity of a galaxy lying between the quasar and Earth. This can make the quasar look as if it is in four different positions at the same time – an effect that is called Einstein's Cross.

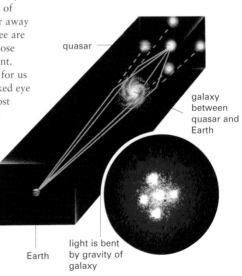

quasar

galaxy between quasar and Earth

light is bent by gravity of galaxy

Earth

The Universe

WHAT IS A BLACK HOLE?

A black hole is a region of space with such high gravity that nothing escapes its grip, not even light. When you jump up, it is the Earth's gravity that pulls you back down to the ground. To escape the Earth's gravity, you would need to jump at a speed of 11 km (7 miles) per second. Because the Sun's gravity is 30 times more powerful than Earth's, its escape speed is 11 km (384 miles) per second. The stronger gravity pulls, the harder it is for you to escape from it.

A black hole is a region of space where gravity pulls so hard that even light travelling at 300,000 km (186,000 miles) per second cannot escape. No light comes out, so a black hole appears black.

Any gas that is close to a black hole will be pulled first into a disc around it, which shines brilliantly as the gas then plunges in. So the area surrounding a black hole is, in fact, anything but black.

A black hole forms when a massive star collapses at the end of its life because it cannot produce any more energy. The black hole itself is tiny, but the area from which light cannot escape – called the Schwarzschild radius – is usually several miles across.

It is difficult to talk about the actual size of a black hole, as it is only a mass, rather than a solid object. However, it is believed that most of the black holes that are actually out there were produced by the deaths of massive stars, and so we expect those black holes to weigh about as much as a massive star. A typical mass for such a stellar black hole would be about ten times the mass of the Sun.

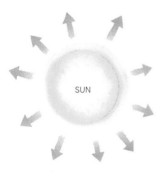

ABOVE: Light easily leaves the surface of the Sun because it travels much faster than the speed needed to escape the Sun's gravity.

RIGHT: Any light inside a region around a black hole called its event horizon cannot escape at all – the escape speed there is greater than the speed of light.

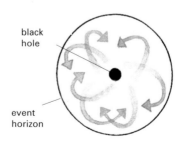

black hole

event horizon

The Universe

THE POWER AT THE CENTRE

Active galaxies, such as radio galaxies and galaxies containing quasars, produce far more energy than their stars can make. Some of the gas swirling around the black hole in the middle of an active galaxy is squirted out to form a pair of high-speed jets. These jets create the great radio clouds detected to either side of radio galaxies and some quasars. Apart from the jets, there is other evidence that something dramatic is going on. In many active galaxies we can see matter swirling around the central region at immense speeds. In a few cases we can also detect a pancake shape of hot gas spinning at the centre. This makes astronomers think that active galaxies probably contain gigantic black holes.

Located at the centre of a galaxy, a black hole sucks in matter of all kinds, including stars and gas. As the matter plunges towards the black hole, some of it is sent spinning around in a disc. Some matter bounces back before reaching the black hole, making the bright jets above and below the disc.

The central black hole pulls material towards itself by gravity. As stars and gas plunge headlong towards this black hole, enormous amounts of energy are given off. In the most powerful galaxies, the black hole has grown to a few billion times the mass of the Sun.

As the gravity pull of a black hole is so intense, it would be quite excusable to believe that nothing could escape this intense pull. Of course this is not true, because if it were the whole Universe would get sucked into it. It is only when something (including light) gets within a certain distance of the black hole, that they actually get sucked into the centre. Stars and planets at a safe distance will circle around the black hole, much like the motion of the planets around the Sun.

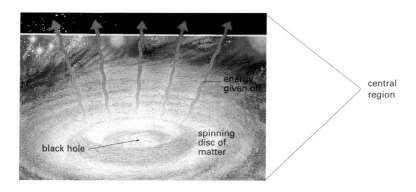

energy given off

central region

black hole

spinning disc of matter

The Universe

THE MILKY WAY

On dark, clear nights, when there is no Moon, you can see a hazy band of light spanning the dome of the heavens and this is called the Milky Way. The Milky Way passes through some of the most brilliant constellations: Cassiopeia, Cygnus, Perseus, Auriga and Aquila in the Northern hemisphere, and Puppis, Vela, Carina, Crux, Centaurus, Scorpius and Sagittarius in the Southern hemisphere. It varies noticeably in brightness. In the Northern hemisphere it is brightest in Cygnus and Aquila, while in the Southern hemisphere, in Scorpius and Sagittarius. The Milky Way also varies in width, in places only being about 5 degrees across, while in others approaching 30 degrees.

But what exactly is the Milky Way? No one knew until Galileo turned his telescope to the heavens nearly 400 years ago. He was amazed at what he saw, as we are today when we look at it through binoculars. The milky white band resolves into a mass of faint stars that are beyond number. In places the Milky Way is split by dark rifts where there appear to be scarcely any stars at all. The stars are there, but intervening clouds of dust are blotting out their light.

The Milky Way represents a cross-section of the great star system, or galaxy, to which our Sun and all the other stars in the sky belong. It takes the form of a disc with a bulge at the centre (or the

The Universe

nucleus). From the nucleus, a number of arms spiral out, carrying the various stars. The whole galaxy rotates and, viewed from afar, would perhaps present the appearance of a Catherine Wheel firework.

The size of the Milky Way is astounding – it measures 100,000 light years across and is made up of at least 100,000 million stars. However, it is nothing special among galaxies, it is a typical spiral galaxy of the Sb type (*see page 37*). There are many larger galaxies, including the Great Spiral in Andromeda.

The Sun is located on one of the spiral arms about 30,000 light years from the centre of the Milky Way. Like the other stars, it rotates around the galactic centre, completing one orbit in 225 million years – a period called the cosmic year.

There is far more to the Milky Way Galaxy than we can see, and its stars appear to move as if they are attracted by something. There does seem to be a huge amount of invisible material surrounding the galaxy, but no one really knows what the dark matter is.

Milky Way Trivia
- To Native American Seminoles, the Milky Way is the path that leads good souls to heaven.
- To the Norse, it is a road leading to Valhalla (literally, hall of the slain; the palace of immortality, inhabited by the souls of heroes slain in battle).
- Chinese and Arab myths represent the Milky Way as a river.
- The name Milky Way comes from the ancient Greeks and their belief that the band was a spray of milk, or 'gala', from which the word galaxy originated.

The Milky Way Galaxy would appear something like this if we were able to see it from the outside. A huge disc with a bulge in the centre makes up the main part of the galaxy, which is crowded by stars. Other stars surround the centre in a ball-shaped halo.

The Universe

CROSS-SECTION OF THE MILKY WAY

We are now starting to appreciate the Milky Way as a cross-section of our home galaxy being about 100,000 light years in diameter. It is noticeable that a conspicuous dark line runs through the centre of the Milky Way, and many reddish nebulae are scattered around it. Although dust clouds hide much of the Milky Way from our view, astronomers are able to map it by detecting radio and other waves coming from the material in its spiral arms.

If we looked at the Milky Way from the outside we would see that it is shaped like a very thin pancake with an enormous bulge at its centre. Spiral arms, made up of dust, gas and young stars, emerge from this central bulge. The Milky Way contains billions of stars which are packed much closer together in the bulge than in the spirals. The Sun lies a little more than halfway from the centre to the edge of the disc, and it is the disc that is the most prominently visible part of our galaxy. The galaxy itself rotates, and the Sun takes 220 million years to make one complete circuit.

If it were possible to slice through the edge of the Milky Way, we would be able to see that the Sun is almost exactly on the central line. At this point the disc is about 1,300 light years thick. The centre of the Milky Way is hidden from view by dust clouds, and these clouds create a dark bank called the Great Rift.

In the central bulge and halo of the Milky Way are old stars, which formed billions of years ago. In the spiral arms are young stars, together with gas and dust from which new stars are continually forming.

Beyond the star-filled disc of the Milky Way there exists an extensive yet diffuse halo of hydrogen gas. The halo is about 100,000 parsecs in diameter which is about twice the diameter of the disc. Astronomers, with the help of powerful telescopes, have ascertained that, unlike the Earth's atmosphere, which is hot enough to hold itself up against the force of gravity, the hydrogen in the halo is too cool to support itself against the gravitational pull of the Milky Way.

MILKY WAY FACT FILE

Size of the Milky Way Galaxy:
100,000 light years across
Distance from Sun to centre of galaxy:
28,000 light years
Thickness of disc:
1,000 light years
Central bulge:
10,000 light years thick
15,000 light years across
Number of stars:
100 billion
Time taken for Sun to orbit around centre of galaxy:
220 million years

The Universe

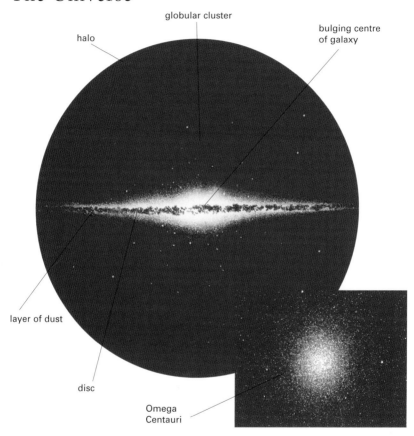

globular cluster

bulging centre
of galaxy

halo

layer of dust

disc

Omega
Centauri

Pictured above is the largest ball of stars in our galaxy. About 10 million stars orbit the centre of this globular cluster – named Omega Centauri – as it orbits our galactic centre. Omega Centauri is by far the most massive of the known globular clusters in the Milky Way. Omega Centauri spans about 150 light years across, lies about 15,000 light years away, and can be seen without visual aid towards the constellation of Centaurus. The stars in globular clusters are generally older, redder and less massive than our Sun. Studying globular clusters tells us not only about the history of our Galaxy but also gives us more information about the age of the Universe.

THE STARS

A star is just a huge ball of hot gas, which is heated from the inside by nuclear energy. This enormous energy in their interior is radiated into space and on a clear dark night can be visible to the naked eye. Even though each individual star is unique, all stars share much in common. All stars, with the exception of one, lie millions of miles from Earth. The Sun, which is the source of virtually all light, heat and energy reaching the Earth, is in fact our nearest star.

THE SUN

Without the Sun, the Earth would be a dark, frozen, lifeless ball with a temperature just barely above absolute zero. For these reasons, it is important for humans to study our Sun. Although the Sun is very special to our survival on Earth, in the Universe as a whole it is not very important. By comparison to the other stars it is not very big and it is not very bright. Because the Sun is only 150 million km (93 million miles) away, astronomers have been able to find out far more about it than any other star. We know that it is similar to a bubbling cauldron, and that enormous quantities of energy seep out into space from its surface. We also know that it has an extremely powerful magnetic field that causes some dramatic effects, such as flares and sunspots.

The Sun is actually made up of gas which is composed of about 70 percent hydrogen and 28 percent helium. Since the Sun formed around 5 billion years ago, it has used up about half of its initial hydrogen supply.

Astronomers study the Sun using special instruments which can analyse how and why the amount of light from the Sun varies over time, the effect of the Sun's light on the Earth's climate, spectral lines, the Sun's magnetic field, the solar wind and many other solar phenomena. The outer regions of the Sun (the corona) are studied during solar eclipses.

SUN FACT FILE
Mass (amount of matter it contains):
   333,000 times Earth's mass
Radius:
   696,000 km (433,000 miles), 109 times
   Earth's radius
Surface temperature:
   5,500°C (10,000°F)
Central temperature:
   15 million°C (27 million°F)
Composition:
   70% hydrogen, 28% helium, 2%
   mixture of other materials
Age:
   5 billion years

The Stars

HEAT FROM THE SUN

The surface of the Sun is called the photosphere, and its temperature is around 5,500°C (10,000°F). Above the surface there is an even hotter layer of atmosphere which is called the chromosphere, which has a temperature of 15,000°C (27,000°F). The outermost layers of the atmosphere are called the corona, which extends for millions of miles and its temperature closest to the Sun is 1 million°C (2 million°F). Gases from the corona stream off into space as solar wind, which blow with a speed of 800 km (500 miles) per hour.

The Sun pours out into space an enormous amount of energy, not only as light and heat (infrared rays), but also as many other kinds of radiation, such as gamma rays, X-rays, ultraviolet rays and radio waves. It has been emitting this energy since the day it was born, around 4,600 million years ago and will continue to do so for at least another 5,000 million years.

Like all stars, the Sun generates nuclear energy and deep inside its core, the temperature is a searing 15 million°C (27 million°F). At this temperature, the particles of gas that make up the Sun react with one another to turn hydrogen into helium and energy. As this energy is released, the Sun loses mass, in fact it can lose as much as 4 million tons every second.

Many changes to the Sun are linked to its magnetic field. Because it is made up of gas, the Sun rotates faster at its equator than at its poles. The magnetic field in the gas stretches and winds itself around the Sun, very much like an elastic band. When it can stretch no further, the magnetism breaks up and releases energy, which we can see on Earth as solar activity.

Tongues or arches of hot gas called prominences are often seen over the Sun's surface. While some may last for many weeks, others surge up violently and last only a few hours. It is possible for these flares to leap tens of thousands of miles into space.

The Stars

LIGHT FROM THE SUN

The Earth is bathed in light from the Sun, which warms our planet and makes life possible. Visible light is a form of electromagnetic radiation (E-M), but not all types of E-M can penetrate the surface of the Earth. For example, ultraviolet light, which can damage DNA, cause mutation, and with enough exposure skin cancer, if it managed to reach the Earth's surface unabated, most forms of animal and plant life would not survive. Luckily for us it is mostly blocked out by the ozone layer of the atmosphere. The light of the Sun is a very precarious thing, too little and the Earth would be a cold, lifeless place, while too much and life would be destroyed. Below is a chart which shows the effects of the various forms of electromagnetic radiation emitted by the Sun, and whether or not they penetrate the atmosphere.

FORMS OF SOLAR ELECTROMAGNETIC RADIATION

Gamma Rays and X-Rays

These are completely blocked by the atmosphere. They are produced in the corona of the Sun and were only observable with the advent of the space age. The X-rays that doctors use are produced by X-ray machines. Only recently have we been able to observe the X-rays that are produced by the Sun.

Visible Light

This makes it through the atmosphere unimpeded and this is the light that we see. Along with infrared light, it is responsible for keeping the planet warm and driving the weather system. Most life is ultimately based on the energy of incoming visible light utilized by plants.

Microwaves

These are the same as the microwaves used in a microwave oven, although those are generated electronically, not by the Sun. The atmosphere absorbs some microwaves, but others reach the Earth, where they are useful for studying the Sun.

Ultraviolet Light

This is mostly absorbed by the ozone layer. The little that makes it through is important to life forms. In humans it is crucial to the production of vitamin D.

Infrared Light

Although mostly absorbed by water vapour, carbon dioxide and methane in the atmosphere, it is responsible for keeping the planet warm along with the visible light and for driving the weather system.

Radio Waves

Radio waves penetrate unimpeded to the surface. They have very little influence on Earth, but humans generate radio waves for communication, such as television and radio.

The Stars

SUNSPOTS

Dark spots, some as large as 50,000 miles in diameter, move across the surface of the Sun, contracting and expanding as they go. These strange and powerful phenomena are known as sunspots. As early as 28 BC, astronomers in ancient China recorded systematic observations of the cycles of what looked like small, changing dark patches on the surface of the Sun. There are also some early references to sunspots in the writings of Greek philosophers from the fourth century BC, but none of the early observers could explain what they were seeing.

Although sunspots appear dark in photographs of the Sun, in fact they are quite bright – they are just dark compared to the rest of the Sun. Sunspots are about the size of the Earth and frequently occur in groups. Sunspots occur when a concentrated portion of the Solar magnetic field pokes through the surface. This field slows energy from entering the sunspot region, causing sunspots to appear cooler, darker and lower than the surrounding surface. Sunspots typically last a few days before dissipating. The number of sunspots is always changing, and varies enormously over a cycle lasting 11 years. Sometimes an extra bright area, called a facula, can be seen nearby. The temperature of a facula is higher than that of its surroundings.

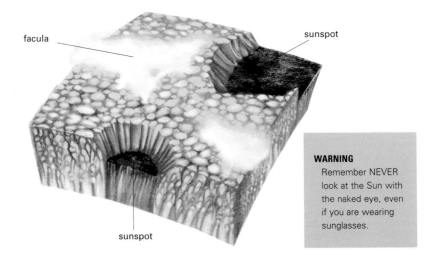

facula

sunspot

sunspot

WARNING
Remember NEVER look at the Sun with the naked eye, even if you are wearing sunglasses.

The Stars

SOHO SPACECRAFT

The Solar and Heliospheric Observatory (SOHO) was launched on December 2, 1995, with 12 instruments on board. It orbits the Sun 1.5 million km (930,000 miles) nearer the Sun than the Earth, at a

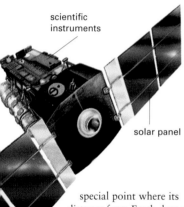

scientific instruments

solar panel

special point where its distance from Earth does not change very much. SOHO was designed to study the solar wind and the Sun's atmosphere. It can also detect movements in the Sun's surface layers, which help astronomers work out what the inside of the Sun is like.

The observations made with SOHO's Michelson Doppler Imager (MDI) provided long-duration, highly detailed and well calibrated time-lapse movies of the magnetic fields on the visible surface or 'photosphere' of the Sun. These revealed the rapidly changing properties of the Sun's 'magnetic carpet', a sprinkling of tens-of-thousands of magnetic concentrations. These concentrations have both north and south magnetic poles, which are the 'foot points' of magnetic loops extending into the solar corona.

Just like field biologists who study the populations and life cycles of animals, the SOHO researchers analysed the appearances and disappearances of large numbers of the small magnetic concentrations on the solar surface.

SOHO is unable to see the far side of the Sun directly, but the MDI instrument can form an image of far-side active regions by analysing ripples on the Sun's surface. Sound waves reverberating through the Sun generate the ripples, which are analysed by computer to form an image of the far side and the solar interior.

In 2002 SOHO recorded video images of powerful solar flares over the course of eight days, indicating stormy weather on the far side of the Sun. The flares came from sights of violent activity on the Sun called active regions.

These days, space weather experts watch the Sun more closely than ever because modern systems are much more vulnerable to solar disturbances than old technology. The experts can still be taken by surprise because the Sun rotates, bringing the effects of hidden active regions to bear on Earth. However, scientists using SOHO had advance warning that stormy weather was brewing on the Sun.

The Stars

OBSERVING SOLAR ECLIPSES

Of all the natural phenomena we witness on Earth, perhaps the most spectacular or awe-inspiring is a total eclipse of the Sun. During an eclipse, day turns suddenly into night, the air becomes suddenly cool, and the birds stop singing and think it is time to roost.

A total eclipse of the Sun is that special celestial event where the Moon passes exactly in front of the solar disc. During a fleeting few minutes of totality, some fortunate people, who are located within the path of the Moon's dark shadow, can witness the wondrous shimmering solar corona sharing the sky with stars and bright planets.

Eclipses of the Sun happen because of a strange astronomical coincidence. The Sun is 400 times further away from the Earth than the Moon, but its diameter is 400 times greater than that of the Moon. The consequence of this is that both the Sun and the Moon appear much the same size in the sky.

Occasionally, as the Moon travels in its orbit around the Earth, it lines up exactly with the Sun and the Earth. When it comes between them, it blots out the Sun's light and casts a shadow on Earth. That is when we have an eclipse of the Sun, or a solar eclipse. When the Moon is on the other side of the Earth from the Sun, it enters the shadow cast by the Earth, and we have an eclipse of the Moon, or a lunar eclipse.

On average, solar eclipses occur about

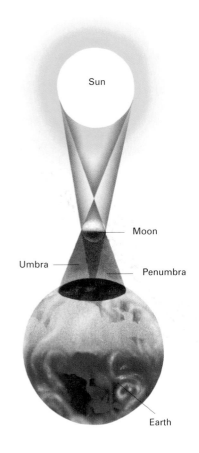

Sun

Moon

Umbra

Penumbra

Earth

The Stars

twice a year, but they are not always total. Sometimes they are partial, and this is when the Moon is only covering part of the Sun's disc. Sometimes they are annular, with the Moon covering up all of the Sun except for an annulus, or ring, around the edge.

PHASES OF AN ECLIPSE

If you are lucky enough to be in the path of totality the eclipse begins with a partial phase in which the Moon gradually covers more and more of the Sun. This typically lasts for about an hour until the Moon completely covers the Sun and the total eclipse begins. The duration of totality can be as short as a few seconds, or as long as about eight minutes, depending on the conditions at the time.

As totality approaches the sky becomes dark and what can be described as an eerie twilight begins to descend. Just before totality waves of shadows rushing rapidly from horizon to horizon may be visible. In the final moments before totality, light shining through valleys in the Moon's surface gives the impression of beads on the periphery of the Moon (something that is known as *Bailey's Beads*). The flash of light from the surface of the Sun as it disappears from view behind the Moon gives the appearance of a diamond ring and is called the *diamond ring effect*.

As totality begins, the extended outer atmosphere of the Sun (the solar corona) blazes into view. The corona is a million

ABOVE: For a few minutes the Moon covers the Sun and we can see the Sun's outer atmosphere, called the corona, around the disc of the Moon.

times more faint than the surface of the Sun, and so it is only when the eclipse is total that it can be seen. At this point the sky is sufficiently dark that planets and some of the brighter stars become visible. Also, if the Sun is active, it is possible to see solar prominences and flares around the outside of the Moon, even without the aid of a telescope.

The period of totality ends when the motion of the Moon begins to uncover the surface of the Sun, and the eclipse proceeds through partial phases for approximately an hour, until the Sun is once again completely uncovered.

The next total solar eclipse that will be visible from land will be in the year 2006. This eclipse crosses northern Africa and enters the Asian continent through Turkey.

The Stars

ABOVE: Star formation can be triggered in a cloud of gas and dust by the shock waves from a supernova explosion.

Shooting stars
A shooting star, or a meteor as they are more commonly known, is the streak of light produced when a lump of dust and rock burns up in the Earth's atmosphere. It looks like a star falling towards us as it momentarily flashes above us.

THE BIRTH OF A STAR

Protostars are stars that are about to be born. They are glowing clouds of interstellar gas and dust, which look like dark spots in the midst of light. Gravity causes every atom and every bit of dust to pull on every other one and they all move towards the centre, causing the protostar to collapse. Having started with a diameter of say 1.5 trillion km, the protostar now shrinks at a very rapid rate about 1,000 years, to a diameter of around 80 million km. Because the atoms move faster and faster as they fall towards the centre, friction is created as they rub together and their temperature rises. This increased heat causes the protostar to glow, and it gives off even more light than the Sun even

though it is not nearly as hot. After about 10,000 years, the protostar's surface temperature is so high that it is now 100 times as luminous as the Sun, and all the while it is still shrinking.

A star is actually born when a protostar stops shrinking in size. At this time the core temperature of the protostar has reached 27 million°F and a reaction, called nuclear fusions, begins in the centre. Nuclear fusion is the joining, or fusing, of small atomic nuclei to create larger ones. The nuclei of two hydrogen atoms join to form the nucleus of one helium atom and when this happens there is a great release of energy. As the protostar starts to shine, its heat blows the remaining gas and dust away, leaving behind only what has already formed into

The Stars

other stars or planets. We see and feel this energy in the form of light and heat from the Sun. All stars give off this energy but they are too far away from Earth for us to feel the effects. The fusion in a star continues for around 90 percent of its life, but this cannot go on forever and the star will eventually fade. As a star grows larger and larger it starts to become red in colour, and it is for this reason that it is called a 'red giant'.

Astronomers have located a number of red giants in the Universe. Alderbaran is in the constellation Taurus, Antares in Scorpio, Arcturus in Bootes and Betelgeuse in Orion. Most of the red giants are found in globular clusters, which are groups of up to 1 million stars that move together through space.

STELLAR NURSERIES

Stars form in clusters rather than on their own. A cluster might contain anything from a handful to hundreds of stars. When we see a cluster of stars in the sky, we know they all formed together. After stars have formed, their presence can set off a new wave of star birth nearby. Over time, the stars in a cluster gradually drift apart. All the stars now scattered through our galaxy were once in clusters.

1 A cluster of brilliant young stars has just emerged from the dark cloud of gas and dust from which they formed.

2 Hot gas from the young stars triggers the formation of more stars just inside the nearby cloud.

3 The first cluster spreads out. The second cluster emerges and sets off the formation of yet another cluster.

The Stars

THE ORION CLOUD

In the direction of the constellation Orion, there drifts a giant cloud of interstellar gas and dust within the Milky Way, the Orion Cloud. This cloud was formed when a density wave, related to the galaxy's spiral structure, moved through the galactic disc. It is about 1,600 light years away from Earth and several hundred light years across.

This enormous cloud, or complex of clouds, of interstellar matter and young stars contains, besides M42 and M43, a number of famous objects – Barnard's Loop, the Horsehead Nebula region and a reflection nebulae.

Within this cloud, stars have recently formed, and are still in the process of formation. These young stars make up the so-called Orion OB1 Association – OB because the most massive, most luminous, and hottest of these stars belong to the spectral types O and B. Because these stars are so luminous they use up their nuclear fuel very quickly and have only a short lifespan.

The Orion Nebula is the only part of this immense cloud that is actually visible. It is a place where a group of very hot, young stars have blown a bubble in the dark cloud. These stars are giving out strong ultraviolet light, which makes the inside of the bubble glow. Because the bubble was near the edge of the Orion Cloud, it broke through and burst open. Now it is possible to see the stars inside and the bright inner surface of the bubble. There are many other clouds in our galaxy where stars are being created but the Orion Cloud is the largest known.

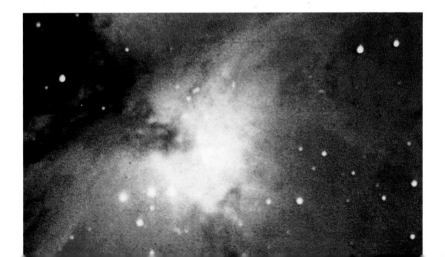

The Stars

THE EAGLE NEBULA

The Eagle Nebula is a region of our galaxy where stars are currently forming out of dusty hydrogen gas. Ultraviolet light from newly-formed stars in the vicinity of the nebula is pumping energy into these gas clouds, causing them to glow in visible light.

These eerie, dark, pillar-like structures are actually columns of cool interstellar hydrogen gas and dust that are also incubators for new stars. The pillars protrude from the interior wall of a dark molecular cloud like stalagmites from the floor of a cavern. They are part of the Eagle Nebula (also called M16), a nearby star-forming region 7,000 light years away, in the constellation Serpens. The ultraviolet light from hot, massive, newborn stars is responsible for illuminating the convoluted surfaces of the columns and the ghostly streamers of gas boiling away from their surfaces, producing the dramatic visual effects that highlight the three-dimensional nature of the clouds. This image was taken on April 1, 1995 with the aid of the Hubble Space Telescope Wide Field Planetary Camera 2. The colour image is constructed from three separate images taken in the light of emission from different types of atoms. Red shows emissions from singly-ionized sulphur atoms, green shows emissions from hydrogen and blue shows light emitted by doubly-ionized oxygen atoms.

From afar, the whole thing looks like an eagle. A closer look of the Eagle Nebula, however, shows the bright region is actually a window into the centre of a larger dark shell of dust.

The Stars

DOUBLE STARS

Most of the stars you see at night have companions, a great many obviously double even when viewed through a modest telescope. The components of some double stars are nearly equal in mass and brightness. More commonly, one dominates the other, sometimes to the point where the smaller star is not really visible at all, and detectable only with the most sophisticated techniques. At the lowest end, we have stars with low-mass brown dwarfs for companions. The stars of some doubles are so far apart that they take thousands of years to orbit; others are so close that they revolve around each other in only days or even hours.

Gravitational theory allows us to measure the masses of the stars from the orbits' characters; indeed such measurements are the only way in which we can find stellar masses. Examples of visually-seen double stars are Alpha Centauri, Acrux, Almach, Albireo and Mizar.

The spectral lines of a double star split in two when the two stars move in opposite directions. The Doppler shift shows each star's speed and size of orbit, and because heavy stars orbit differently to light stars, astronomers can work out each star's mass.

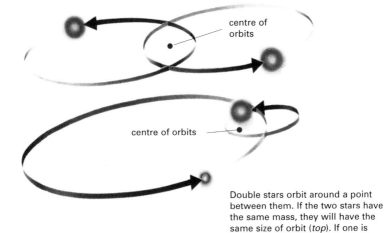

centre of orbits

centre of orbits

Double stars orbit around a point between them. If the two stars have the same mass, they will have the same size of orbit (*top*). If one is smaller, its orbit is larger (*left*).

The Stars

CATEGORIZING STARS

Stars are categorized according to their magnitude, colour, luminosity and temperature. The magnitude of a star depends on how bright it is and the scale ranges from one to six (one being the brightest). The colour of a star can actually tell us its temperature because, just like a piece of heated metal, it first glows dull red then changes to bright orange. If the temperature of a star continues to increase, then its colour turns first to yellow and then eventually to a bluish white. The same thing works with the gas at the surface of a star, so that we can ascertain what temperature it is.

Red stars are the coolest, bluish stars are the hottest, while the temperature of the yellow sun is somewhere in between.

The size of a star is also important. Our Sun is an ordinary star and is small compared with stars ten or hundreds of times larger. However, there are also some strange stars that are truly mini-dwarfs if put alongside the Sun. Sometimes balls of gas in space are so small that they never develop into proper stars at all, and astronomers call these brown dwarfs. White dwarfs are in fact old, dying stars that have used up all of their fuel. Inside a white dwarf, there is as much material as there is in the Sun, but it has been squashed into a ball that is around the size of Earth.

Lower mass stars create planetary nebulae and white dwarfs, while higher mass stars make supernovae that result in neutron stars or black holes. Double stars make novae and a different kind of supernovae. All these changes send out newly-made chemical elements into the interstellar stew, out of which new stars are formed and as a result the heavy element content of the galaxy increases with time. Ancient main sequence stars, the 'subdwarfs' have a low abundance of metals, while younger stars like the Sun have higher metal contents, which allows us to track the oldest and youngest stars and to determine the age of the galaxy.

STAR FACT FILE

Nearest star:
Proxima Centauri, red dwarf, distance 4.25 light years

Brightest star in the sky:
Sirius, white star, radius 1.7 Suns, distance 8.7 light years, true brightness 25 Suns

Star of very high true brightness:
Eta Carinae, thought to have the brightness of about 4 million Suns but is hidden behind a dust cloud. It is also one of the most massive known stars at about 100–150 times the mass of the Sun. Distance 8,000 light years

A very cool, dim star:
Gliese, located 19 light years from Earth in the constellation Lepus, estimated temperature 2,300°C (4,200°F), true brightness 0.0001 of the Sun

Hottest known stars
Temperatures of around 250,000°C (450,000°F)

The Stars

GIANT AND DWARF STARS

Stars come in an assortment of sizes and brightness, from the smallest ones, called dwarfs, larger stars called giants, to the biggest of them all called supergiants. The Sun itself is 20 times larger than a white dwarf star, while the supergiants are hundreds of times the size of the Sun.

Red dwarf stars can range in size from 100 times smaller than the Sun, to only a couple of times smaller. Because of their small size these stars burn their fuel very slowly, which allows them to live trillions

of years before they run out of fuel. Because red dwarf stars only burn a small amount of fuel at a time, they are not very hot compared to other stars, and, just like a fire, the coolest part at the top of the flame glows red, the hotter part in the middle glows yellow, while the hottest part near the fuel glows blue. Stars work in exactly the same way, which means that their temperature determines what colour they will be. This means that we can determine how hot a star is just by looking at its colour. Red dwarf stars are

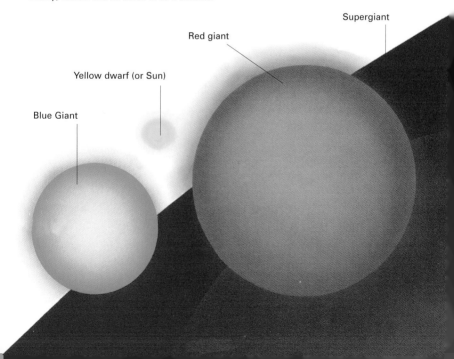

Supergiant

Red giant

Yellow dwarf (or Sun)

Blue Giant

The Stars

by far the most common type of star seen in outer space.

Like the Sun, medium-sized stars are yellow because they have a medium temperature, which causes them to burn their fuel faster. This means they will not live as long as the dwarf stars, only about 10 billion years or so, and near the end of their lives, these medium-sized stars will swell in size.

Because blue stars are so large and compact, they burn their fuel very rapidly, which gives them a very high temperature. These stars often run out of fuel in only 10,000 to 100,000 years. A blue giant is exceptionally bright and can shine across a vast distance. Even though blue giant stars are rare, they make up many of the stars we see at night. The death of a blue giant star is quite spectacular because instead of shrinking and forming a planetary nebula they explode into what is called a supernova. Supernova explosions can be brighter than an entire galaxy, and can be seen from a long distance away.

A giant star is simply one that started out about the size of the Sun and expanded. As a sun-sized star gets old, it starts to run out of its hydrogen fuel, and when the burning of hydrogen in the star's core starts to slow down, the core gets more and more compact. As the centre gets smaller and smaller it starts to heat up again, and when it gets hot enough it will start to burn a new fuel called helium. Once ignited, helium burns

much hotter than hydrogen and this additional heat pushes the outside of the star much further than it used to be, making the star much larger.

A supergiant star is exactly the same thing as a giant star, only bigger. Supergiant stars differ from giant stars in much the same manner that giant stars differ from main sequence stars – they have depleted their helium core fuel, and go on to burn carbon. It is important to remember that the more massive a star is, the faster it burns out its fuel.

White dwarf
  Radius: 0.02 of the Sun
  True brightness: 0.005 of the Sun
  Surface temperature: 25,000°C (45,000°F)
Brown dwarf
  Radius: 0.1 of the Sun
  True brightness: 0.00001 of the Sun
  Surface temperature: 720°C (1,300°F)
Red dwarf
  Radius: half of the Sun
  True brightness: 0.05 of the Sun
  Surface temperature: 6,000°C (3,300°F)
The Sun (Yellow dwarf)
  Radius: 1 Sun
  True brightness: 1 Sun
  Surface temperature: 5,500°C (10,300°F)
Blue giant
  Radius: 10 Suns
  True brightness: 800,000 Suns
  Surface temperature: 45,000°C (80,000°F)
Red supergiant
  Radius: 500 Suns
  True brightness: 40,000 Suns
  Surface temperature: 3,400°C (6,100°F)

The Stars

STAR DISTANCES

Two things affect how bright a star appears, one is its true brightness – the brightness with which it shines in space – and the other is the distance. To compare the true brightness of stars, we would have to view them from the same distance. This is the basis of the scale of true or absolute magnitude that astronomers use. They define the absolute magnitude of a star as the magnitude they would observe if the star were at a distance of 10 parsecs (1 parsec equals approximately 3.3 light years). Once the distance to the star is known, it is quite straightforward to calculate its true brightness or luminosity. For example, the North Pole Star, Polaris, is not especially bright but it is 680 light years away. Since Polaris is so remote and yet can still be seen with the naked eye, it must be extremely luminous. In fact, the true brightness of Polaris is 10,000 Suns.

No matter how powerful a telescope you have, you can never see the stars other than as pinpoints of light. That is because they are so far away that their light takes years to reach us. For example, the light from Sirius takes 8.8 years to reach us, so we can say that Sirius is 8.8 light years away – one light year being the distance light travels in a year.

In this book we mainly express stellar distances in light years, but professional astronomers prefer to use the unit called the parsec. Because of the Earth's revolution around the Sun, near stars

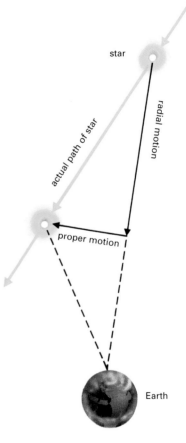

ABOVE: All the stars are moving relative to Earth. For just a few stars we are able to detect their proper motion, or motion across our line of sight.

The Stars

seem to shift their position against the further stars and this is called parallax shift (*see diagram*). By observing the distance of the shift and knowing the diameter of the Earth's orbit, astronomers are able to calculate the parallax angle across the sky.

The smaller the parallax shift, the further away from Earth the star is. This method is only accurate for stars within a few hundred light years of Earth. When the stars are very far away, the parallax shift is too small to measure.

The method of measuring distance to stars beyond 100 light years is to use Cepheid variable stars. These stars change in brightness over time, which allows astronomers to figure out the true brightness. Comparing the apparent brightness of the star to the true brightness allows the astronomer to calculate the

distance to the star. This method was discovered by American astronomer Henrietta Leavitt in 1912 and used in the early part of the century to find distances to many globular clusters.

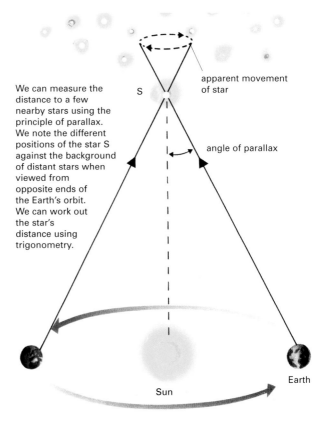

apparent movement of star

S

angle of parallax

We can measure the distance to a few nearby stars using the principle of parallax. We note the different positions of the star S against the background of distant stars when viewed from opposite ends of the Earth's orbit. We can work out the star's distance using trigonometry.

Earth

Sun

The Stars

NEAREST STARS

The information we can learn from the stars closest to our planet is vast, for example:

- We live very close (500 light seconds) to a star. This is probably a necessary condition for the origination and maintenance of life
- Stars are very far apart (average about 8 light years for the closest dozen), compared to their size (about 2 light seconds for the Sun); by a factor of 250 million or so
- Many stars occur in multiple systems, shown here by the suffixes A, B and C from brightest to dimmest. In fact, about 55 percent of stars in this list are in multiple systems. The nearest star is a triple. And we may be missing many dim stars
- Most of the nearby stars are dimmer (higher numbers for absolute magnitude) than our Sun, by factors of 100 to 10,000.

Nearest star	Distance (light years)	Proper motion ('/year)	App. magnitude	Absolute magnitude	Spectral type
Proxima Centauri	4.3	3.9	11.1	15.5	M5
α Centauri A	4.3	3.7	−0.3	4.4	G2
α Centauri B	4.3	3.7	1.3	5.7	K5
Barnard's Star	5.9	10.3	9.5	13.3	M5
Wolf 359	7.6	4.7	13.5	16.7	M8
Lalande 21185	8.1	4.8	7.5	10.5	M2
Sirius A	8.8	1.3	−1.5	1.4	A1
Sirius B	8.8	1.3	8.7	11.6	A
Luyten 726-8A	8.9	3.4	12.5	15.3	M5
UV Ceti	8.9	3.4	13.0	15.8	M6
Ross 154	9.4	0.7	10.6	13.3	M4
Ross 248	10.3	1.6	12.3	14.8	M6
ε Eridani	10.8	1.0	3.7	6.1	K2
Luyten 789-6	10.8	3.3	12.2	14.6	M7
Ross 128	10.8	1.4	11.1	13.5	M5
61 Cygni A	11.1	5.2	5.2	7.6	K5
61 Cygni B	11.1	5.2	6.0	8.4	K7
ε Indi	11.2	4.7	4.7	7.0	K5
Procyon A	11.4	1.3	0.4	2.7	F5
Procyon B	11.4	1.3	10.7	13.0	F
Struve 2398 A	11.5	2.3	8.9	11.2	M4
Struve 2398 B	11.5	2.3	9.7	12.0	M5

The Stars

VARIABLE STARS

Most of the stars we see in the sky shine steadily, but variable stars brighten and dim periodically. This behaviour allows them to be used as cosmic yardsticks out to distances of a few tens of millions of light years.

In 1912, Henrietta Leavitt noted that 25 stars, called Cepheid stars, in the Magellanic Cloud would brighten and dim periodically. Leavitt was able to measure the period of each star by measuring the timing of its ups and downs in brightness. Leavitt's work using this method of distance determination greatly increased the scientific knowledge of the physical universe.

CEPHEIDS

Cepheids are one of the most important kind of variable stars. They take their name from the star Delta Celphei, which takes five days and nine hours to complete its cycle of change. Going from minimum to maximum, it doubles in brightness, and this can take anything from one to about fifty days. All Cepheids are giant yellow stars which are several thousand times more brilliant than the Sun. A Cepheid varies because the whole star pulses in and out like a beating heart and the size of the Delta Celphei varies between 32 and 35 times that of the Sun.

Cepheids are important to astronomers because they help them measure distances to galaxies beyond our

own. To work out a galaxy's distance, astronomers need to compare how bright its stars seem from Earth with their true brightness. Cepheids are ideal for this because the number of days it takes a Cepheid to vary is always linked to the amount of its true brightness.

Around 700 Cepheids have been discovered in our galaxy and astronomers working with the Hubble Space Telescope are looking for Cepheids in other galaxies. With the help of Cepheids, astronomers can measure some galaxy distances extremely accurately and from there they can go on to discover the size of the entire Universe.

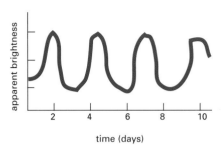

RIGHT: Henrietta Leavitt.

The Stars

In the outer layers of some red supergiant stars, tiny dark particles form, rather like the soot you get from a candle flame. When a lot of soot has collected, it makes the star look very much dimmer. However, the dark material eventually blows off the surface of the star and it returns to its normal brightness. The variations of stars like these are very irregular.

1   A red supergiant star shines at normal brightness.

2   The star dims when dark particles like soot form in its outer layers.

3   (*opposite*) The star blows away the dark material and returns to normal.

The Stars

MIRA VARIABLES

Perhaps the best-known type of variable stars are the Mira variety, named after the star Mira in the constellation of Cetus. Mira was the first variable star ever to be discovered.

In 1596, before the telescope had been invented, a Dutch astronomer noticed that Mira was a bright star that was visible with the naked eye. A few months later, however, it seemed to have disappeared, although it did eventually come back. This star was subsequently given the name Mira Stella, which literally means 'wonderful star', and now all stars that behave

in that way are called Mira variables.

Mira itself is a big red giant star that pulses in and out like a Cepheid. However, it takes much longer than a Cepheid to go through its cycle – about 332 days – and it does not behave in a regular way. Mira's visible light fades by a huge amount when the star expands and cools down a little. But all the time the star is giving out most of its energy as infrared rays, which are invisible to the human eye.

Most Mira variables are surrounded by shells of dust. This dust is produced in the cool outer layer and blown outwards by radiation pressure from the star. This dust can be observed directly at infrared wavelengths.

NOVAE

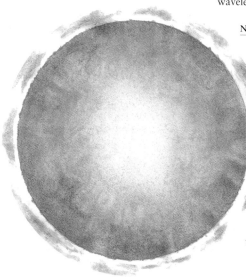

Sometimes a bright new star will appear in the sky and this is called a nova (which literally means 'new'). In fact, it is not a new star at all, but an existing dim star that has suddenly increased in brightness by many thousands of times. The most dramatic new star occurrences are the supernovae. These happen when supergiant stars blast themselves apart in their death throes.

The Stars

BINARY STARS

There are two basic types of binary stars: Visual Binaries and Optical Doubles.

Visual binaries are stars that are clearly associated with one another through gravitational pull. They orbit each other around a common centre called a *barycentre*. It is possible to view visual binaries through a telescope, but only a very small portion of binary stars are visual binaries. In order to see a visual binary, the stars must be separated by fairly wide distances, and the orbital periods are usually very long.

Optical doubles are stars that appear to lie close together, but in reality are a long way apart. They only appear to be close together because that is how we observe them from Earth. One of the stars in the pair is actually behind the first star and very far away. The stars of an optical double are not bound by gravity.

In 1782 William Herschel made an important discovery by comparing a close star to the more distant star in an optical double. He concluded that a pair of stars known as Castor were orbiting one another. This was the first time that observational evidence clearly showed two objects in orbit around each other outside of the influence of our own Sun and solar system.

SPECTROSCOPE

It is also possible to detect binary stars using an instrument called a spectroscope.

A star's spectrum is a rainbow crossed by dark lines.

A spectrum of gas is dark crossed with bright lines (hydrogen above and sodium below).

If two stars are orbiting each other they will produce a spectrum. If the stars are close to being the same brightness then it is possible to see different spectral lines from both stars. Stars will appear red shifted when receding away from Earth and blue shifted as they approach. This effect is caused by the Doppler effect which distorts arriving light waves from the stars depending on the direction in which they are moving. A spectroscopic binary will alternate between blue and red shifted spectral lines.

spectrum

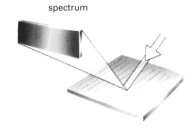

Inside a spectroscope

The Stars

ECLIPSING BINARY STARS

Because of the angle of some binary stars in space, we can see them cross in front of each other as they orbit. This causes their total brightness to vary. The most famous eclipsing binary is Algol which is in the constellation Perseus, and is probably so because it can be observed with the unaided eye. Another reason is because it has a relatively short period of less than three days. This means that a new observer can go out each night and see a complete cycle of Algol in their first week of observing if the star is visible at night in their location.

Algol is 93 light years away and the main star is three times as large as our Sun and its secondary star is a K2-type subgiant. Together they rotate around each other.

The two stars of Algol circle each other every 2.87 days, crossing alternately in front of each other. The brighter star is blue-white and the dimmer one is yellow.

1 The blue star is hidden and the total brightness dips strongly over a few hours.

2 The blue star comes out from behind the yellow star, and the light of both stars is seen.

3 The blue star moves in front of the yellow star, reducing the total light by a tiny amount.

4 The blue star moves from in front, and both stars show all their light again.

The Stars

DOUBLE STARS AND BLACK HOLES

Astronomers have discovered that the behaviour of a few unusual double stars can only be explained if one of the stars is a star-sized black hole. A star-sized black hole contains at least as much matter as three Suns, all crammed into a ball several kilometres, or a few miles, across. A black hole itself cannot be seen, so a black hole on its own in space would be hard to find. However, the effects of a black hole's powerful gravity on a partner in a binary system are extremely powerful. It drags across streams of gas from its partner, which spiral around before eventually falling into the black hole. A famous example of this is Cygnus X-1.

Astronomers have been fascinated and puzzled by this strange phenomenon for over 20 years, because it is expelling streams of particles at more than 48,000 miles a second – a quarter of the speed of light. That's far faster than any velocities seen near other objects in the Milky Way.

Astronomers have now discovered that Cygnus X-1 is a supergiant that may be 11 times more massive than the Sun. The star is whipping around a black hole in the centre of the disc and the gravitational force from the black hole is stripping gas away from the star at a rate that would consume the entire Sun in just 10,000 years. As the black hole is unable to

blue giant star

black hole

gas blowing off the star

disc of gas collecting around the black hole

digest all of the gas it is ejected at incredible speeds into violent jets. The disc around a black hole can be seen because matter sucked into the centre is accelerated at high velocities and heated so that it gives off X-rays and light.

The Stars

THE LIFE OF A NOVA

Occasionally we can see a star in the night sky that suddenly increases in brightness by about 10,000 times. This is called a nova – an explosion in a double star where one partner is a white dwarf and the other is a more ordinary red dwarf. Understanding the nature of novae is essential to understanding the details of how our galaxy achieved its chemical composition.

Nova explosions are not completely destructive phenomena. In fact, after the explosion occurs the star recovers and starts shining again. Until recently, astronomers didn't know how long this recovery took, but new data analysed from ESA's XMM-Newton X-Ray satellite in October 2002, revealed that one particular exploding star repaired itself in less than three years. This is quite surprising, given the fact that the original explosion released around 100,000 times the energy given out by our Sun in a single year.

1 This pair of stars will eventually make a nova explosion. The red star is being overheated by the powerful energy from its white dwarf companion.

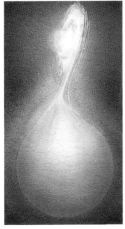

2 The red star distorts into a pear shape as the strong gravity of the white dwarf draws a stream of gas from it. The gas swirls into a disc then down on to the white dwarf's surface.

3 The white dwarf cannot take the pressure of all the new material. It gets hotter and hotter until a huge and massively bright nuclear explosion takes place on its surface.

The Stars

DYING STARS

A star, just like the Sun, shines steady for about 10,000 million years, but even a star cannot shine forever. There comes a time in a star's life when the source of its power simply starts to run out. When this happens its central core gradually starts to collapse inwards, causing its temperature to rise as it does so. Some of the heat energy released causes the remainder of the star to expand outwards, and it becomes a giant or a supergiant. When stars are finally dead all that remains are the cores that used to be their power sources.

DEATH OF A NORMAL STAR

After a star exhausts the supply of hydrogen in its core, there is no longer any source of heat to support the core against the force of gravity. The core of the star collapses under gravity's pull until it reaches a high enough density to start burning helium to carbon. In the meantime, the star's outer covering expands and the star evolves into a red giant. Eventually the Sun will lose all of the mass in its outer covering and leave behind a hot core of carbon imbedded in a nebula of expelled gas. Radiation from this hot core will ionize the nebula, producing a 'planetary nebula', similar to the nebulas seen around the remnants of other stars. The carbon core will eventually cool and become a white dwarf, the dense dim remnant of a once bright star.

DEATH OF A MASSIVE STAR

Because massive stars burn much brighter they perish more dramatically than the lower mass stars. When a star ten times larger than the Sun uses up all the helium in its core, the nuclear burning cycle continues. The carbon core contracts even further and reaches a high enough temperature to burn carbon into oxygen, neon, silicon, sulphur and finally to iron. Iron is the most stable form of nuclear matter and there is no energy to be gained by burning it to any heavier element.

Without any source of heat to balance the gravity, the iron core collapses until it reaches nuclear densities. This high density core resists further collapse causing the infalling matter to literally 'bounce' off the core, and it is this bounce that causes a supernova explosion.

For one brilliant month, a single star burns brighter than a whole galaxy of a billion stars. Supernova explosions inject carbon, oxygen, silicon and other heavy elements, including iron, into interstellar space. Supernova are also the sites where most of the heavier elements are produced. These heavier elements, incorporated with gas, will form into future generations of stars and planets. Without the supernova, the fiery death of massive stars, there would be no carbon, oxygen or indeed any other elements, that make life here on Earth possible.

The Stars

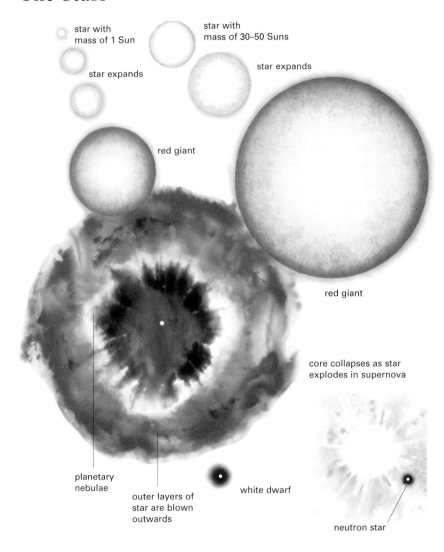

star with mass of 1 Sun

star expands

star with mass of 30–50 Suns

star expands

red giant

red giant

planetary nebulae

outer layers of star are blown outwards

white dwarf

core collapses as star explodes in supernova

neutron star

The Stars

PULSARS AND BLACK HOLES

A star may not be destroyed completely even following the enormous force of a supernova explosion. Part of the star can still be left as a mysterious object called a neutron star, which may go on to become an even stranger object – a black hole.

A neutron star forms because gravity pulls the centre of the massive star in on itself, causing the particles inside the atoms to cram closer and closer together. The atoms are unable to stand the strain and they collapse, forming neutrons in the core of the star. Because the mass has collapsed, the star also shrinks and instead of being many thousands of miles across, it is now only about 16 to 24 km (10 to 15 miles) in size. Neutron stars have the strongest magnetic fields in the known Universe, and the strongest neutron star fields are nearly 100 trillion times stronger than those of Earth.

PULSARS

A pulsar is a neutron star whose magnetic field sweeps through the Earth's line of site. When a neutron star shrinks, it spins faster – instead of turning once every few weeks like a full-sized star, it may turn many times a second. As it spins faster and faster the pull of the star's magnetic field also gets stronger. The magnetic field picks up electrons from the surface of the star which in turn are carried away out of the star's magnetic poles, creating beams of radio waves.

Astronomers are able to track these waves using radio telescopes, which detect radio waves rather than light waves. As the star turns, its radio waves sweep across space, and when a beam from a neutron star shines into a radio telescope, it produces a pulse in the telescope's receiver. Pulsars pulse because the rotation of the neutron star causes the radiation generated within the magnetic field to sweep in and out of our line of sight with a regular period.

BLACK HOLES

If the dying star is very massive, something even more peculiar happens. Because the weight of its outer layers is so great, it just goes on and on shrinking until eventually it becomes infinitely dense (or tightly packed) and far smaller even than the pupil in a human eye.

Because light is affected by gravity, as the dying star shrinks, the light has to struggle harder and harder against the star's gravity in order to leave it. Once the star shrinks past a certain size, no light can escape at all – in fact, nothing can get out and it becomes a black hole. Black holes can rotate very rapidly, dragging along the space around them. When more material falls in, it swirls and struggles wildly before being swallowed up. Astronomers have witnessed this violence, including the ejection of jets, with radio and X-ray observations, but they are not able to see the black hole itself.

The Stars

FORMATION OF A BLACK HOLE

A black hole forms when a massive star collapses at the end of its life because it cannot produce any more energy. Just as a rocket will fall back to Earth if it does not have enough power to beat the pull of gravity, light from a black hole will not be able to escape. The black hole itself is tiny, but the area from which light cannot escape – called the Schwarzschild radius – is usually several miles across.

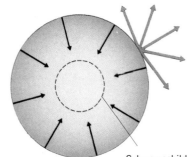

When a star shines, it gives off light in all directions.

Schwarzschild radius

Interesting facts about black holes

- The known closest black hole to Earth is Cygnus X-1, located about 8,000 light years away.
- Black holes can suck up other black holes when they come in close proximity. Usually the larger one will suck up the smaller one. Depending on the size of the matter that is making up the black holes, the size of the black hole created will differ. Direct collisions between black holes are rare, as black holes are very small for their mass. Black holes may also merge.
- At the centre of a black hole, space time has infinite curvature and matter is crushed to infinite density under the pull of 'infinite' gravity.
- Space and time cease to exist as we know them at the centre of a black hole.

As a dying star shrinks, the pull of its gravity gets stronger and light finds it increasingly hard to escape.

As the star nears the Schwarzschild radius, only light coming straight out can escape the pull of gravity.

When the star is smaller than the Schwarzschild radius, nothing can escape and the star becomes a black hole.

THE SOLAR SYSTEM

Until the sixteenth century, people believed that the Earth was fixed at the centre of the Universe, and that all the other planets circled around it. This was the claim of the Greek philosopher Ptolemy in about AD 150. However, certain astronomers were not satisfied with this belief, one of them being Nicolas Copernicus. Copernicus proposed an alternative theory – that the Earth was a planet orbiting the Sun, and that all planets moved in circles, one inside the other. Mercury and Venus had the smallest circles, smaller than that of the Earth, and therefore their position in the sky was always near the Sun's. Copernicus was very cautious about voicing this theory, and it was not until the end of his life that he actually saw his ideas published.

THE SUN'S FAMILY

The solar system consists of the Sun; nine planets, more than 130 satellites of the planets, a large number of small bodies (comets and asteroids) and the inter-planetary medium. There are, of course, probably many more planetary satellites that have not yet been discovered.

The inner solar system contains the Sun, Mercury, Venus, Earth and Mars. While the planets of the outer solar system are Jupiter, Saturn, Uranus, Neptune and Pluto.

The orbits of the planets are ellipses with the Sun at one focus, though all except Mercury and Pluto are very nearly circular. The orbits of the planets are all more or less in the same plane (called the ecliptic and defined by the plane of the Earth's orbit). The ecliptic is inclined only 7 degrees from the plane of the Sun's equator. Pluto's orbit deviates the most from the plane of the ecliptic with an inclination of 17 degrees. The diagram below shows the orbit of the four inner planets to scale, illustrating that they all orbit in the same direction (counter-clockwise).

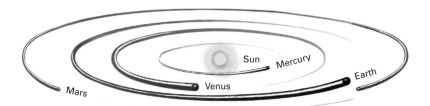

The Solar System

How the solar system was formed

The planets, asteroids and comets in the solar system are purely loose particles of debris left over from the formation of the Sun. Originally, the gas and dust that would become the Sun, was the core of a cloud much larger than the solar system, probably several light years across. This core rotated slowly at first, but as it collapsed it started to spin faster, and this prevented the material at the core's equator from collapsing as fast as material at the poles, until eventually the core became a spinning disc.

Gas and dust in the disc spiralled gradually into the centre, where it

1 The Sun, the planets and everything in the solar system formed 4.6 billion years ago from the same slowly rotating cloud of gas and dust in space. Drawn together by gravity, material collected in a disc around the young Sun.

2 Small clumps came together in the disc. Some collided hard and smashed apart again. Others gently merged to make larger clumps, which were bombarded by the debris that was left.

3 Over millions of years, these larger clumps became the planets we know today. Many smaller chunks of material became comets and asteroids.

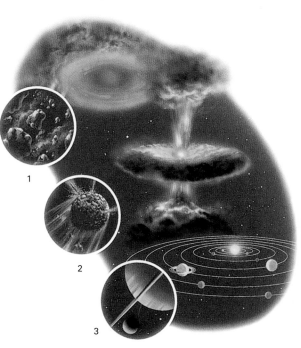

The Solar System

accumulated to form the Sun. However, because dust is denser than gas, some of the dust settled to the mid-plane of the disc. These dust particles stuck together to make clumps, then clumps stuck together to make rocks, then rocks collided to make planets. In the case of the planets, Jupiter, Saturn, Uranus and Neptune, the rocky cores were massive enough to also attract some of the gas – the outer layers of these planets are made up of hydrogen and other gases. So, in simple terms, the Sun is the collapsed core of an interstellar gas cloud, and the planets, asteroids and comets are small lumps of dust or ice chunks which stayed in orbit instead of spiralling into the Sun. The planets all formed within a very short period, probably a few million years, about 5 billion years ago.

THE PLANETS IN ORBIT

The Sun's gravity is pulling everything in the solar system towards it, but planets do not fall into the Sun because of their constant movement in orbit and it is their speed that balances the pull of the Sun's gravity. The Earth completes one rotation about its axis every 24 hours, but it completes one complete revolution around the Sun every 365 days. Just as the Moon orbits the Earth because of the pull of Earth's gravity, the Earth orbits the Sun because of the pull of the Sun's gravity.

The Earth actually travels in an elliptical orbit around the Sun, and this is because the Earth has a velocity in the direction perpendicular to the force of the Sun's pull. If the Sun wasn't there, the Earth would simply travel in a straight line. But because the Sun's gravity alters its course, it causes the Sun to travel in a shape very near to a circle.

Even when the solar system first formed, everything was circling in the huge, turning disc of gas and dust that surrounded the newborn Sun. The further away a planet is from the Sun, the slower it orbits. Pluto, the planet furthest from the Sun, is ten times slower than Mercury, which is the closest. Pluto also has a lot further to travel on its circuit because it is 100 times further from the Sun than Mercury, which means that Pluto takes more than 1,000 times longer to make an orbit than Mercury.

RIGHT: The Jupiter family.

The Solar System

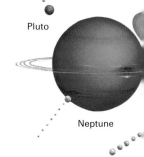

Pluto

Neptune

PLANETS AND THEIR MOONS

Seven of the planets orbiting the Sun have moons of their own, and the image on the right shows the planets and their moons to scale.

Mercury is the nearest planet to the Sun at a mean distance of 93.3 million km and travelling at about 48 km/s, it takes Mercury about 88 days to make one complete orbit. Mercury has no moons.

Venus is the second planet from the Sun at a mean distance of 108 million km and travelling at about 35 km/s, it takes Venus about 224.7 days to make one complete orbit. Venus has no moons.

The Earth is the third planet from the Sun at a mean distance of 150 million km and travelling at about 30 km/s, it takes Earth about 365.25 days to complete one orbit. The Earth has one moon, *the* Moon, and is the only planet known to support life for sure.

Mars is the fourth planet from the Sun and at a means distance of 228 million km and travelling at about 24 km/s, it takes Mars about 687 days to make one complete orbit. Mars has two irregularly shaped moons, Phobos (22 km across) and Deimos (13 km across).

Jupiter is the fifth planet from the Sun and the first of the gas giants. At a mean distance of 778 million km and travelling at about 13 km/s, it takes Jupiter about 11.86 years to orbit the Sun once. Jupiter has a narrow and faint ring system of very fine grained dust particles and 16 known moons. The largest moons, the

Galilean moons, are Io, Europa, Ganymede and Calisto. Io is known to be volcanically active, while Europa's icy surface layers are thought to hide underlying oceans of water which might support some form of life.

Saturn is the sixth planet from the Sun and the second of the gas giants. At a mean distance of 1.427 million km and travelling at about 10 km/s, it takes Saturn about 29.46 years to complete one orbit. Saturn has at least 18 confirmed moons, but possibly as many as 24, the largest of which is Titan (about 5,000 km across) and it has a thick, nitrogen-dominated atmosphere.

Discovered in 1781, Uranus is the seventh planet from the Sun and the third of the gas giants. At a mean distance of 2,871 million km and travelling at about 7 km/s, it takes Uranus about 84.01 years to complete one orbit. Uranus has a faint ring system made out of the darkest material known in the solar system and has 15 known moons, all of which are named after Shakespearean characters – the main ones being Miranda, Ariel, Umbriel, Titania and Oberon. The most interesting moon geologically is Miranda. Even though it is only 500 km in diameter, it shows surface geological features that are as varied as any site in

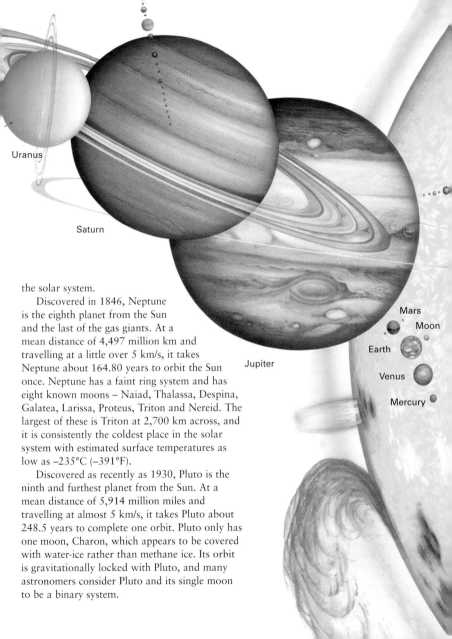

Uranus

Saturn

Jupiter

Mars

Moon

Earth

Venus

Mercury

the solar system.

Discovered in 1846, Neptune is the eighth planet from the Sun and the last of the gas giants. At a mean distance of 4,497 million km and travelling at a little over 5 km/s, it takes Neptune about 164.80 years to orbit the Sun once. Neptune has a faint ring system and has eight known moons – Naiad, Thalassa, Despina, Galatea, Larissa, Proteus, Triton and Nereid. The largest of these is Triton at 2,700 km across, and it is consistently the coldest place in the solar system with estimated surface temperatures as low as –235°C (–391°F).

Discovered as recently as 1930, Pluto is the ninth and furthest planet from the Sun. At a mean distance of 5,914 million miles and travelling at almost 5 km/s, it takes Pluto about 248.5 years to complete one orbit. Pluto only has one moon, Charon, which appears to be covered with water-ice rather than methane ice. Its orbit is gravitationally locked with Pluto, and many astronomers consider Pluto and its single moon to be a binary system.

The Solar System

THE ROCKY PLANETS

The inner planets Mercury, Venus, Earth and Mars, as well as Earth's moon, are known as the rocky planets. This is because they are mainly made up of iron and rock and have cratered surfaces. When the planets first formed, about 4.6 billion years ago, there were many chunks of left-over ice and rock circling around the Sun. For millions of years thereafter, there was a period called 'runaway growth', during which these giant rocks collided and merged to form just a few dozen huge planetary embryos. Initially the new planets were extremely hot, mainly due to the force of their impacts, and inside they were hot enough for the rock and metal to melt. Eventually these embryos joined forces to create the inner four 'terrestrial' planets – Mercury, Venus, Earth and Mars. Although the cores of Mercury, Mars and the Moon have now cooled and hardened, the inner cores of Venus and Earth are still liquid.

SHAPED BY VOLCANOES

All the rocky planets, including the Moon, has a heavy core of rock or iron, and a layer of lighter rock called the mantle, which surrounds the core. On the outside there is a solid crust which is made up of strong rock a few miles thick. Just as they have on Earth, volcanoes have played a powerful role in shaping other worlds in our solar system. For example, Venus is covered with volcanoes, and many of them are still very young. These were detected by the Magellan spacecraft and although it is likely that Venus has active volcanoes, there has been no evidence of present-day eruptions.

Mars also has many distinctive volcanic features, including the largest volcano in the solar system – Olympus Mons – which towers 26 km (16 miles) over the Martian landscape.

Volcanoes also shaped Mercury, where volcano activity appears to have stopped

Maxwell Montes, Venus
12 km (7 miles) high

Mauna Kea, Hawaii,
Earth, 9 km (5 miles)
high from the sea bed

Earth's sea level

The Solar System

early in the planet's history, billions of years ago. On the Moon, also, volcanoes were active until around 3 billion years ago.

On Jupiter's moon, Europa, volcanoes may still be active under the fractured outer surface of ice. There is also evidence that Jupiter's moon Io, which is about the size of our Moon, is the most volcanically active body in the solar system. Recent images that were obtained by NASA's Galileo spacecraft have revealed that there are around 100 active volcanoes, each comprising of many large volcanic depressions (or *calderas*). Io's craters are remarkably hot, and measurements taken prove that the temperatures are far hotter than any active volcano on Earth.

At some time all the inner planets and the Moon have had volcanic activity, which caused deep fissures to open in the crust and hot molten rock, called lava, to flood out from the mantle underneath. The Moon, Mercury and Mars, have since cooled down and become solid, so their volcanoes are now totally inactive. However, lava, ash and gas still belch out of volcanoes on Earth and Venus. Volcanic eruptions over billions of years allow gas trapped inside a planet to escape to the surface, and this is how the atmospheres of Earth, Venus and Mars first formed. However, over the last 3.5 billion years, the atmosphere on Earth has changed considerably due to the effect that plant and animal life has had on our planet.

Giant volcanoes
Venus, Earth and Mars all have mountainous volcanoes, but those on Mars are the largest. Mars is smaller than Earth or Venus, so it has weaker gravity and lets mountains build up higher. In addition, its crust does not move about, so volcanic eruptions tend to happen again and again in the same place, with each lava flow piling on top of the last. Mars has the highest volcano in the solar system, Olympus Mons.

Olympus Mons, Mars, 42 km (26 miles) high

The Solar System

COMPARING THE ROCKY PLANETS AND EARTH'S MOON

The terrestrial planets are the small rocky planets, which may or may not have any atmosphere. The Earth's moon can be thought of as a terrestrial planet, even though it is technically a moon, because it orbits a planet rather than the Sun. Planets have a steadily decreasing source of heat from the decay over time of natural radioactive elements at their core. The larger the planet the slower they cool down, and this is mainly because they have less surface area. A geologically active planet has volcanoes and earthquakes which help to renew

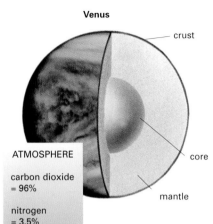

Venus

crust

core

mantle

ATMOSPHERE

carbon dioxide = 96%

nitrogen = 3.5%

other gases = 0.5%

The thick atmosphere on Venus contains about 100 times as much gas as Earth's atmosphere. It has dense clouds.

Mercury

crust

core

mantle

Mercury has no real atmosphere, but there is a very tiny amount of gas (mainly sodium and helium) around it.

the surface of the planet.

Whether or not a planet has atmosphere depends on many things, for example, the mass of the planet, the distance of the planet from the Sun and the amount of volcanic activity that has occurred. Atmospheres can help to shield the planet from meteor and comet impacts, erode the surface, shield the surface from harmful light like ultraviolet, trap heat and moderate temperature, as well as provide gases that are essential for plants and animals to breathe. A geologically young planet means that the surface has been altered by the effect of

The Solar System

volcanoes or erosion, in such a way as to erase evidence of its past, such as craters from meteorite impact. All the planets in the solar system have been hit by many meteorites and comets since they formed billions of years ago, and many show the scars from those multitudes of impacts.

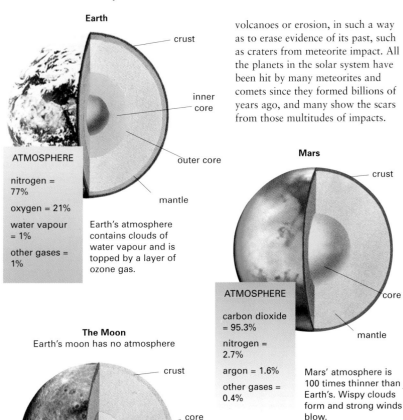

Earth

crust

inner core

outer core

mantle

ATMOSPHERE

nitrogen = 77%

oxygen = 21%

water vapour = 1%

other gases = 1%

Earth's atmosphere contains clouds of water vapour and is topped by a layer of ozone gas.

Mars

crust

core

mantle

ATMOSPHERE

carbon dioxide = 95.3%

nitrogen = 2.7%

argon = 1.6%

other gases = 0.4%

Mars' atmosphere is 100 times thinner than Earth's. Wispy clouds form and strong winds blow.

The Moon
Earth's moon has no atmosphere

crust

core

lower mantle

upper mantle

The Solar System

MERCURY

Mercury, named for the fast-footed Roman messenger of the gods, is the closest planet to the Sun. Mercury is also the smallest planet in the solar system after Pluto. Because it is so close to the Sun it is a difficult planet to study, although it is possible to see for a little while low in the evening sky just after sunset. Again, because of its close proximity to the Sun its orbit is much faster than other planets, and only takes 88 days to make a complete orbit. However, in contrast Mercury spins very slowly, and takes 59 of our days to make one entire spin. That means that it spins only three times for every two journeys it

MERCURY FACT FILE
Atmosphere:
  None
Temperature:
  −200°C to 425°C or −330°F to 797°F
Rotation period:
  59 days ($^2/_3$ of a Mercurian year)
Geologically old surface:
  Covered with impact craters
Water:
  None, except possibly ice at poles, so no life
Size:
  About 40% the diameter of Earth
Mass:
  Much lower than the Earth's (about 6% of the Earth's mass)
Gravity at the surface:
  37% of the Earth's gravity
Distance from the Sun:
  About 40% of the distance between the Earth and the Sun
Distance from the Earth:
  Moderately far away (60% of the distance between Earth and the Sun)

Directly opposite the Caloris Basin is a jumbled landscape called 'weird terrain' that may have been formed by shock waves from the impact that produced the basin. Similar terrain is found opposite huge impact basins on the Moon.

The Solar System

makes around the Sun, and this has a very strange effect on the length of its day. Days and nights are long on Mercury. The combination of a slow rotation relative to the stars and a rapid revolution around the Sun means that one Mercury solar day takes 176 Earth days or two Mercury years – the time it takes the innermost planet to complete two orbits around the Sun.

Mercury appears to have a crust of light silicate rock like that of Earth. Astronomers believe that Mercury has a heavy iron rich core making up slightly less than half of its volume. That would make Mercury's core proportionally larger than the Moon's core or those of any of the other planets.

Mercury is one of the most cratered objects in the solar system, and its surface has been shaped over the years by the many impacts and volcanic eruptions. Shortly after all the craters formed, Mercury shrank in size as its surface cooled, which had the effect of making the crust wrinkle up in certain places. One of the craters discovered on the surface of Mercury is huge. It is called the Caloris Basin and measures more than 1,287 km (800 miles) across and is surrounded by a bull's-eye of several rings of mountains, covering over 3,701 km (2,300 miles).

MARINER 10

Until Mariner 10 little was known about the planet Mercury. Even the best telescopic views from Earth showed Mercury as an indistinct object lacking in any surface detail. But this is because the planet is so close to the Sun that it is normally lost in solar glare. Even when Mercury is visible from Earth, just after sunset or before dawn, it is obscured by the haze and dust in our atmosphere. Only radar telescopes gave any hint of Mercury's surface conditions.

The primary objective of Mariner 10, was to obtain close-up images of Mercury. It was launched on November 3, 1973, from the Kennedy Space Center in Florida and, after a journey of nearly five months, including a fly-by of Venus, the spacecraft passed within 703 km (437 miles) of the solar system's innermost planet on March 29, 1974.

The photographs Mariner 10 radioed back to Earth revealed an ancient, heavily cratered surface, with huge cliffs crisscrossing the planet. These cliffs are as high as 3 km (2 miles) and as long as 500 km (310 miles).

The complex instruments carried on Mariner 10 discovered that Mercury has a weak magnetic field and a trace of atmosphere – a trillionth the density of Earth's atmosphere – and composed chiefly of argon, neon and helium. When the planet's orbit takes it closest to the Sun, surface temperatures range from 467°C (872°F) on Mercury's sunlit side to –183°C (–298°F) on the dark side. This range in surface temperature is the largest for a single body in the solar system. Mercury literally bakes and freezes at the same time.

The Solar System

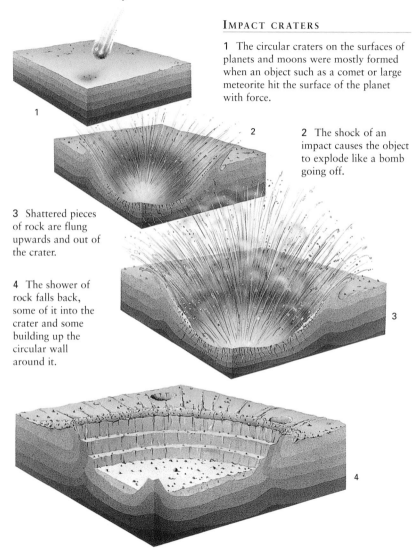

IMPACT CRATERS

1 The circular craters on the surfaces of planets and moons were mostly formed when an object such as a comet or large meteorite hit the surface of the planet with force.

2 The shock of an impact causes the object to explode like a bomb going off.

3 Shattered pieces of rock are flung upwards and out of the crater.

4 The shower of rock falls back, some of it into the crater and some building up the circular wall around it.

The Solar System

VENUS

Venus is the second planet from the Sun in our solar system and its orbit brings it within 42 million km (26 million miles) of Earth, closer than any other planet. It is the hottest planet in our solar system and its surface is covered with fast-moving sulphuric acid clouds which help to trap the heat from the Sun. It has a thick atmosphere which mainly consists of carbon dioxide. Venus has an iron core but only a very weak magnetic field. The bright surface that is visible on Venus is merely hiding a hot, inhospitable, volcanic world. Nothing could survive the conditions on this planet. It would simply asphyxiate in the poisonous atmosphere, be cooked in the extreme heat or crushed by the enormous atmospheric pressure.

Venus is also known as the 'morning star' or 'evening star' since it is visible and quite bright at either dawn or dusk. These are the only times that it is visible as it is closer to the Sun than Earth, and the Sun obscures our vision. Just like the Moon, Venus' appearance from Earth changes as it orbits around the Sun. It goes from full to gibbous to crescent to new and back again.

Venus is about 12,104 km (7,521 miles) in diameter and is about 95 percent of the diameter of Earth. Venus is the closest to Earth in size and mass than any of the other planets.

The gravity on Venus is 91 percent of that on Earth, which means a 45-kg (100-lb) person would only weigh 41 kg (91 lb) on Venus.

Venus rotates very slowly, and each day on Venus takes 243 Earth days, and 224.7 Earth days for Venus to complete its orbit of the Sun. The same side of Venus always faces Earth when the two planets are closest together. Venus rotates clockwise, which is the opposite direction to Earth and the other planets. The first spacecraft to reach Venus was *Venera 3* from the USSR and was launched on November 16, 1965. On March 1, 1966, the spacecraft arrived at Venus and a capsule parachuted down to the planet, but contact was lost just before entry into the atmosphere.

The Solar System

ATMOSPHERE AND SURFACE

The atmosphere on Venus is exceptionally hot and dry and contains about 100 times as much gas as Earth's atmosphere. The atmospheric pressure – the weight of the atmosphere pressing down on the planet's surface – is about 90 times greater than on Earth. Because of Venus' extremely thick atmosphere, the planet suffers from a runaway greenhouse effect. Energy from the Sun passes through the atmosphere to the planet's surface, where it is absorbed and radiated at longer wavelengths as infrared. Venus' atmosphere traps these longer wavelengths so they cannot escape into space, and the trapped energy builds up, so the planet grows hotter and hotter.

With a surface temperature of almost 480°C (900°F), Venus is hot enough to melt lead and because of Venus' heavy atmosphere, the planet's surface pressure is very high. Pressure is defined as the weight of the atmosphere pressing down on you per unit area. On Earth, we don't notice the air pressure at all, but on Venus the thick atmosphere would make it difficult to see objects very far away

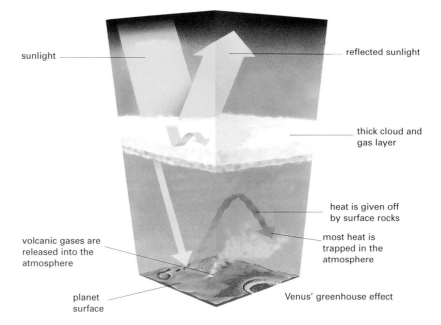

sunlight

reflected sunlight

thick cloud and gas layer

heat is given off by surface rocks

most heat is trapped in the atmosphere

volcanic gases are released into the atmosphere

planet surface

Venus' greenhouse effect

The Solar System

from you. Since carbon dioxide is poisonous to humans, you would not be able to breathe on Venus.

Although the gravity on Venus is about the same as on Earth, the weight of the atmosphere would crush you. There are always thunderstorms somewhere on the planet, and lightning flashes about 25 times every second somewhere in Venus' atmosphere. This atmosphere consists mainly of carbon dioxide, which is a gas that is not breathable and, in addition, the clouds of Venus contain drops of sulphuric acid, which is a poisonous chemical.

Despite the thick atmosphere, there is hardly any wind to wear away the mountains, volcanoes and craters that are a feature of the surface of Venus. In fact the surface features have not changed at all since they formed millions of years ago. Venus has literally hundreds of thousands of volcanoes, some of which are extremely large, but most are about 3 km (2 miles) across and about 90 metres (300 feet) high. The thin, rocky skin on Venus' surface literally floats on top of hot molten rock, which tries to burst out wherever it can.

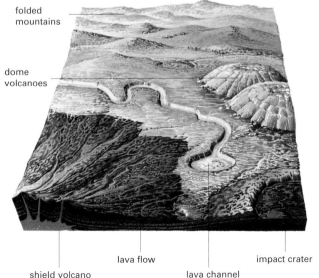

folded mountains

dome volcanoes

shield volcano

lava flow

lava channel

impact crater

Volcanoes are common on Venus. Repeated lava flows built up shield volcanoes, while the pancake-shaped dome volcanoes – which are unique to Venus – were made by single eruptions of very sticky lava. Folded mountains rose where the planet's crust moved and got squeezed. The planet also has nearly 900 impact craters.

The Solar System

The volcanic surface has been hit by many meteorites and these have left craters, most of which are at least 10 km (6 miles) across, because any smaller rocks would simply have been destroyed by the planet's atmosphere. Some bounced off the surface, while others slowed down or burnt up in the thick atmosphere before they struck the surface. Large craters are not as common on Venus as say on the Moon or Mercury, because many of them that were made by large rocks crashing into the planet when the solar system was first formed, would long since have been covered by the flows of volcanic lava.

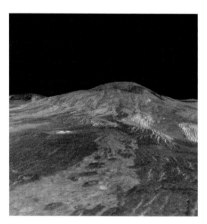

ABOVE: Pictures of the surface of Venus came from the Magellan spacecraft (*see opposite page*), which orbited the planet from 1990 to 1994. It used radar to look through the clouds, and an altimeter to measure the height of the surface.

VENUS FACT FILE

Atmosphere:
Very dense (90 times as dense as the Earth's, with a pressure equal to $1/2$ mile under water) carbon dioxide, with small amounts of nitrogen and sulphur dioxide.

Temperature:
377°C to 487°C or 711°F to 909°F

Rotation period:
243 days (almost equal to the 224.7 day Venus year)

Geologically old surface:
With many impact craters compared to the Earth, but very few compared to the Moon

Surface age:
Half a billion years or so

Water:
None, so no life

Size:
Approximately the same as Earth

Mass:
Approximately the same as Earth

Gravity at the surface:
88% of the Earth's gravity

Distance from the Sun:
About 72% of the distance between the Earth and the Sun

Number of known moons:
None

Distance from the Earth:
Moderately far away (28% of the distance between Earth and the Sun)

Distinguishing features:
Poisonous clouds totally cover a once volcanic surface

The Solar System

THE MAGELLAN MISSION

Before *Magellan*, more than 20 spacecraft from the United States and the USSR had already probed the surface of Venus. Magellan was launched from Cape Canaveral on May 4, 1989, aboard the space shuttle *Atlantis*. The spacecraft arrived at Venus on August 10, 1990, after travelling more than 1.3 billion km (806 million miles) in a path that took the probe around the Sun one and a half times.

Because Venus is hidden from our view by clouds, the Magellan spacecraft was sent into orbit around the planet to make a map of its surface using radar. Radar uses radio waves which easily penetrate the clouds, and Magellan bounced radar pulses off the surface of Venus and beamed the reflected pulses back to Earth. From these, a computer worked out what Venus' surface must look like. Each time Magellan circled the planet, it mapped a strip 24 km (15 miles) long and it took three years to build up a complete picture of the planet beneath the clouds.

The images and data collected from the Magellan mission substantially increased scientists' knowledge of Venus. The mission came to an end in 1994 and Magellan changed course in a gradual drive towards Venus so that scientists could collect data about the planet's atmosphere. Magellan was the first spacecraft to purposefully crash, but the radio signal was lost on October 12, 1994, and the spacecraft was presumed lost the following day.

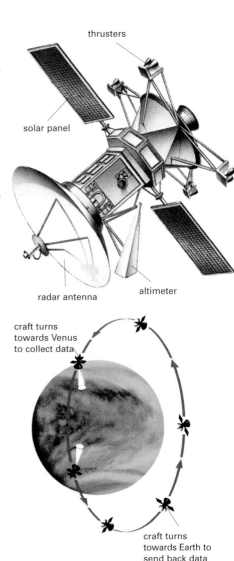

thrusters

solar panel

radar antenna

altimeter

craft turns towards Venus to collect data

craft turns towards Earth to send back data

The Solar System

THE EARTH

Earth is the third planet from the Sun and the fifth largest. Although Earth can be studied without the aid of spacecraft, it was not until the twentieth century that we had maps of the entire planet. Pictures that have been taken from space are of considerable importance, for example, they are an enormous help in weather prediction and especially in the tracking and predicting of hurricanes.

The Earth is divided into several layers: the crust, upper mantle, transition region, lower mantle, 'D' layer, outer core and inner core. The crust varies considerably in thickness, it is thinner under the oceans, and thicker under the continents. The inner core and crust are solid, while the outer core and mantle layers are semi-fluid. Most of the mass of the Earth is in the mantle with most of

the remainder in the core. The part of Earth that we actually inhabit is only a tiny fraction of the whole mass.

The majority of the Earth is inaccessible and we have to rely on seismic techniques and samples obtained from the upper mantle in the form of lava from volcanoes. This gives us some idea of what goes on at the centre of Earth, the temperature of which is hotter than that of the surface of the Sun.

Unlike the other terrestrial planets, Earth's crust is divided into separate solid plates which float around independently on top of the hot mantle below. The theory that describes this is known as plate tectonics. Plate tectonics is a relatively new theory that has revolutionized the way geologists think about the Earth. In simple terms, the size and position of the plates change over time. The edges of these plates, where they move against each other, are sites of intense geologic activity, such as earthquakes, volcanoes and mountain building. Plate tectonics is actually a combination of two earlier ideas, continental drift and sea-floor spreading. Continental drift is the movement of continents over the Earth's surface and in their change in position relative to each other. Sea-floor spreading is the creation of new oceanic crust at mid-ocean ridges and movement of the crust away from the mid-ocean ridges.

LEFT: A view of Earth from space.

The Solar System

A PLACE TO LIVE

We are able to live on Earth because of its thick atmosphere, which provides us with air to breathe but also shields us from radiation from space. The atmosphere on Earth is 77 percent nitrogen, 21 percent oxygen, with traces of argon, carbon dioxide and water. There was probably a very much larger amount of carbon dioxide in the atmosphere when Earth was first formed, but it has since been consumed by living plants, dissolved in the oceans and incorporated into carbonate rocks. Oxygen is what we breathe to keep us alive, and as you go higher the atmosphere starts to thin out – there is less of it so it is harder to breathe.

The atmosphere also acts like a blanket helping to keep the planet warm. It raises the surface temperature by 30°C (54°F) – without the atmosphere our planet would simply freeze. Earth is the only planet that has liquid water on the surface which, together with the heat and light from the Sun makes it the only planet in the solar system, as far as we know, that can sustain life.

HOW IT ALL STARTED

Earth had an atmosphere soon after it was formed, around 4.5 billion years ago, but it did not contain oxygen as it does today. The atmosphere was made up of carbon dioxide, water vapour and nitrogen released from volcanoes. Gradually the Earth began to cool, and as it did so the water vapour turned to rain. The rain eventually formed the oceans that now cover three-quarters of the Earth's surface. This was where the first tiny forms of life began, in the oceans around 4 billion years ago.

Water is able to hold carbon dioxide and early life in the seas used up this gas to survive and form shells. The first green plants on our planets also used up the carbon dioxide, and in so doing released oxygen into the atmosphere. Around 2 billion years ago plant and animal life had removed the majority of the carbon dioxide from the air and at the same time produced large amounts of oxygen. If this had not happened the carbon dioxide would have caused the Earth to be boiling hot, similar to Venus.

THE OZONE LAYER

About 50 km (30 miles) above the surface of the Earth is a special atmosphere called the ozone layer. This layer forms a thin shield in the upper atmosphere, protecting life on Earth from the Sun's ultraviolet rays. In the 1980s, scientists began accumulating evidence that the ozone layer was gradually being depleted due to pollution from the Earth's surface. Depletion of the ozone layer results in increased ultraviolet radiation reaching the Earth's surface, which in turn can lead to a greater chance of overexposure to ultraviolet radiation and the related health effects of skin cancer, cataracts and immune suppression.

The Solar System

Ozone is a naturally occurring gas that is found in two layers of the atmosphere. In the layer surrounding the Earth's surface the troposphere ground-level or bad ozone is an air pollutant that is a key ingredient of urban smog. The troposphere extends up to the stratosphere, which is where good ozone protects life on Earth by absorbing some of the Sun's ultraviolet rays. Stratospheric ozone is most concentrated between 9 to 48 km (6 to 30 miles) above the Earth's surface.

THE WEATHER

Earth's weather and its liquid interior make it the most changeable planet in the solar system. Large storms can cause massive floods, moving billions of tons of rocks and soil. Flood waters wear away the land quickly and carry soil and rock into the oceans. Even more dramatic are the effects of volcanoes and earthquakes, which are caused by movements in the plates of rock in the Earth's crust. Volcanic eruptions build new land from lava and ash, and pump steam, carbon dioxide and poisonous gases into the atmosphere. Earthquakes are just as devastating as they shake the land, sometimes violently, enough to open huge cracks in the surface.

The air on Earth is constantly on the move, creating winds and storms. The pull of gravity from the Moon and the Sun cause tides, which raise and lower the sea level twice a day. When there is a big storm at high tide, strong winds whip up giant waves and send them crashing to the shore with destructive force.

THE AURORA

Around the Earth's North and South poles, the skies at night are lit up by amazing auroras. They are caused by the

Each aurora forms a ring of about 4,023 km (2,500 miles) around one of the Earth's magnetic poles. The thicker air lower down in the atmosphere glows green, and the upper air glows red. The beautiful aurora to be seen in the north is called the Northern Lights or *aurora borealis (left)*, while the one in the south is the Southern Lights or *aurora australis (right)*.

The Solar System

solar wind, which is made up of protons and electrons which are given off by the Sun. Protons and electrons are affected by magnetism and, unlike gravity, magnetism only affects certain things such as some metals. The Earth has a magnetic field surrounding it and this is strongest towards the Earth's North and South poles. The particles of the solar wind passing Earth are attracted to these magnetic fields, and they collide with Earth's upper atmosphere at speeds of up to 2,011 km (1,250 miles) per second. This makes the gases in the thin air start to glow, and streams of these particles cause the beautiful auroras.

EARTH FACT FILE
Atmosphere:
  Composed of nitrogen, oxygen, carbon
  dioxide and trace gases
Temperature:
  –88°C to 58°C or –127°F to 136°F
Rotation period:
  24 hours
Geologically young surface:
  Has volcanoes, weather, erosion and
  very few remaining impact craters
Diameter at equator:
  12,756 km (7.926 miles)
Title of axis on which it spins:
  23.44 degrees
Distance from the Sun:
  92 million miles
Gravity at the surface:
  The amount of gravity tugging down at
  any point of the Earth is proportional to
  the amount of mass sitting at that
  point. This means, the more mass an
  area has, the stronger the gravitational
  force will be at that point.

From our journeys into space, we have learned much about our home planet. The first American satellite, *Explorer 1*, was launched from Cape Canaveral in Florida on January 31, 1958, and discovered an intense radiation zone, now called the Van Allen radiation belts, surrounding Earth. Since then, other research satellites have revealed much about our planet and its constant changes.

The Solar System

THE SEASONS

The reason that we experience seasons on our planet is because the Earth spins on its axis, which produces night and day. However, not only does it spin on its axis it also moves around the Sun in an elliptical (or elongated) circle; an orbit that takes about 365.25 days to complete. The Earth's spin axis is tilted with respect to its orbital plane and this is what causes the seasons. When the Earth's axis points towards the Sun, it is summer for that hemisphere. When the Earth's axis points away, it will be winter. Since the tilt of the axis is 23.5 degrees, the North Pole can never point directly at the Sun, but on the Summer Solstice it points as close as it can, whereby on the Winter Solstice as far as it can. Midway between these two times, in spring and autumn, the spin axis of the Earth points 90 degrees away from the Sun. This means that on this date, day and night have about the same length – 12 hours each, more or less.

To try and explain further why we are affected by the Earth's tilt, imagine that the Sun is directly overhead, which means that the light is falling straight on you, and so more light (and subsequently more heat) hit each square centimetre of the ground. When the Sun is lower in the sky, the light gets more spread out over the surface of the Earth, and so less heat per square centimetre can be absorbed. Since the Earth's axis is tilted, the Sun is higher when you are on the part of the Earth where the axis points towards the Sun,

and lower on the part of the Earth where the axis points away from the Sun.

In the Northern hemisphere, the axis points most towards the Sun in June – specifically around June 21 – and away from the Sun around December 21. This corresponds to the Winter and Summer Solstice, or the midpoints of winter and summer. For the Southern hemisphere, of course, it is reversed. The word solstice is the Latin word for 'the sun stands'.

For both the hemispheres, the Earth is 90 degrees away from the Sun around March 21 and then again around September 21 and this corresponds to the Autumn and Spring Equinox. Everywhere in the world has about 12 hours of daylight and 12 hours of night. The word equinox is Latin for 'equal night'.

Predicting the seasons

The ability to predict the seasons – by tracking the rising and setting points of the Sun throughout the year – was key to survival in ancient times. Babylonians, Mayans and other cultures developed complex systems for monitoring seasonal shifts. But it took centuries more to unravel the science behind the seasons.

The Solar System

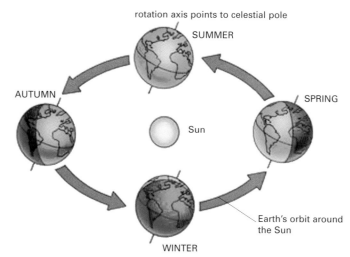

rotation axis points to celestial pole

SUMMER

AUTUMN

Sun

SPRING

Earth's orbit around the Sun

WINTER

Earth's axis tilts 23.5 degrees

celestial axis tilts 23.5 degrees

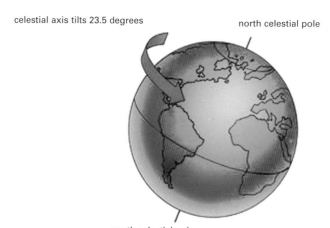

north celestial pole

south celestial pole

The Solar System

THE MOON

The Moon is the constant companion to Earth as it travels through space and is its only natural satellite. Although the Moon is relatively small, it dominates the night sky because it is so much closer than any other planet, and it is the only other world that humans have ever visited. The Moon lies about 384,000 km (239,000 miles) away from Earth and takes about one month to complete its orbit.

THE MOON'S PHASES

As the Moon circles our planet, we can see it go through different phases, with more or less of its surface lit up. The Moon, like every other planet and satellite in the solar system, shines not with its own light but with the reflected light of the Sun. This means that at any point in time one half of the Moon is lit while the other half is in darkness. As the Moon revolves around the Earth, over a period of about 29 days, a varying proportion of the illuminated half can be seen from Earth. The boundary between the light and dark halves, called the terminator, migrates from east to west across the lunar surface and, because the Moon is spherical, creates the familiar phases – crescent, full, quarter etc.

The Moon rises and sets in roughly the same directions as the Sun, but about 49 minutes later each night than the night before. The cycle of phases begins with a new moon, when the Moon passes close

The Moon looks much bigger when it is low in the sky, but this is just an illusion because we are comparing it with objects on the horizon. When it is higher, there is nothing familiar to compare it with.

to the Sun and so cannot be seen against its overwhelming glare.

A couple of evenings later the Moon has moved away from the Sun. It sets a little after sunset, and so can be briefly observed as a thin crescent low in the west. The phase of the Moon facing the Earth is always the exact opposite of the phase of the Earth facing the Moon, so although very little of the sunlit portion of the Moon is visible from the Earth there is quite a lot of earthshine on the dark portion. Sometimes this is enough to faintly reveal the Moon's whole disc.

The Solar System

Over successive nights it becomes easier to see as it sets progressively later and as its phase becomes larger (called waxing). About a week after the new moon the phase has reached a semicircle. Despite the shape, this a called the first quarter, because it marks one quarter of a lunation. This is the phase most often seen during the daytime, as it rises around noon, sets at about midnight and is highest around 6 p.m.

As the waxing continues, the next phase is called gibbous – a disc with just a crescent missing from it. Then, some 14 days after the new moon, we see a Full Moon – the Sun and the Moon are on opposite sides of the Earth, and when one sets the other rises.

From this point onwards for the remainder of the lunation the Moon's phase becomes thinner again, called waning. It passes through gibbous phase, then roughly three weeks after new, it becomes a half circle again, the mirror of the First Quarter, called the Last Quarter.

The last phase is a crescent again, ending with another chance to see the effect of earthshine. Then, about 29 days after the last new moon, another takes place, with the Sun and Moon rising and setting at much the same times, and the whole process repeats.

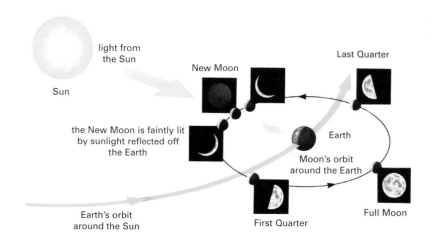

light from the Sun

Sun

the New Moon is faintly lit by sunlight reflected off the Earth

New Moon

Last Quarter

Earth

Moon's orbit around the Earth

Full Moon

Earth's orbit around the Sun

First Quarter

The Solar System

HOW DID THE MOON FORM?

The main key to the origin of the Moon came from the rocks brought back by Apollo astronauts. They found that the chemical make-up of the rocks on the Moon and those of the Earth are very similar. This means that the Earth and the Moon formed together somehow.

The leading theory for the formation of the Moon is that a large object about the size of Mars hit the Earth early in the history of the solar system. The glancing blow blasted pieces of the Earth into orbit, where they quickly (within a few days) reassembled to form the Moon. The rest of the Mars-like object merged with the Earth. While this theory may sound far-fetched, computer simulations have shown that it works very well in explaining the known facts about the Earth/Moon system.

1 Soon after Earth formed, it may have been struck by another rocky planet as large as Mars.
2 & 3 Using supercomputers, astronomers have shown what might have happened. Rocks from Earth's outer layers and from the object that hit it were smashed into a great plume of debris.
4 Some of the pieces clumped together to make the Moon.

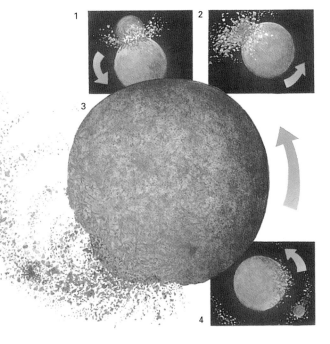

The Solar System

THE MOUNTAINS AND SEAS

When our ancestors stared up at the Moon, they never saw the mountains, nor the huge impact craters or long rift valleys, but they did believe they saw one kind of formation similar to the Earth – they believed they saw seas.

However, the seas didn't actually exist, even though today, we still call these areas 'seas'. These seas, known by names each beginning with the latin word for sea, 'Mare'. are: Mare Tranquillitatis, Crisium, Imbrium, Nectaris, Nubium, Humorum, Serenitatis, Vaporum, Fecunditatis and Oceanus Procellarum. The size of the Maria added together make up about 17 percent of the half of the surface of the Moon visible from Earth.

What we are really seeing are dark mares, which are the dark, smooth regions of the lunar surface. For a long time, astronomers were unsure as to the nature of these areas. Some thought they were large fields of dust blown by millions of years of micro-meteorite erosion on the Moon. Others believed that vast quantities of tiny asteroids had struck the mountains of the Moon, slowly causing them to erode, spreading dust for hundreds of miles across the lunar surface. However, although we now know there is micro-meteorite erosion on the Moon, and in fact the only kind of erosion, it is still not responsible for the formation of the Maria of our sister

ABOVE: The near side of the Moon showing the seas with their English names.

world. Further investigation has now revealed them to be majestic stretches of solidified lava, covered by several inches of Moon dust.

Unlike Earth, where some of the mountains are the youngest landforms, the mountains on the Moon are the oldest part of its surface that we can see. The Moon has now cooled and become almost completely solid inside. The Moon always keeps the same face to Earth, but photographs sent back from spacecraft show that the side turned away from us is covered by cratered mountains.

The Solar System

DUST AND CRATERS

The surface of the Moon is covered by a fine, crunchy dust and every time the surface was hit by a meteorite it crushed a patch of surface into even finer dust. It is these impacts that formed all the craters that we can see on the surface of the Moon. The explosion and excavation of materials at the site of impact created piles of rock (called ejecta) around the circular hole, as well as bright streaks of target material (called rays) which were thrown for great distances.

By recording the number, size and extent of erosion of craters, lunar geologists can determine the ages of different areas on the Moon and can piece together a geologic history. Some of the craters that have been examined are extremely large, for example, Tycho is 85 km (53 miles) across and has a peak in the centre 2.3 km (7,500 feet) high, while Copernicus is 93 km (58 miles) wide. Both of these craters have bright rays around them where debris was scattered over an enormous area. The largest crater is called Bailly and measures 295 km (183 miles), but smaller craters are much more common.

Impact craters are not unique to the Moon, they are also found on all the terrestrial planets and on many moons of the outer planets.

Most of the craters on the Moon were formed around 4 billion years ago, soon after the Moon and the Earth solidified. Back then we believe the solar system was full of left-over bits of rock and ice that hadn't yet been incorporated into planets. The rate of meteorite strikes was much, much higher than it is today. The Moon has probably gained three or four new craters within the last million years.

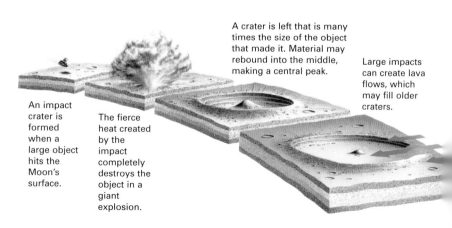

A crater is left that is many times the size of the object that made it. Material may rebound into the middle, making a central peak.

Large impacts can create lava flows, which may fill older craters.

An impact crater is formed when a large object hits the Moon's surface.

The fierce heat created by the impact completely destroys the object in a giant explosion.

The Solar System

OUTSTANDING FEATURES ON THE NORTHWEST QUADRANT

Most of the northwest quadrant is occupied by three seas, the sprawling Oceanus Procellarum, Mare Imbrium and in the north, Mare Frigoris. Oceanus Procellarum is the largest sea on the Moon and, unlike most of the others, it has no definite boundary. Among the craters that grace this quadrant, Copernicus, Kepler and Aristarchus are outstanding, being at the hub of spectacular ray systems at full moon.

Archimedes (75 km, 47 miles) is the largest of a prominent trio of craters, the others being Autolycus and Aristillus. All have flat, lava-filled floors.

Aristarchus is only 37 km (23 miles) across, but is the brightest feature on the Moon. Nearby is a deep, winding fault called Schroter's Valley.

Copernicus (97 km, 60 miles) is one of the most conspicuous lunar craters. It has a classic profile: high terraced walls and central mountain peaks. At Full Moon it is surrounded by bright crater rays.

Eratosthenes is a two-thirds size replica of Copernicus and lies at the end of the Apennine chain.

Kepler is small (35 km, 22 miles) but stands out prominently on Oceanus Procellarum at Full Moon because of its sparkling crater rays.

Lansberg (42 km, 26 miles) on the lunar equator, stands out clearly on Oceanus Procellarum. It is a near-twin of Reinhold

to the northeast.

Otto Struve (160 km, 100 miles) is one of the largest craters in this quadrant, but it is difficult to see because it lies close to the western edge.

Pico is an isolated mountain near the edge of Mare Imbrium, just south of Plato. It rises to about 2,400 m (8,000 feet).

Plato (97 km, 60 miles), on the edge of the Alps, is a circular crater, noted for its flat, very dark floor.

Reinhold (48 km, 30 miles) lies between Copernicus and Lansberg. Like the latter, it has a deep floor.

Straight Range is an isolated mountain range near the northern edge of Mare Imbrium, close to Plato. It measures about 60 km (40 miles) long and has peaks up to about 1,800 m (6,000 feet).

ABOVE: The crater Kepler as pictured by Apollo 12 from its lunar orbit.

The Solar System

OUTSTANDING FEATURES ON THE SOUTHWEST QUADRANT

Oceanus Procellarum spills into this quadrant, merging into Mare Cognitum, which adjoins Mare Nubium and Mare Humorum. Among the many craters that dot the quadrant are a number of huge walled plains, craters whose floors have been flooded with lava relatively recently. None is finer than Ptolemaeus. The real showpiece crater, however, is Tycho, which becomes dazzlingly prominent at Full Moon. Two of the six Apollo landings were made in this quadrant.

Alphonsus (125 km, 80 miles) is the middle of three large walled plains near the 0° longitude line. Rilles and mountains cross its floor. It is best seen at First Quarter.

Bailly is the largest crater on the Moon, with a diameter of 295 km (183 miles). Unfortunately, it is right on the edge and is difficult to see at any time.

Bullialdus (50 km, 31 miles), on the edge of Mare Nubium, is a perfectly formed crater with intact walls and central peaks.

Clavius is the largest lunar crater that we can see well from Earth, with a diameter of 232 km (144 miles). Its walls and floor are covered with craters.

Gassendi (89 km, 55 miles) bordering Mare Humorum, is one of the many fine walled plains this quadrant has to offer. Its floor shows interesting detail.

Grimaldi (193 km, 120 miles) lies a few degrees south of the equator, close to the western edge. It has low walls, but it is always easy to spot because of its dark floor. It is the darkest area of the Moon.

Longomontanus (145 km, 90 miles) is one of the trio of large craters in the south, the others being Clavius and Maginus. Like them, it has partly ruined walls.

Maginus (177 km, 110 miles) lies due east of Longomontanus. These two craters, together with Clavius to the south and Tycho to the north, make a kind of lunar 'southern cross'.

Pitatus (80 km, 50 miles), at the southern edge of Mare Nubium, has a dark floor with a low central peak.

Ptolemaeus is the first and largest of the string of large craters extending north–south near the 0° longitude line, which are particularly prominent at First Quarter. Close to the Moon's centre, it is a walled plain with a dark floor measuring 148 km (92 miles) across.

Riccioli (160 km, 100 miles) lies just south of the equator near the western edge. Like its neighbour and near-twin Grimaldi, it has a very dark floor.

Schickard (200 km, 124 miles) is a fine walled plain, with low surrounding walls.

Tycho vies with Copernicus for being the finest lunar crater. Though not big (84 km, 52 miles), it becomes truly spectacular at Full Moon as the centre of a bright crater-ray system, whose shining spokes extend in all directions, as far as Oceanus Procellarum to the northwest and Mare Nectaris to the northeast.

The Solar System

OUTSTANDING FEATURES ON THE NORTHEAST QUADRANT

Three seas dominate this quadrant, the circular Mare Serenitatis and Mare Crisium, and the rather shapeless Mare Tranquillitatis. To the public at large, the latter is the best known of all the lunar seas, since it was the site of the first Apollo landing in July 1969. This quadrant also features part of the Apennines and also the Caucasus mountain range bordering Mare Imbrium, which lies mainly in the northwest quadrant. The Haemus Mountains to the south are a much lower range. They give way in the east to an area of low hills and small craters, of which the largest is Plinius. The surface of the mare is noticeably wrinkled, but features only one prominent crater, Bessel. The most distinctly circular sea in this quadrant is Mare Crisium on the eastern edge.

Alpine Valley A valley that cuts through the Alps, in effect linking Mare Imbrium with Mare Frigoris. It looks very much like a river valley on Earth, but is actually a particularly straight geological fault.
Aristillus (56 km, 35 miles) is one of a pair (with Autolycus) of small but prominent craters near the eastern edge of Mare Imbrium. It has a deep floor and a central range.
Aristoteles (97 km, 60 miles) is one of another pair (with Eudoxus) of craters north of Mare Serenitatis.
Atlas (89 km, 55 miles) and Hercules form yet another pair of craters in the north of the quadrant.
Autolycus (36 km, 22 miles) forms a conspicuous pair with Aristillus.
Bessel (19 km, 12 miles) is the only notable crater on Mare Serenitatis and therefore easy to spot. It is associated with a crater ray.
Cleomedes (126 km, 78 miles) is a large crater just north of Mare Crisium and looks splendid just after Full Moon, along with the smaller Geminus and Messala further north.
Eudoxus (64 km, 40 miles) forms a conspicuous pair with Aristoteles.
Gauss (136 km, 85 miles) is one of the largest craters in this quadrant, but is difficult to see because it is right on the edge in the northeast.
Hercules (72 km, 45 miles) forms a pair with Atlas.
Hyginus Rille One of the most prominent rilles on the Moon, running from the south of Mare Vaporum towards Mare Tranquillitatis.
Manilius (36 km, 22 miles), a relatively small crater on the edge of Mare Vaporum, has highly reflective walls, making it one of this quadrant's brightest spots.
Menelaus (32 km, 20 miles) lies on the other side of the Haemus Mountains from Manilius and is also exceptionally bright.
Posidonius (96 km, 60 miles) on the edge of Mare Serenitatis, is a beautiful crater with fascinating walls and well placed for detailed study.

The Solar System

OUTSTANDING FEATURES ON THE SOUTHEAST QUADRANT

This quadrant contains a relatively small area of seas. Mare Tranquillitatis extends into it from the north, as does Mare Fecunditatis. The only sea wholly in this quadrant is the small Mare Nectaris. The terrain consists mainly of rugged highlands, but high mountain ranges are noticeably absent. There are more craters here than in any of the other quadrants, with a spectacular chain of large craters in the east.

Albategnius (129 km, 80 miles) is an ancient walled plain south of Hipparchus. It shows up well at First Quarter, when it is on the terminator. It has a central range, and in the southwest has a deep crater, Klein, embedded in its walls.
Aliacensis (84 km, 52 miles) is the largest of a chain of craters in the west. It forms a distinct pair with its neighbour, the slightly smaller Werner.
Fabricus (89 km, 55 miles) spoils the large ruined plain Janssen and adjoins the similar-sized crater Metius.
Fracastorius (97 km, 60 miles) is a badly ruined crater almost obliterated during the formation of Mare Nectaris, of which it now forms a bay.
Hipparchus (145 km, 90 miles) is an ancient walled plain close to the Moon's centre. It forms a pair with Albategnius, but it is more ruined. It has low walls and is not easy to spot except when on the terminator.

Langrenus (137 km, 85 miles) is the most prominent of the chain of large craters that more or less follow the 60° longitude line in the east.
Maurolycus (109 km, 68 miles) is an example of an ancient crater, badly eroded by later impacts.
Petavius (170 km, 106 miles) is one of the 'big three' craters (with Langrenus and Vendelinus) on the 60° longitude line in the east. It is magnificent around Full Moon, sending out bright rays that meet those coming from Tycho in the adjacent quadrant.
Piccolomini (80 km, 50 miles) lies at the southern edge of the Altai range. It stands out because there are no large craters nearby.
Rheita (68 km, 42 miles) is close to one of the finest crater chains on the Moon, the 160-km (100-mile) long Rheita Valley.
Theophilus (100 km, 62 miles) is the largest of the arc of craters west of Mare Nectaris. It has well-terraced walls and a deep floor with a central range.
Vendelinus (165 km, 103 miles) lies between Langrenus and Petavius in the string of large craters in the east. It is undoubtedly more ancient than the others and has low walls. It is much less prominent than the other two.
Walter (129 km, 80 miles) lies right on the 0° longitude line and is the southernmost of a string of large craters that lies just in the southeast quadrant (Ptolemaeus, Alphonsus, Arzachel, Purbach, Regiomontanus).

The Solar System

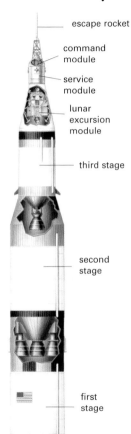

escape rocket

command module

service module

lunar excursion module

third stage

second stage

first stage

MISSIONS TO THE MOON

On July 20, 1969, Neil Armstrong became the first human being to set foot on the Moon. The first step on to the lunar surface from the Apollo 11 Lunar Module, *the Eagle*, fulfilled the promise of President John F. Kennedy that the US would land a man on the Moon before the end of the decade. It was the highlight of an extended US programme to study and map the Moon, beginning with *Ranger 7* impacting the Moon on July 31, 1964 and culminating with Apollo 17, which left the Moon on December 14, 1972. The scientific return from these missions was immensely important and included nearly complete high-resolution imaging of the lunar surface, lunar samples, topographic, seismic and gravity data and information on the lunar environment. These data, as well as data from the Galileo, Clementine and many Soviet missions, have helped us understand exactly what our nearest planet is like.

There were 17 Apollo launches, but it was only the last seven that set out to land their crews on the Moon. Each mission took two and a half days to reach the Moon, but Apollo 13 did not land because of an explosion in its oxygen tank. A Lunar Rover was carried aboard Apollos 15, 16 and 17 to allow the astronauts to explore a wider area than was possible on foot. Using the Lunar Roving vehicle the astronauts were able to take valuable samples of rock from various places on the Moon's surface. The vehicles were left on the Moon's surface after use.

The *Saturn 5* rocket used for the Apollo missions was the most powerful rocket ever built. It had three stages. The lower two dropped away during the launch, but the third went into Earth's orbit carrying the Command, Service and Lunar Excursion modules.

The Solar System

ROCKS AND SOILS FROM THE MOON

Between 1969 and 1972 six Apollo missions brought back 382 kg (842 lb) of lunar rocks, core samples, pebbles, sand and dust from the lunar surface. The six space flights returned 2,200 separate samples from six different exploration sites on the Moon. In addition, three automated Soviet spacecraft returned important samples totalling 300 g ($^3/_4$ lb) from three other lunar sites. The lunar sample building at Johnson Space Center is the chief repository for the Apollo samples. Within the space center is a laboratory where lunar samples are prepared for shipment to scientists and educators, and nearly 1,000 samples are distributed each year for research and teaching projects.

Study of rock and soil samples from the Moon continues to yield useful information about the early history of the Moon, the Earth and the inner solar system. Scientists have been able to work out the chemical composition of the Moon, derived from studies of lunar rocks which gives us much more idea of how the Moon was originally formed.

THE MOON FACT FILE
Diameter:
  3,476 km (2,160 miles)
Atmosphere:
  None (trace gases from capture of solar wind)
Temperature:
  −200°C to 100°C or −330°F to 212°F
Rotation period:
  27 days (about one month)
Geologically old surface:
  Covered with impact craters
Water:
  None (except frozen at the poles)
Size:
  About one quarter the diameter of Earth
Mass:
  Much lower than the Earth's (about 1.2% of the Earth's mass)
Gravity at the surface:
  16% of the Earth's gravity
Distance from the Sun:
  Same distance as the Earth, 92 million miles
Distance from the Earth:
  384,400 km (238,900 miles)
Time taken to spin once:
  27.32 Earth days

RIGHT: This sample of Moon rock brought back to Earth by the Apollo 16 astronauts, is a typical volcanic rock containing many vesicles, or cavities, made by gas escaping when the molten rock cooled and set. Unlike rocks on Earth, Moon rocks are dry and contain hydrocarbons or carbonates.

The Solar System

MARS

Of all the planets in the solar system, Mars is the planet most like our own, although it is only half the size. At first glance, the landscape on Mars looks just like a desert on Earth and wispy clouds and patches of mist form in its thin atmosphere. There are rocks, dust dunes and mountains and, with its axis tilted at about the same angle as Earth's, Mars has similar, although longer, seasons. The martian day, which is called a 'sol', is only a little over 24 hours long.

Because Mars is further from the Sun, its surface is cold, and the temperature is well below freezing for most of the time. The Martian atmosphere, like that of Venus, is primarily carbon dioxide. Nitrogen and oxygen are present but only in very small percentages. Martian air contains only about 1/1,000 as much water as our own air, but even this small amount can condense out, forming clouds that ride high in the atmosphere or swirl around the slopes of towering volcanoes. There is evidence that in the past a denser atmosphere may have allowed water to flow on Mars. Physical features closely resembling shorelines, gorges, riverbeds and islands, all suggest that great rivers once marked the surface of the planet.

The lowest temperature ever recorded on Mars was –120°C (–184°F), and this

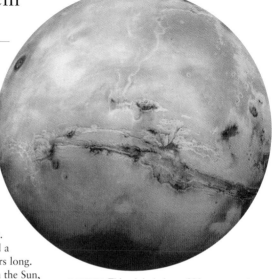

ABOVE: This global view of Mars was put together from many images taken by the orbiting Viking spacecraft between 1976 and 1980. The huge complex of the Mariner Valley stretches a quarter of the way around the planet.

was taken on the northern side of the planet from the Viking Lander 2 weather station. Near-hurricane speed winds were also measured during global dust storms, but because the atmosphere is so thin on Mars, the wind force was minimal. Patches of frost have also been observed on Mars, most probably water-ice, and this was during the second winter on the planet. The volcanoes on Mars are now extinct, and one of them, Olympus Mons, is the largest volcano in the solar system, rising 24 km (15 miles) above the desert.

The Solar System

A DRY AND LIFELESS PLANET

Based on the science fiction classic *War of the World* by H. G. Wells, people once believed in the tale of little green men from Mars invading our planet. Another reason for scientists to expect life on Mars had to do with the apparent seasonal colour changes on the surface of the planet. This phenomenon led to speculation that the conditions might be able to support some form of martian vegetation during the warmer months.

In truth, Mars is a dry planet that has no liquid water left on its surface. There are signs that this was not always the case, but today the heavily-cratered highlands cover most of Mars' Southern hemisphere. Over the remainder of its surface are plains of volcanic lava with fewer craters. In the region of Mars called Tharsis, there are four huge extinct volcanoes which bulge out from the surface. When this bulge first swelled up, it opened a deep fissure in the crust called the Mariner Valley, and this valley is long enough to stretch across the entire United States.

So far, six American missions to Mars have been carried out. Four Mariner spacecraft, three flying by the planet and one placed into martian orbit, surveyed the planet extensively before the Viking Orbiters and Landers arrived. They returned pictures to Earth of Mars' surface, which showed landscapes littered with rocks and a layer of fine, reddish soil, which is rich in iron. Dried up water channels on Mars were carved out long ago by falling rain and gushing floods. Since then the climate has changed dramatically. When Mars first formed it must have had a much thicker atmosphere, but gas gradually escaped into space because the gravity on Mars is not very strong. As the atmosphere became thinner so the temperature dropped and all the remaining water froze. Evidence shows that it has not rained on Mars for about 3 billion years.

Mars is so cold in places that carbon dioxide in the atmosphere freezes into frosty crystals of dry ice. Even in summer it is bitterly cold on Mars and a number of experiments carried out on the soil on Mars has failed to prove any existence even of microscopic life.

ABOVE: The Hubble Space Telescope took this picture of Mars in 1997. It shows clouds of ice crystals near the North Pole, and dust clouds just north of Mars *Pathfinder*'s landing site which is marked with a +.

The Solar System

THE MOONS OF MARS

Mars has two small moons – Phobos and Deimos. These moons of Mars were not formed in the same way as the Earth's Moon, they are probably fragments of larger objects broken apart in a collision. Such moons may be formed from collisions of objects originally in orbit around the planet, or they might also have been captured gravitationally at some point in the past. There are many such small moons around the giant planets like Jupiter and Saturn.

These two moons are examples of what are called minor satellites – small chunks of rock in orbit around planets as compared with large satellites like the Earth's Moon. As the images below show, they are very irregular in shape. Phobos is 24 km (15 miles) long in its longest dimension and Deimos is 16 km (9 miles) long in its longest dimension.

Both are cratered and orbit the planet in rather low orbits. Phobos is only about 4,828 km (3,000 miles) above the Martian surface and orbits in a little over seven hours (thus it makes more than three orbits in a single Martian day). This makes the moon appear to rise in the west and set in the east. Phobos is heavily cratered with interesting parallel grooves about 150 m (492 feet) long and 25 m (82 feet) deep. The grooves seem to radiate from the largest crater to an oddly-shaped area on the other end of the Moon. Because of this it is presumed that the grooves may have formed with the impact of the largest crater.

Deimos is a little further out and orbits in about 30 hours. Deimos appears to have little surface detail because it is covered with a thick layer of dust. The dust fills craters and covers some surface detail. Both moons are probably about 2 billion years old and appear to have a composition very similar to carbonaceous chondrites (meteorites rich in water and organic content). Since carbonaceous chondrites form in the asteroid belt, it is considered highly probable that both Phobos and Deimos are captured asteroids.

Deimos is the smaller of the two Martian moons. It shines at about mag. 13 and orbits Mars every 30 hours.

Phobos orbits Mars in little more than seven hours and, like Deimos, it is thought to be an asteroid that was captured by Mars' gravity.

The Solar System

MARS FACT FILE
Diameter:
  4,218 miles (0.53 Earths)
Atmosphere:
  Thinner than Earth's, mostly carbon dioxide
Temperature:
  −127°C to 17°C or −197°F to 63°F
Rotation period:
  24 hours (about the same as Earth)
Geologically old surface:
  Covered with impact craters in Southern hemisphere
Distance from the Sun:
  141.6 million miles
Mass:
  0.11 Earths
Time taken to orbit the Sun:
  687 Earth days
Moons:
  Two

MISSIONS TO MARS

Mariner 4 was launched in late 1964 and flew past Mars on July 14, 1965, within 9,846 km (6,118 miles) of the surface. It transmitted back to Earth 22 close-up pictures of the planet. This was followed by *Mariners 6* and *7* in the summer of 1969, and they returned 201 pictures of the planet.

On May 30, 1971, the *Mariner 9* Orbiter was launched on a mission to make a year-long study of the Martian surface. The spacecraft arrived five and a half months later, only to find Mars in the middle of a planet-wide dust storm that made surface photography impossible for several weeks. However, once the storm had cleared, *Mariner 9* took 7,329 pictures which revealed previously unknown features about Mars.

In August and September 1975, the *Viking 1* and *2* spacecraft took off from the Kennedy Space Center. The mission was primarily designed to prove whether or not life existed on Mars. *Viking Lander 1* became the first spacecraft to successfully touch down on another planet when it landed on July 20, 1976. The Viking Landers became weather stations, recording wind velocity and direction as well as atmospheric pressure and temperature. Because of these two stations we now know far more about Mars than any other planet – except Earth, of course.

Viking Lander
spacecraft

The Solar System

ASTEROIDS – THE MINI PLANETS

On January 1, 1801, astronomer Giuseppe Piazzi discovered an object which he first thought was a new comet. However, after studying its orbit he discovered that it was not a comet at all, but more like a small planet. Piazzi named it Ceres, after the Sicilian goddess of grain, and it is by far the biggest at 975 km (605 miles) in diameter. In the next few years three other small bodies were discovered, Pallas, Vesta and Juno, and by the end of the nineteenth century there were several hundred. These small planets became known as asteroids, and they are purely small chunks of rock that orbit the Sun. They are all too faint to be seen without a telescope.

The majority of asteroids circle the Sun in an area between the orbits of Mars and Jupiter called the asteroid belt. More than 90 percent of asteroids exist in the

Ida

asteroid belt and some 7,000 of these have been identified. It is possible to find them in other parts of the solar system, and a group known as the Trojans follows the orbit of Jupiter. Asteroids take between three and six years to orbit the Sun.

Asteroids are small bodies that were left over when the solar system formed. All of them clumped together contain less than one thousandth the amount of material in planet Earth. The next largest asteroid after Ceres are Pallas and Vesta, with diameters of just 500 km (310 miles). Next up in size are around 15 that are larger than 500 km (150 miles) across. Spacecraft have taken images of three fairly small asteroids – Gaspra, Ida and Mathilde – which showed them to be uneven-shaped rocks pitted by craters where smaller rocks have collided with them.

Asteroids are not all made out of the same material – although most are dark

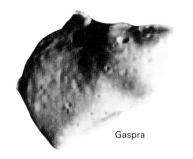

Gaspra

The Solar System

and dull, some appear quite shiny. Some are made up of light-coloured rock, while the shiniest ones are made up mainly of metal. This metal probably came from the core of a very small planet that formed in the asteroid belt and was then smashed apart again.

Asteroids sometimes pass within close proximity of Earth and in 1994 a small rock about 10 metres (30 feet) across passed only 105,000 km (65,000 miles) away. That is less than one third the distance to the Moon.

A large number of asteroids have been found in an area of our solar system known as the Kuiper Belt. The largest of these asteroids so far discovered is 2002 LM60, or 'Quaoar'. This asteroid is about half the size of Pluto and is larger than the four primary asteroids combined.

CHIRON

One of the most unusual asteroids in the solar system is Chiron, which was discovered by Charles Kowal in 1977. Orbiting between Saturn and Uranus, its own orbit is elliptical and eccentric. It takes approximately 50 years for Chiron to complete its orbit. In 1988 astronomers were surprised when Chiron suddenly became much brighter, but on closer observation they discovered that Chiron was surrounded by a cloud of gas and dust that had come off its surface, making it look like the bright coma of a comet. Asteroids and comets are similar in a lot of ways, except for the fact that comets

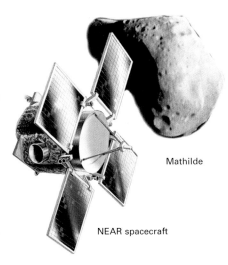

Mathilde

NEAR spacecraft

ABOVE: The asteroid Eros is the main target of the Near-Earth Asteroid Rendezvous (NEAR) mission, however, on its way the spacecraft passed close by another asteroid, Mathilde. NEAR sent back images which showed that Mathilde is made of dark rock and is about 52 km (32 miles) in diameter.

have a lot of ice. Chiron seems to be halfway between an asteroid and a comet.

In the early 1990s it was discovered that Chiron was not alone in its orbit, and this new group of asteroids became known as the Centaurs with Chiron as the leader. There are now known to be at least 41 of them. The first new one to be discovered was named Pholos, followed by Nessus, Asbolus, Chariklo and Hylonome.

The Solar System

MYSTERIOUS VESTA

The Hubble Space Telescope first observed Vesta in 1994, when Vesta was at a distance of 251 million km (156 million miles) from Earth. Vesta has a diameter of 525 km (326 miles) and it rotates about its axis in 5.34 hours.

Vesta is the most geologically diverse of all the asteroids, and the only one known to have distinctive light and dark areas, very similar to the face of our Moon. The Hubble images revealed a diverse world with ancient lava flows and a gigantic impact basin that is so deep, it exposed the asteroid's mantle. It appears that after the formation of Vesta, molten rock flowed on to the asteroid's surface.

This happened more than 4 billion years ago, and since then the surface has remained unchanged, with the exception of an occasional meteorite impact. One or more large impacts broke away some of Vesta's crust, revealing a deeper mantle of olivine, a substance which is believed to constitute most of the Earth's mantle.

In October 1960, two fence workers in Western Australia, observed a fireball heading towards the ground, and it wasn't until ten years later that the pieces of fallen meteorite were found. The fragments stood out from the area's reddish, sandy soil because they had a shiny, black fusion crust, which was produced by their fiery entry through Earth's atmosphere.

1 As the solar system formed, small chunks of material collected together to make asteroid Vesta and it became extremely hot.

2 Molton iron and nickel sank to the centre of the hot asteroid. Lava from the interior flowed out through the crust on to the surface.

3 After Vesta had cooled and become solid, other rocks crashed on to the surface and dug out large craters in the crust revealing the mantle underneath.

The Solar System

THE ASTEROID BELT

The asteroid belt lies between about 275 and 550 million km (170 and 340 million miles) from the Sun between the orbits of Mars and Jupiter.

Some of the asteroids stray a long way from the main belt, as the diagram below shows. Two groups of asteroids, the Trojans, travel in the same orbit as Jupiter, locked in place by the planet's gravity.

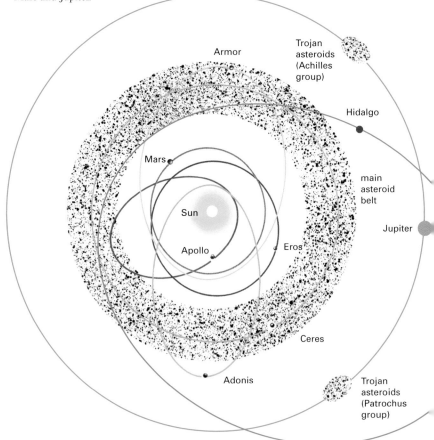

The Solar System

ASTEROID FACT FILE

The Largest Asteroids

Name	Year discovered	Approximate average distance	Distance from Sun (Earth = 1)
Ceres	1801	975 km (605 miles)	2.77
Pallas	1802	535 km (330 miles)	2.77
Vesta	1807	525 km (325 miles)	2.36
Hygeia	1849	425 km (265 miles)	3.14
Davida	1903	325 km (200 miles)	3.18
Interamnia	1910	325 km (200 miles)	3.06
Cybele	1861	280 km (175 miles)	3.43
Europa	1858	280 km (175 miles)	3.10
Sylvia	1866	270 km (170 miles)	3.49
Patientia	1899	270 km (170 miles)	3.06

Much of our understanding about asteroids comes from examining pieces of space debris that fall to the surface of Earth. Asteroids that are on a collision course with Earth are called meteoroids. When a meteoroid strikes our atmosphere at high velocity, friction causes this chunk of space matter to incinerate in a streak of light known as a meteor. If the meteoroid does not burn up completely, what is left strikes Earth's surface and is called a meteorite.

Of all the meteorites examined, 92.8 percent are composed of silicate (stone), and 5.7 percent are composed of iron and nickel; the rest are a mixture of the three materials. Stony meteorites are the hardest to identify since they look very much like terrestrial rocks.

Because asteroids are material from the very early solar system, scientists are interested in their composition. Spacecraft that have flown through the asteroid belt have found that the belt is really quite empty and that asteroids are separated by very large distances. Before 1991 the only information obtained on asteroids was through Earth-based observations. Then in October 1991 asteroid 951 Gaspra was visited by the Galileo spacecraft and became the first asteroid to have high-resolution images taken of it, giving us more information about what asteroids really are.

The Solar System

THE GIANT PLANETS

The four giant planets in our solar system – Jupiter, Saturn, Uranus and Neptune – are very different from the rocky planets nearer the Sun. They are known as the 'gas giants' because they are giant globes of dense gas, with little or no rocky material. The gas includes vast amounts of hydrogen and helium, which are the main gases that make up the Sun. Beneath their clouds, there is no solid surface, they are virtually all atmosphere. This means that it will never be possible for any type of spacecraft to land on these planets, so our knowledge of these giants is somewhat limited.

These giants were formed in cooler parts of the solar system and so their gases and ices were preserved. They take from almost 12 years to 165 years to circle the Sun, but they spin on their axes remarkably quickly, in 10 to 16 hours, rather than in days or months.

On the planets Jupiter and Saturn, we can see spectacular banded patterns of swirling, brilliantly coloured clouds. These clouds, being at such an incredibly high altitude, are probably composed of frozen ammonia crystals. At the lower altitudes, Jupiter's clouds are probably made up of water and complex molecules.

Saturn

Jupiter

The Solar System

The atmospheres of the far-away planets, Uranus and Neptune, are very hard to study, but they do show faint traces of clouds as well.

Because of our limited knowledge we can only make informed guesses about condition. Currents circulating in the metallic fluids of Jupiter and Saturn have generated powerful magnetic fields that then surround the two planets in space. These magnetic fields trap atomic particles from the solar wind that streams

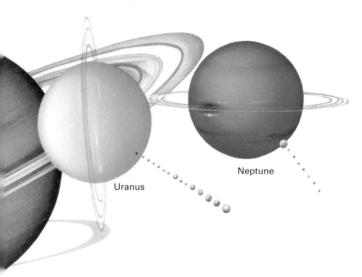

Uranus

Neptune

the interiors of these giant planets. They may possibly have small rocky cores, but if they do they would certainly be surrounded by layers of solid ice. Around this ice, in Jupiter and Saturn, the enormous pressure of the overlying material has reduced the hydrogen gas to a liquid state in which the gas behaves electrically, similar to a metal.

In Uranus and Neptune, the hydrogen is dense but may not reach the metallic

outwards from the Sun.

The gas giants have solid moons orbiting around them. Not just one or two moons, like Earth and Mars, but whole families; in fact, Jupiter and Saturn have more than a dozen moons each.

Each planetary world is unique, but each also has something in common with the others, so that by studying one, it is possible to discover information that relates to them all.

The Solar System

THE RING SYSTEMS

The origin of the rings of the giant planets is unknown. Though they may have had rings since their formation, the ring systems are not stable and must be regenerated by ongoing processes, probably the breakup of larger satellites. It is only Saturn's rings of shiny ice particles that are broad and bright enough to be easily visible from Earth. Spaceprobes have shown that Saturn is surrounded by a complex system of rings and ringlets, with tiny moons orbiting in the outer rings. The three main rings are visible through a telescope from Earth, as is the gap that separates two of them. This gap is called the Cassini Division, after Giovanni Cassini, who discovered the gap in 1675. It is about 4,800 km (2,980 miles) wide. The three rings may appear small from Earth but they are vast and their diameter would stretch two-thirds of the distance from Earth to the Moon. The thickness of the rings, however, is less than 2 km (1.24 miles).

Uranus and Neptune have narrow rings made up of dark particles. Jupiter's rings are fine dust, rather like smoke. Although the rings look continuous from the Earth, they are actually composed of innumerable small particles each in an independent orbit. They range in size from a centimetre or so to several metres.

The ring particles, themselves, seem to be composed primarily of water-ice, but they may also include rocky particles with icy coatings.

To make the comparison easier, the planets in the diagram below have been drawn to the same size.

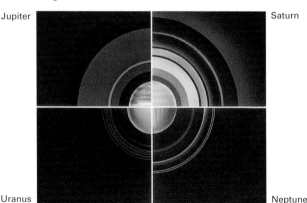

Jupiter

Saturn

Uranus

Neptune

The Solar System

THE VOYAGER MISSIONS

The most successful mission to the giant planets was the *Voyager* spacecraft. Two spacecraft sent back close-up pictures of Jupiter, Saturn, Uranus, Neptune and many of their moons. Both *Voyager 1* and *Voyager 2* were launched within a few days of one another in 1977. *Voyager 1* sent back pictures of Jupiter as it flew past the planet in 1979, and then went on to visit Saturn in 1980.

Voyager 2 took a slower route to Jupiter, reaching it four months after *Voyager 1*, and then arrived at Saturn in 1981. It passed Uranus in 1986, and finally, after 12 years in space, it reached Neptune in 1989.

Each spacecraft carried cameras as well as detectors to measure such things as magnetic fields and solar wind particles in space. Also, because the Voyagers may at some time in the future be found by other civilizations, they carry on board records with different sounds from Earth, together with pictures of its peoples and cultures.

The Voyager mission, now in its 26th year, continues its quest to push the bounds of space exploration. The twin *Voyager 1* and 2 spacecraft opened new vistas in space by greatly expanding our knowledge of Jupiter and Saturn. *Voyager 2* then extended the planetary adventure when it flew by Uranus and Neptune, becoming the only spacecraft ever to visit these worlds. *Voyager 1*, now the most distant human-made object in the Universe, and *Voyager 2*, close on its heels, continue their ground-breaking journey with their current mission to study the region in space where the Sun's influence ends and the dark recesses of interstellar space begin.

The Solar System

JUPITER – THE SUPERPLANET

Jupiter is heavier than all the other planets of the solar system put together, and it is by far the largest. Jupiter is a beautiful sight seen with the naked eye on a clear night, but it is only when you look through a telescope that it begins to reveal its magnificence.

The most prominent features of Jupiter are alternating light and dark bands, running parallel to the equator and subtly shaded in tones of blue, yellow, brown and orange, which are spread all around the planet by immensely strong winds. The *Galileo* probe into Jupiter's atmosphere measured wind speeds of up to 650 km (400 miles) per hour, which is many times faster than any winds on Earth. These winds are caused by the rapid speed of Jupiter's spin. The giant planet spins so fast that a Jovian day is less than half as long as a day on Earth, averaging just under ten hours.

These bands, however, are not the only conspicuous markings on this planet. In 1664 the English astronomer Robert Hooke first reported seeing a large oval spot on Jupiter, and additional spots were noted as telescopes became more advanced. As the planet rotates on its axis, such spots are carried across the disc and can be used to measure Jupiter's speed of rotation.

Jupiter's atmosphere is made up of about 90 percent hydrogen and 10 percent helium, with traces of methane, water,

ABOVE: The Hubble Space Telescope gave us this picture of Jupiter's cloud patterns. The dark spot is the shadow of Io, one of Jupiter's moons. Io itself is visible to the right of its shadow. The red and blue colouring around Jupiter is not real but due to the way the picture was made through coloured filters.

The Solar System

ammonia and rock. Our knowledge of the core of Jupiter is very limited because the data from *Galileo*'s atmospheric probe has only penetrated about 150 km (93 miles) below the cloud tops. Jupiter probably has a core of rocky material which amounts to something like 10 to 15 Earth-masses.

Three distinct layers of clouds are believed to exist, consisting of ammonia ice, ammonium hydrosulphide and a mixture of ice and water. The vivid colours seen in these clouds are most probably the result of chemical reactions of the trace elements in Jupiter's atmosphere. These colours correlate with the cloud's altitude – blue lowest, followed by browns and whites, with reds the highest.

The high velocity winds of Jupiter are confined in wide bands of latitude and blow in opposite directions in adjacent bands. There are slight chemical and temperature differences between these two bands and they are responsible for the coloured bands that dominate the planet's appearance. The light coloured bands are called *zones*, and the dark ones *belts*.

Jupiter has an enormous magnetic field, much stronger than that of Earth. This field, or magnetosphere, extends more than 650 million km (404 million miles), past even the orbit of Saturn. The environment surrounding Jupiter contains high levels of energetic particles which are trapped by Jupiter's magnetic field. This radiation is similar to, but far more intense, than that found within Earth's

Van Allen belts.

Jupiter has rings like Saturn's, but they are much fainter and smaller. These rings are dark and are probably composed of very small grains of rocky material and, unlike Saturn's, seem to contain no ice. The particles within the Jupiter rings probably don't stay there for long due to the atmospheric and magnetic drag, and the *Galileo* probe found clear evidence that the rings are continuously resupplied by dust formed by micrometeor impacts on the four inner moons.

Although the face of Jupiter is constantly changing, some spots and other cloud features have actually survived for years, far longer than even the largest storms on Earth. Imagine a hurricane that lasted for 300 years – Jupiter's Great Red Spot indeed seems to be a giant hurricane-like storm system rotating with the Jovian clouds. The record for longevity goes to the Great Red Spot. This gigantic red oval, larger than the planet Earth, was first seen more than three centuries ago. Over the decades it has changed in both size and colour, and for nearly 50 years in the late eighteenth century, no sightings at all were reported. However, since about 1840, the Great Red Spot has been the most prominent feature on the disc of Jupiter. Still today, details of how and why the Great Red Spot changes its shape, size and colour remain a mystery. A better understanding of the weather on Jupiter may help contribute to a better understanding of weather here on Earth.

The Solar System

MOONS OF JUPITER

Jupiter has 16 moons and they divide into four different groups. The four nearest to Jupiter are very small, next come the four large Galilean moons and then, much further out, are two clusters of four small, dark moons.

The four large Galilean moons, Ganymede, Callisto, Europa and Io all have their own distinctive characteristics: *Ganymede* is the seventh and largest of Jupiter's known moons and orbits 1,070,000 km (664,867 miles) from the main planet. Ganymede is the largest satellite in the solar system, even larger than the planet Mercury. Ganymede has a very old, highly cratered, dark region and younger, lighter regions which are distinctly marked by an extensive array of grooves and ridges. The craters on Ganymede, unlike the Moon, are quite flat and lacking any ring mountains and central depressions, and this is probably due to the weak nature of the moon's icy crust. *Callisto* is the eighth of Jupiter's known satellites and the second largest. It is the outermost of the Galilean moons and orbits 1,883,000 km (1,170,041 miles) from Jupiter. Unlike Ganymede, Callisto seems to have little internal structure and is mainly made up of 40 percent ice and 60 percent rock/iron. Callisto's surface is covered entirely with craters, and has the oldest, most cratered surface of any body yet observed in the solar system. This is because it has undergone very minimal change other than the occasional impact in the last 4 billion years. The largest craters on Callisto are surrounded by a series of concentric rings which look like huge cracks which have been smoothed out over time by the slow movement of the ice. The largest of these has been named *Valhalla,* which is nearly 3,000 km (1,864 miles) in diameter. *Valhalla* is a dramatic example of a multi-ring basic which was the result of a massive impact. Like Ganymede, Callisto's ancient craters have collapsed, lacking high ring mountains, radial rays and central depressions. Another interesting feature about Callisto is *Gipul Catena*, which is a long series of impact craters that are in an almost straight line. This was probably caused by an object that was tidally disrupted as it passed close to Jupiter. *Io* is the fifth of Jupiter's satellites, the third largest, and the innermost of the Galilean moons. Io is slightly larger than the Earth's Moon and orbits 422,000 km (262,218 miles) from Jupiter. In contrast to most of the moons in the outer solar system, both Io and Europa are similar in composition to the terrestrial planets, being primarily composed of molten silicate rock. Recent data sent back from *Galileo* indicates that the core of Io is mostly iron mixed with iron sulphide, with a radius of at least 900 km (559 miles). Io's surface is radically different to any other body in the solar system as there are few, if any, impact craters, which means that its surface is very young. Instead of having craters, Io has hundreds of volcanic calderas, some of which are active. Images sent back from the Voyager missions show actual

The Solar System

eruptions with plumes as high as 300 km (186 miles), and this was the first real proof that the interiors of other terrestrial bodies are actually hot and active. Unlike the other Galilean satellites, Io has little or no water and its thin atmosphere is composed largely of sulphur dioxide and perhaps some other gases.

Europa is the sixth of Jupiter's moons and the fourth largest. It is slightly smaller than the Earth's Moon and orbits

The surface of Europa resembles images of sea ice on Earth, and beneath this is a layer of liquid water, which is possibly as deep as 50 km (31 miles). Europa's most striking aspect is a series of dark streaks which crisscross the entire globe. The larger ones are about 20 km (12 miles) across with diffuse outer edges and a central band of lighter material. It is believed that they were produced by a series of volcanic eruptions or geysers.

Ganymede

Europa

Callisto

Io

670,900 km (416,878 miles) from Jupiter. Although Europa is similar in composition to Io, it differs in that it has a thin outer layer of ice. Europa's surface is unlike any other body in the inner solar system because it is exceedingly smooth. There are very few craters on Europa, in fact only three craters larger than 5 km (3 miles) in diameter have been found.

The Solar System

THE GALILEO MISSION

Galileo was launched in October 1989 from Space Shuttle Atlantis. The spacecraft was named in honour of the first modern astronomer – Galileo Galilei. The spacecraft and probe travelled as a single unit for almost six years, and in July 1995 the probe was released to begin a solo flight into Jupiter.

Five months later the probe managed to penetrate Jupiter's atmosphere at 170,590 km per hour (106,000 miles per hour). As it approached the surface, it reduced its speed, released its parachute and finally dropped its heat shield. As the probe descended through the 59 km (95 miles) of the top layers of Jupiter's atmosphere, it collected 58 minutes of data about the local weather. This data was sent back to the spacecraft overhead, which in turn was transmitted back to Earth. Towards the end of its 58 minute descent, the probe measured winds of 724 km per hour (450 miles per hour), far stronger than anything ever experienced on Earth. The probe was finally melted and vaporized by the intense heat of Jupiter's atmosphere.

Galileo travelled around Jupiter in elongated ovals and each orbit lasted about two months. These orbits enabled the spacecraft to sample different parts of the planet's extensive magnetosphere, and also managed to negotiate close fly-bys of Jupiter's largest moons. To keep track of *Galileo*'s journey, each orbit was numbered and named for the moon that the spacecraft encountered at closest range. For example 'C-3' – the third orbit around Jupiter passed close by the moon Callisto.

The data that was collected on Jupiter and its moons was stored on an onboard tape recorder. The information gathered during its initial orbits was so intriguing that *Galileo*'s mission was extended.

The *Galileo* spacecraft's 14-year journey eventually came to an end on Sunday, September 21, 2003, when the spacecraft passed into Jupiter's shadow then disintegrated in the planet's dense atmosphere.

The Solar System

SATURN – THE RINGED PLANET

Perhaps one of the most beautiful sights through a telescope, is that of Saturn surrounded by its spectacular set of rings. Saturn is the sixth planet from the Sun and is the second largest in the solar system, with a diameter of 119,300 km (74,130 miles). Much of what is known about Saturn is due to the Voyager explorations of 1980–81.

Saturn is visibly flattened at the poles and this is a result of the very fast rotation of the planet on its axis. A day on this planet lasts 10 hours, 39 minutes, and it takes 29.5 Earth years to complete its orbit of the Sun.

The atmosphere on Saturn is primarily composed of hydrogen with small amounts of helium and methane. The upper atmosphere of Saturn is prone to violent storms, and the wind blows at exceptionally high speeds. Near the equator it reaches velocities of 500 metres a second or 1,100 miles an hour.

Saturn is the least dense of all the planets, it has a specific gravity of 0.7, which is less than that of water. Saturn's interior is similar to Jupiter's, consisting of a rocky core, a liquid metallic hydrogen layer, and a molecular hydrogen layer. Traces of various ices have also been found present.

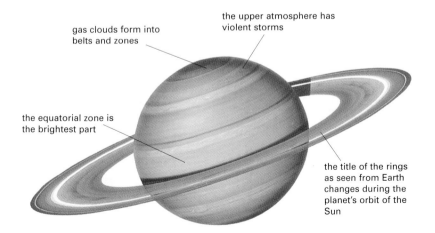

the upper atmosphere has violent storms

gas clouds form into belts and zones

the equatorial zone is the brightest part

the title of the rings as seen from Earth changes during the planet's orbit of the Sun

The Solar System

SATURN'S RINGS

Saturn's rings system makes the planet one of the most beautiful objects in the solar system. The rings are divided into a number of different parts, which include the bright A and B rings and a fainter C ring. The ring system has various gaps which look like empty spaces, but space probes have shown there are smaller rings within these gaps. The most notable gap is the Cassini Division, which separates the A and B rings. This gap was named after Giovanni Cassini who discovered it in 1675. The Encke Division, which splits the A ring, is named after Johann Encke, who discovered it in 1837. Space probes have shown that the main rings are really made up of a large number of narrow ringlets.

The origin of these rings is rather obscure, but it is thought that they may have been formed from larger moons that were shattered by comet or meteoroid impacts. Although the ring composition is not known for certain, they do show a significant amount of water. They may possibly be composed of icebergs and snowballs that vary tremendously in size from just a few centimetres to several metres. Much of the elaborate structure

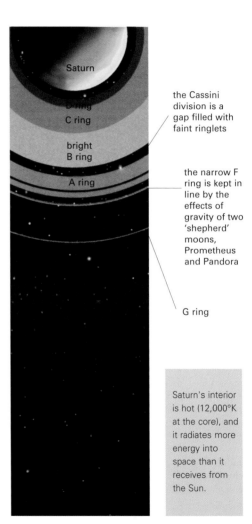

Saturn

D ring

C ring

bright B ring

A ring

the Cassini division is a gap filled with faint ringlets

the narrow F ring is kept in line by the effects of gravity of two 'shepherd' moons, Prometheus and Pandora

G ring

Saturn's interior is hot (12,000°K at the core), and it radiates more energy into space than it receives from the Sun.

The Solar System

Saturn's rings are made up of millions of individual moonlets. They are like dirty snowballs, mostly made up of frozen water, with some dust and rock mixed in. The smallest chunks are about the size of a golf ball, while the largest may be as big as 1 km (half a mile) across.

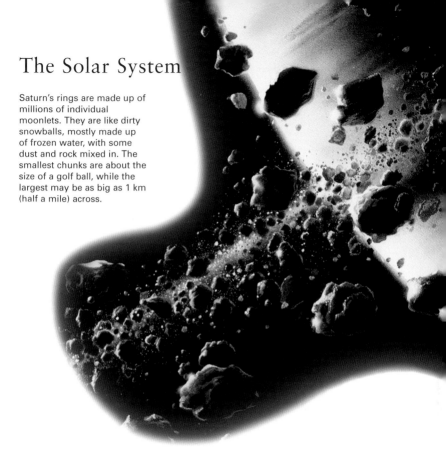

of some of the rings is due to the gravitational effects of nearby satellites. This phenomenon is demonstrated by the relationship between the F ring and two small moons that shepherd the ring material, Prometheus and Pandora.

The Voyager missions also discovered radial, spoke-like features in the broad B ring. These features are believed to be composed of fine, dust-sized particles. The spokes were seen to form and dissipate in the time-lapse images taken by the spacecraft. Although electrostatic charging may create spokes by levitating dust particles above the ring, the exact cause of the formation of the spokes is not yet understood. One thing that is known about the rings of Saturn, though, is that they are extremely thin; though they are 250,000 km (155,342 miles) or more in diameter, they are less than 1 km (0.62 miles) thick.

The Solar System

THE TILTING RINGS

As Saturn and Earth move around the Sun, the view we have of the planet and its rings changes. The ring system can be edge-on to our line of sight, or we can view it from below and above. The complete cycle of views takes 29.5 years.

These changes are normally quite easy to see with a small telescope, but every 15 years they seem to close up then open out again. When the rings are exactly edge-on to us, we cannot see them. In September 2000 Saturn was in an excellent position for viewing, being within a couple of degrees of maximum tilt to the north.

SATURN FACT FILE

Diameter:
120,540 km (74,900 miles), although rings increase this to 270,000 km (167,770 miles)

Average distance from the Sun:
1,427,000,000 km (886,696,691 miles)

Average temperature:
-180°C (-292°F)

Surface gravity (Earth equals 1):
1.16

Atmosphere:
Hydrogen, helium with small amounts of ammonia and methane

Length of year (in Earth days/years):
29.5 years

Period of rotation (length of a day):
10 hours, 39 minutes

Number of known moons:
18

Speed planet travels at around the Sun (Average orbital velocity):
9.7 km a second (6 miles a second)

The Solar System

MOONS OF SATURN

Saturn has 18 officially recognized and named satellites – Pan, Atlas, Prometheus, Pandora, Epimetheus, Janus, Mimas, Enceladus, Tethys, Telesto, Calypso, Helene, Dione, Rhea, Titan, Hyperion, Iapetus and Phoebe. In addition to these there are other unconfirmed satellites. One circles in the orbit of Dione, a second is located between the orbits of Tethys and Dione, and a third is located between Dione and Rhea.

Each satellite is individual, though they are all made up of a mixture of ice and rock. The largest, Titan, is bigger than the planet Mercury and is the only moon in the solar system that has a thick atmosphere. The surfaces of Saturn's other moons are mostly dotted with craters, although many of the craters on Enceladus have been covered over by ice. The huge Herschel crater on Mimas was made by an impact that nearly shattered the whole moon. A massive canyon cuts three-quarters of the way around Tethys.

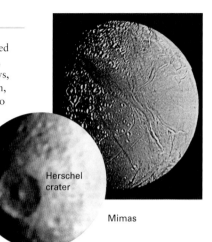

Enceladus

Herschel crater

Mimas

Saturn is the second largest planet in the Solar System after Jupiter. It is so big that Earth could fit into it 755 times.

The atmosphere surrounding Titan is four times thicker than that of Earth, and is mainly made up of nitrogen. No one has ever seen Titan's surface because it is always hidden by an orange-coloured haze. In 2004, the *Cassini* spacecraft will release a probe that will parachute down on to Titan. The probe will carry six instruments to send back pictures and data.

Titan

The Solar System

THE MOONS OF SATURN FACT FILE

Moon	Discovered	Diameter kilometres	Diameter miles
Pan	1985	20	12
Atlas	1980	40	25
Prometheus	1980	80	50
Pandora	1980	100	62
Janus	1966	190	118
Epimetheus	1980	120	75
Mimas	1789	394	245
Enceladus	1789	502	312
Tethys	1684	1048	651
Telesto	1980	25	16
Calypso	1980	25	16
Dione	1684	1120	696
Helene	1980	30	19
Rhea	1672	1530	951
Titan	1655	5150	3200
Hyperion	1848	270	168
Iapetus	1671	1435	892
Phoebe	1898	220	137

EARLY DISCOVERIES OF SATURN

Galileo Galilei was the first to view Saturn's system of rings in the year 1610. Because he happened to be viewing their edge, he failed to recognize them as rings.

In 1655, a Dutch astronomer named Christiaan Huygens was able to discern what Galileo had thought to be moons as rings. Huygens benefited from a much improved telescope than that used by Galileo.

In 1671, a second moon of Saturn called Iapetus was found by the Italian astronomer Cassini. He also discovered, in 1675, that Saturn had more than one ring, that is a concentric pair of rings.

A third ring was discovered by Johann Franz Encke in 1837 using a telescope at the Berlin Observatory.

Until *Pioneer 11* approached Saturn in September of 1979, the planet was thought to have only three rings.

The *Pioneer* Saturn fly-by in 1979 made several new discoveries about the size and consistency of the rings.

The Solar System

THE CASSINI SPACECRAFT

The *Cassini* spacecraft was launched on October 15, 1997 via a Titan IV-Centaur rocket from Cape Canaveral in Florida, and is still heading for Saturn.

The main objectives of *Cassini* are:

1. to determine the three-dimensional structure and dynamical behaviour of the rings;
2. to determine the composition of the satellite surfaces and the geological history of each object;
3. to determine the nature and origin of the dark material on Iapetus' leading hemisphere;
4. to measure the three-dimensional structure and dynamical behaviour of the magnetosphere;
5. to study the dynamical behaviour of Saturn's atmosphere at cloud level;
6. to study the time variability of Titan's clouds and hazes;
7. to characterize Titan's surface on a regional scale.

On July 1, 2004, the *Cassini* spacecraft will fire its main engine to reduce its speed. This will allow the spacecraft to be captured by Saturn's gravity and enter orbit. The spacecraft will then begin a four-year tour of the ringed planet, its mysterious moons, the stunning rings, and its complex magnetic environment.

During the Saturn Tour, *Cassini* will complete 74 orbits of the ringed planet, 44 close fly-bys of the mysterious moon Titan and numerous fly-bys of Saturn's other icy moons.

If all goes well during the mission, there should be enough fuel and power for the spacecraft to continue to take data and relay it back to Earth for many years (just as the *Voyager* still does). Cassini will continue to orbit Saturn, and will be placed in an orbit that minimizes its chances of colliding with any of the other satellites.

The Solar System

NEPTUNE

Uranus and Neptune are often thought of as a pair, because of their great distance from the Sun and their similarities in size and colour. But already scientists expect that Neptune will be vastly different from any of the other planets yet studied.

Neptune was named after the Roman god of the sea, and was the first planet to be located using mathematical predictions rather than through systematic observations of the sky. Neptune is the eighth planet from the Sun being 4.5 billion km (2.8 billion miles) away. Neptune is a giant gas planet that is so far away that it is only a tiny, blurred image even in the strongest telescope. It is invisible to the naked eye because it orbits in the outer regions of the solar system. Because it is so far away Neptune receives nearly 1,000 times less sunlight than Earth, and about two and a half times less than Uranus. However, its overall temperature is about the same as that of Uranus, and consequently scientists believe that Neptune must have some internal heat of its own, just like Jupiter and Saturn.

Neptune has a hazy atmosphere and very strong winds and its beautiful blue colour is caused by the methane in its atmosphere. Because Neptune's rotational axis is tilted about 30 degrees to the plane of its orbit around the Sun (Earth's axis

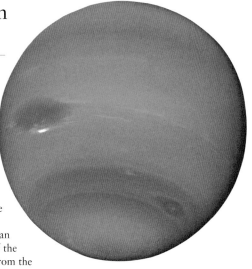

When this picture of Neptune was taken by *Voyager 2* in 1989, the planet had a Great Dark Spot in its Southern hemisphere (left of centre). However, when the Hubble Space Telescope sent back pictures of the planet in 1994, this dark spot had disappeared.

tilts 23.5 degrees), it experiences seasons. Unlike Earth, however, Neptune's seasons last for more than 40 years. This means that the poles are in constant darkness or sunlight for 40 years at a time.

Each day on Neptune takes 19.1 Earth hours and one year takes 164.8 Earth years, which means that it takes almost 165 Earth years for Neptune to orbit the Sun once. Since Neptune was discovered in 1846, it has not yet completed a single revolution around the Sun.

The Solar System

Neptune is mainly made up of water with an atmosphere of hydrogen, helium and methane, but it shows more markings than its companion Uranus. Dark spots come and go, while bright clouds of methane hang high in its atmosphere. Winds rage around the planet at around 965 km (600 miles) per hour, and the Great Dark Spot that was seen by *Voyager 2* was a huge storm in the atmosphere.

RINGS OF NEPTUNE

Neptune's rings were first detected in star experiments from Earth in 1983, but they were very difficult to study until *Voyager 2* sent back its data. The rings of Neptune are very faint and only the two brightest rings show clearly in the image (*right*), but *Voyager 2* did find additional fainter rings. The rings rotate in the same direction as the planet and are nearly in the equatorial plane.

The material in one of the rings is clumpy (more dense in some regions than others). This gave the impression in ground-based observations that the rings were arcs instead of complete rings, but the *Voyager 2* data showed that they were complete rings. The rings of Neptune contain much more dust-size grains than the corresponding rings of Saturn and Uranus, and are quite narrow. Neptune's rings are called: the Adams Ring, the Leverrier Ring, Galle Ring, Lassell and the Arago Ring.

Bright wispy clouds of methane ice appear on Neptune's surface.

Neptune has at least four faint rings

The Great Dark Spot

'Scooter'

In addition to the Great Dark Spot, which is a circular storm the size of Earth, *Voyager 2* also found a smaller dark spot on the surface of Neptune. It also returned images of a fast-moving cloud which became known as 'Scooter'.

Neptune's diameter is almost four times that of Earth.

The Solar System

THE MOONS OF NEPTUNE

Neptune has two large moons that are easily seen from Earth, Triton and Nereid, but *Voyager 2* discovered six additional moons. One of these is actually larger than Nereid, but could not be seen easily from Earth because it orbits close to Neptune.

Triton is the largest moon of Neptune with a diameter of 2,700 km (1,680 miles). It was discovered by William Lassell, a British astronomer, on October 10, 1846, which was scarcely a month after Neptune itself was discovered. Triton is colder than any other measured object in the solar system, with a surface temperature of –235°C (–391°F). It has an extremely thin atmosphere, and nitrogen ice particles form thin clouds a few miles above the surface. The atmospheric pressure on Triton is about 0.000015 times the sea-level surface pressure on Earth.

Triton is the only large satellite in the solar system to circle a planet in a retrograde direction. This means that it travels in the opposite direction to the rotation of Neptune. Triton contains more rock in its interior than the icy satellites of Saturn and Uranus, and its relative high density suggests to scientists that it was most probably captured by Neptune as it travelled through space several billion years ago.

Triton's surface is scarred by enormous cracks. Images sent back by *Voyager 2*, showed active geyser-like eruptions spewing nitrogen gas and dark dust particles several miles into the atmosphere.

In 2003 astronomers announced the discovery of three previously unseen moons orbiting Neptune, which brought the total of satellites around that planet to 11. These new moons are the first found at Neptune since the *Voyager 2* mission in 1989 and the first detected from ground since 1949. Each is roughly 30–40 km (18–24 miles) in diameter.

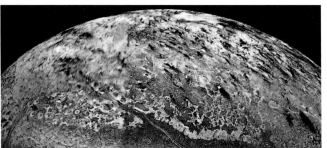

Triton's surface is covered with clear, pinkish ice. Frozen nitrogen below the ice is heated, possibly by the distant Sun, and gushes from cracks forming five-mile-high geysers.

The Solar System

URANUS

Uranus is the seventh planet from the Sun in our solar system. This huge, icy planet is covered with clouds and is encircled by a belt of 11 rings and 22 known moons. Its outer layers are made up of hydrogen, helium and methane, and it is the methane that gives Uranus its slight blue-green colour. Uranus has very few markings, only a few faint bands are visible, but if you were to go deeper you would discover more and more water. Starting off as a thin mist, it gets thicker and thicker until it eventually becomes a warm, dark ocean. Near the centre of this planet, this ocean becomes increasingly hot and sludgy until it becomes solid rock.

Unlike any other planet, Uranus spins on its side. The other planets have poles that point more or less upwards and downwards, while Uranus' poles point sideways, tilted by an angle of 97.9 degrees. This tipped rotational axis gives rise to extreme seasons. At the Summer Solstice (which occurred in 1985), the North Pole is pointed almost directly towards the Sun: the Northern hemisphere of Uranus receives constant sunlight and the Southern hemisphere is in perpetual darkness. At the Autumnal Equinox (happening in 2007) the Sun will rise on the entire planet every 17 hours. At the Winter Solstice (in 2027) the North Pole will be pointed almost directly away from the Sun: the Northern hemisphere will be in perpetual darkness and the Southern

Uranus has thin rings, like Saturn's but much narrower and fainter. The ice particles in them are the colour of coal, while Saturn's are like snow. Uranus' rings are probably much older than those of Saturn.

The Solar System

hemisphere will receive constant sunlight.

During the summer and winter, the uneven heating of the Northern and Southern hemispheres will cause winds to blow in a north-south direction, decreasing the importance of the east-west bands seen on the other Jovian planets. In addition, it is very cold that far out in the solar system, and the sunlight Uranus receives is 370 times weaker than sunlight on the Earth.

Uranus has an orbital period of 84 years and a rotation period of 17 hours. Each day on Uranus takes 17.9 Earth hours, while a year takes 84.07 Earth years.

RINGS OF URANUS

The rings were discovered from the Earth in 1977 when Uranus passed in front of a star, and it was noticed that there were dips in the brightness of the star before and after it passed behind the body of Uranus. This data suggested that Uranus was surrounded by at least five rings. Four more rings were suggested by subsequent measurements taken from Earth, and two additional ones were found by *Voyager 2*, bringing the total to 11.

Most of the rings are not quite circular, and most are not exactly in the plane of the equator. The rings vary in brightness depending on their angle around the moon. The rings are very narrow – some only a few miles across – and no material can be detected in the areas in between the rings.

The brightest ring is termed the

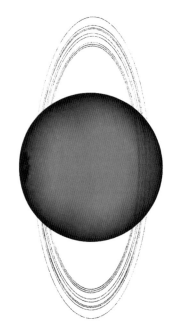

Uranus has a belt of 11 faint, narrow rings which are composed of rock and dust. These rings are only a fraction of the size of Saturn's rings.

Epsilon ring. *Voyager 2* found two small shepherd moons for it, one just inside and one just outside. They appear to be about 20–30 km (12–18 miles) in diameter, and have been named Ophelia and Cordelia.

The Solar System

THE MOONS OF URANUS

Currently, we know that Uranus has at least 21 moons. The five largest are: Miranda, Ariel, Umbriel, Titania and Oberon. The *Voyager 2* mission discovered ten more moons when it visited the planet in 1986 and since then, astronomers have discovered six more.

Miranda Although it is the smallest of the five larger moons of Uranus, Miranda has presented us with a number of puzzles. If you look closely at the picture on the right, you will notice that about half of the moon looks like a lot of the other moons in our solar system. It has lots of craters that tell us that it has been hit by many objects during its long life. The other half of the moon is covered by what appear to be giant cliffs, grooves, gullies and other features a lot like you might find in the American West, although much, much larger. Nobody really knows what has caused all of these unusual features, and the only way we will find out is to send another spacecraft to the distant planet for an extended visit.

The half of Miranda that is covered with canyons, valleys and giant ridges is the most interesting part of this tiny world. Although the moon is a little under 482 km (300 miles) in diameter, there is a ridge on its surface that is taller than Mount Everest here on Earth.

Ariel The second of the large moons of Uranus is Ariel. Ariel, with a diameter of almost 1,158 km (720 miles), is much larger than Miranda and is made up

Miranda is the smallest of Uranus' moons. It seems to have broken up in the past and pieced itself together again, leaving strange patterns on its surface.

mostly of rocky material and ice. It has an interesting surface that shows lots of craters much like our own Moon, but the other side is crisscrossed by what appear to be large grooves of some kind. One explanation of these unusual features is that possibly at some time in the distant past Ariel might have been much warmer than it is now. If this is the case, some of the ice in the moon may have melted and smoothed out the surface of the moon and then more recent geological activity may have formed the long, wide grooves.

Umbriel The third in the family of the five largest moons of Uranus is Umbriel. Although Umbriel is about the same size as Ariel, the family resemblance ends there. Where Ariel shows us a face that has lots of interesting and mysterious features, Umbriel is more like the other moons in the solar system. It does have

The Solar System

lots of impact craters, but other than that, it is a pretty cold, plain place.

The only really interesting feature of this moon is a bright crater. This crater is very large, almost 112 km (70 miles) across, and is also very bright, compared to the surface of the rest of the moon.

Titania At a little over 1,577 km (980 miles) in diameter, Titania is the largest moon of Uranus, as befits its name. Like the other moons of the planet that we have seen, Titania is made up of rocks and ice.

Another thing that Titania has in common with its family members is the fact that part of its surface is heavily cratered, and part of it has lots of ridges, gullies and other features that look like erosion features that we see here on Earth and on Mars.

Oberon The last of the largest moons of Uranus is Oberon. At a little over 1,521 km (945 miles) in diameter, this moon is just a little smaller than Titania. Oberon differs from its other family members in that it has a region that is covered with ridges and gullies. This moon is almost entirely covered by impact craters, much like most of the other moons in the solar system. What is interesting though about

THE MOONS OF URANUS FACT FILE

Moon	Discovered	Diameter kilometres	Diameter miles
Cordelia	11986	26	16
Ophelia	1986	30	19
Bianca	1986	42	26
Cressida	1986	62	39
Desdemona	1986	54	34
Juliet	1986	84	52
Portia	1986	108	67
Rosalind	1986	54	34
Belinda	1986	66	41
Puck	1985	154	96
Miranda	1948	472	293
Ariel	1851	1158	720
Umbriel	1851	1169	720
Titania	1787	1578	980
Oberon	1787	1523	946
S/1997 U2	1997	160	100
S/1997 U1	1997	80	50

The Solar System

Oberon, is that there appears to be a 'mountain' rising from the surface of this moon. This mountain is over 5 km (3 miles) high and is the most fascinating feature on the surface of this moon.

DISCOVERY OF NEW MOONS

In 1997 a team of astronomers discovered two distant moons orbiting the planet Uranus. The new Uranian satellites are the faintest ever detected without the aid of a spacecraft, and their discoveries were made possible by using the large Hale 5-metre Telescope on Palomar Mountain near San Diego, California. The brighter of the two satellites has been given the name Sycorax (S/1997 U2) and the fainter object Caliban (S/1997 U1).

Moons of Uranus have traditionally been named after characters from the poetry of Shakespeare and Pope. Caliban came from a character in Shakespeare's play *The Tempest*, who was the deformed son of the witch Sycorax.

Caliban is approximately 60 km (37 miles) in diameter and orbits Uranus at about 7.1 million km (4.4 million miles). Sycorax is about 120 km (74.5 miles) in diameter and orbits at about 12.2 million km (7.5 million miles) from Uranus.

Caliban and Sycorax are the first moons around Uranus to be called irregular satellites, due to their highly inclined orbits. The other giant planets such as Jupiter, Saturn and Neptune are also known to possess similar irregular moons.

William Herschel

Uranus was discovered by accident on March 13, 1781, by William Herschel (1738–1822) when he was studying stars with a telescope. It was the first planet to be found that could not be seen by the naked eye. Herschel was a professional musician from Hanover, who settled in England. His hobby was building astronomical telescopes. He discovered Uranus using one of his own telescopes (*right*).

The Solar System

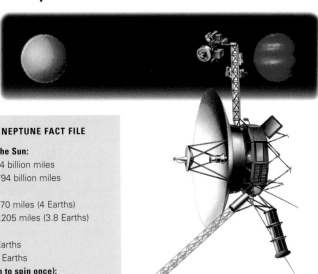

URANUS AND NEPTUNE FACT FILE

Distance from the Sun:
  Uranus: 1,784 billion miles
  Neptune: 2,794 billion miles
Diameter:
  Uranus: 31,570 miles (4 Earths)
  Neptune: 30,205 miles (3.8 Earths)
Mass:
  Uranus: 15 Earths
  Neptune: 17 Earths
Day (time taken to spin once):
  Uranus: 17 Earth hours 14 minutes
  Neptune: 19 Earth hours 12 minutes
Year (time taken to orbit the Sun):
  Uranus: 84 Earth years 4 days
  Neptune: 165 Earth years
Surface temperature:
  Uranus: –346°F
  Neptune: –360°F
Moons:
  Uranus: 21
  Neptune: 11
Maximum magnitude:
  Uranus: 5.5
  Neptune: 7.8

Neptune

Earth

Uranus

VOYAGER 2

After *Voyager 2*'s successful Saturn
encounter, it was reprogrammed to
conduct a Uranus fly-by, and was
subsequently renamed the *Voyager
Neptune Interstellar Mission.*

Voyager 2 encountered Uranus on
January 24, 1986, returning detailed
photos and other data on the planet, its
moons, magnetic field and dark rings.

Both *Voyager 1* and *Voyager 2* are
expected to return valuable data for two
or three more decades. Communications
will be maintained until the *Voyagers'*
nuclear power sources can no longer
supply enough electrical energy to power
critical subsystems.

The Solar System

PLUTO AND BEYOND

At the very edge of the solar system lies
the tiny planet, Pluto, as well as millions
of smaller objects that make up what is
called the Kuiper Belt. Pluto is the ninth
and usually the furthest planet from the
Sun. It is also the smallest planet in our
solar system and the very last to be
discovered. It is the only planet in our
solar system that has not been visited by
any spacecraft, although we do have
blurry pictures of its surface. Even the
Hubble Space Telescope orbiting the
Earth can only get very grainy
photographs because Pluto is so far away.

Pluto was discovered by the American
astronomer, Clyde Tombaugh, in 1930,
following a systematic search for planets
beyond Neptune. His search was carried
out by taking thousands of long-exposure
photographs of the sky and then
comparing images of the same area taken

on different nights. Although a planet at
this distance from Earth would look just
like a star on a photograph, it would
show that it moves from day to day,
unlike a star.

Pluto has one moon, Charon, and it is
unusually large in proportion to its parent
planet. Pluto is 2,390 km (1,485 miles) in
diameter, while Charon at almost half the
size (1,172 km/728 miles), could almost
be called a double planet.

INSIDE PLUTO

Pluto is smaller than the Earth's Moon
and Charon is half the size of Pluto. No
one is certain what Pluto is like inside,
but it is possible that it is a mixture of
ice and rock, covered with a mantle of
water-ice around 200–300 km
(125–200 miles) thick. On the
surface, frozen methane, carbon
monoxide and nitrogen form a layer
of frost, perhaps several kilometres or
miles deep.

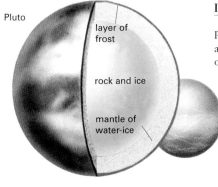

Pluto

layer of
frost

rock and ice

mantle of
water-ice

The Solar System

The atmosphere on Pluto is very thin, but when Pluto is nearest the Sun its atmosphere gets thicker because the increase in warmth releases gases from the frost on the planet's surface. The temperature on Pluto is exceptionally cold and may range from between –238°C to –228°C (–396°F to –378°F), but the average temperature is around –236°C (–393°F).

Each day on Pluto takes 6.39 Earth days. Each year on Pluto takes 247.7 Earth years, which means that it takes 247.7 Earth years for Pluto to orbit the Sun once. Occasionally, Neptune's orbit is actually outside that of Pluto, and this is because of Pluto's highly eccentric (non-circular) orbit. During this time (which is 20 years out of every 248 Earth years),

Neptune is actually the furthest planet from the Sun and not Pluto. Pluto's eccentric orbit means that its distance from the Sun varies a lot during its journey around the Sun. Also to make things even stranger, Pluto also rotates about its axis in the opposite direction from most of the other planets. This is all because Pluto's orbit is tilted at an angle of 17.15 degrees, and this is the largest inclination of any of the planets.

Although Pluto's composition is unknown, it has been determined from density calculations to be made up of about 70 percent rock and 30 percent water. There may also be methane ice together with frozen nitrogen and carbon dioxide on the cold, rocky surface.

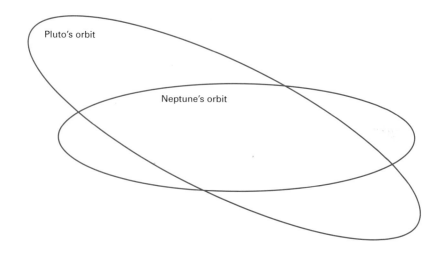

Pluto's orbit

Neptune's orbit

The Solar System

PLUTO'S MOON

Charon was discovered by Jim Christy in 1978 and was named after the mythological demon who ferried people across the mythological river Styx into Hades. Charon orbits 19,640 km (12,203 miles) from Pluto, and is 1,172 km (728 miles) in diameter.

Charon is unusual in that it is the largest moon with respect to its primary planet in the solar system. Pluto and Charon are also unique in that their orbits are gravitationally locked, which means both bodies continually keep the same hemisphere facing one another at all times. Although Charon's true composition is unknown, its low density indicates that it may be similar to Saturn's icy moon, for example Rhea. Its surface does seem to be covered with water-ice, which is quite different to that on Pluto which indicates that Pluto and Charon formed independently. It has been proposed that Charon was formed by a giant impact similar to the one that formed Earth's Moon. Another theory is that Charon could be an accumulation of the lighter materials resulting from a collision between Pluto and another large Kuiper Belt object in the ancient past.

Charon is always in the same place above the surface of Pluto. The Sun looks like a star in Pluto's sky, but it is in fact 250 times brighter than the Earth's Full Moon.

Charon seen from Pluto

The Solar System

THE KUIPER BELT

In 1992 astronomers became aware of a vast population of small bodies orbiting the Sun beyond Neptune. Called 1992 QB1, it appeared to be only about 322 km (200 miles) across. There are believed to be at least 70,000 'trans-Neptunians' ('trans' meaning on the other side of), and they may be the closest members of a belt of material at the outer edge of the solar system. These bodies occupy a ring or belt surrounding the Sun, and this ring is generally referred to as the Kuiper Belt.

The Kuiper Belt is named after the famous Dutch astronomer, Gerald Kuiper (1905–1973), who was a pioneer in solar system research using spacecraft.

This disc-shaped region of icy debris is about 12 to 15 billion km (2.8 billion to 9.3 billion miles) from our Sun. The most recent exciting discovery to come out of the Kuiper Belt is 'Quaoar' (officially known as 2002 LM60, a frozen world orbiting our Sun about 1.6 billion km (a billion miles) beyond the orbit of Pluto. This tiny world's diameter is 1,300 km (800 miles), which is about half the size of Pluto. It is the largest of more than 500 Kuiper Belt objects that have been discovered in the last decade.

Astronomers find the Kuiper Belt fascinating for many reasons. One of these is that the objects of the Belt are likely to be extremely primitive remnants from the early accretional phases of the solar system. The inner, dense parts of the pre-planetary disc condensed into major

planets, probably within a few million years. However, the outer parts were less dense and so accretion progressed slowly and it appears that a great many objects were formed. Another reason for their interest is that it is widely believed that the Kuiper Belt is the source of the short-period comets. It acts as a kind of reservoir for these comets, in the same way that the Oort Cloud (*see below*) acts as a reservoir for the long-period comets.

THE OORT CLOUD

Comets reside in a vast cloud at the outer reaches of the solar system. This has come to be known as the Oort Cloud. It is suggested that there are as many as a trillion comets within this cloud. However, since these individual comets are so small and at such large distances, we have no direct evidence regarding the Oort Cloud. This comet reservoir is named after the astronomer Jan Oort, who first suggested that comets might come from this area of outer space.

PLUTO-KUIPER EXPRESS

Scientists have designed a space mission that is planned to go to Pluto and the Kuiper Belt early in the twenty-first century. This mission is designed to fly by and make studies of the planet Pluto and its satellite Charon in the year 2012, and then fly on to encounter one or more of the large bodies in the Kuiper Belt beyond the orbit of Pluto. The mission is intended to reach Pluto before the tenuous Plutonian atmosphere can refreeze on to the surface as the planet recedes from the Sun. The main objectives of the *Express* are to characterize the geology of Pluto and Charon, map the composition of Pluto's surface, determine the composition and structure of Pluto's atmosphere and make studies of the double-planet system.

The overall structure of the spacecraft is an aluminium, hexagonal bus with no deployable structures. Its total mass will be around 220 kg (485 lb.), 7 kg (15 lb.) of which will consist of scientific instruments. It will be powered by radioisotope thermal generators similar in design to those used on earlier missions, for example on *Galileo* or *Cassini*.

The *Pluto-Kuiper Express* spacecraft will be either launched on a Delta or from the Space Shuttle, and has tentatively been scheduled for December 2004. Current plans are for the spacecraft to obtain a gravity assist from Jupiter in April to June 2006 to obtain sufficient velocity to fly-by Pluto in December 2012. Data would be transmitted back to Earth for a year following the fly-by, and then continue on to the Kuiper Belt.

The Solar System

Comet West was discovered in 1975 by Richard West, and it arrived perpendicular to the planetary plane. With its broad yellowish-white dust tail and bluish gas tail, it was seen to best effect in 1976 (*below*).

COMETS

Comets are small, fragile, irregularly-shaped bodies composed of a mixture of non-volatile grains and frozen gases. They are in theory like 'dirty snowballs' and are only a few kilometres in size. They are the leftovers from the formation of the solar system, and there are millions of them at the very fringes of the present solar system. Comets have highly elliptical orbits that bring them very close to the Sun and send them deeply into space, often beyond the orbit of Pluto. About ten comets are discovered every year, but most of them are very faint. A comet that is easily visible to the naked eye typically appears once every ten to twenty years. Most bright comets turn up unexpectedly and are only seen once, but some come around regularly. The most famous and by far the brightest of these is Halley's Comet, which takes 76 years to orbit the Sun.

HEADS AND TAILS

Comet structures are diverse and very dynamic, but they all develop a surrounding cloud of diffuse material, called a coma, that usually grows in size and brightness as the comet approaches the Sun. Usually a small, bright nucleus (less than 10 km/6 miles in diameter) is visible in the middle of the coma. The coma and the nucleus together constitute the head of the comet.

The Solar System

When a comet nucleus is a long way from the Sun, it has no coma or tail. As it approaches the Sun, its surface temperature goes up and the ice within it starts to evaporate. Gas and dust are released and stream off the nucleus, creating a huge cloud that trails away from the Sun to give the comet two tails – a curved yellowish dust tail and a straight bluish gas tail.

When far from the Sun, the nucleus is very cold and its material is frozen solid within the nucleus. In this state comets are sometimes referred to as a 'dirty iceberg' or 'dirty snowball', since over half of their material is ice. When the nucleus is frozen, it can be seen only by reflected sunlight. However, when a coma develops, dust reflects still more sunlight, and gas in the coma absorbs ultraviolet

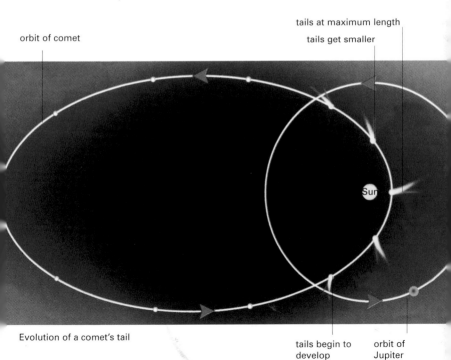

orbit of comet

tails at maximum length

tails get smaller

Sun

Evolution of a comet's tail

tails begin to develop

orbit of Jupiter

The Solar System

radiation and begins to fluoresce.

As the comet absorbs ultraviolet light, chemical processes release hydrogen, which escapes the comet's gravity, and forms a hydrogen envelope. This envelope cannot be seen from Earth because its light is absorbed by our atmosphere, but it has been detected by spacecraft.

ABOVE: Millions of people around the world saw Comet Hale-Bopp in 1997. It was discovered by Alan Hale and Thomas Bopp on July 22, 1995, and became one of the brightest comets of the twentieth century.

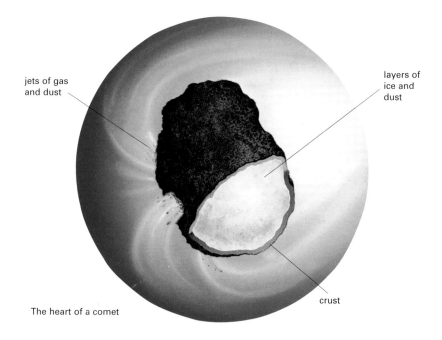

jets of gas and dust

layers of ice and dust

crust

The heart of a comet

The Solar System

PARTS OF A COMET

Nucleus The nucleus is the frozen centre of a comet's head. It is composed of ice, gas and dust. The nucleus contains most of the comet's mass but is very small, about 1 to 10 km (0.62 to 6 miles) across.

Coma The coma is the roughly spherical blob of gas that surrounds the nucleus of a comet; it is about a million kilometres across. The coma is comprised of water vapour, carbon dioxide gas, ammonia, dust and neutral gases that have sublimed from the solid nucleus. The coma and the nucleus form the head of a comet.

Ion Tail A tail of charged gases (ions) always faces away from the Sun because the solar wind pushes it away (it is also called the plasma tail). When the comet is approaching the Sun, the ion tail trails the comet, and when the comet is leaving the Sun, the ion tail leads. The tail fades as the comet moves far from the Sun. The ion tail can be well over 100 million kilometres long.

Dust Tail The dust tail is a long, wide, tail composed of microscopic dust particles that are buffeted by photons emitted from the Sun. This tail curves slightly due to the comet's motion, and then the tail fades as the comet moves away from the Sun.

Hydrogen Envelope Hydrogen gas surrounds the coma of the comet and trails along for millions of kilometres, usually between the ion tail and the dust tail. The hydrogen envelope is about 10 million kilometres across at the nucleus of the comet and about 100 million kilometres long. It is biggest when the comet is near the Sun.

COMETS IN ORBIT

Most comets travel to the inner solar system from about one light year away. They swing around the Sun then disappear far into space for thousands of years. These are called long period comets. If a comet passes close to a giant planet, particularly Jupiter, it can be caught in a smaller elliptical orbit and become a short period comet. Jupiter has trapped several dozen comets, known as Jupiter family comets, which take between five and eleven years to orbit the Sun. A periodic comet is one that is in a closed, elliptical orbit within our solar system. These comets typically have orbital periods of less than 200 years. Perhaps the best-known periodic comet is Halley's Comet, whose orbital period is 76 years.

Comets orbit the Sun in very long, flattened circles called ellipses. Their orbits can take them closer to the Sun than Mercury, and further away than Pluto. They can approach from any direction, unlike the planets, which orbit the Sun in the same plane, just as if they were all orbiting on the same flat surface around the Sun. A comet's gas tail is affected by the solar wind, so it always points away from the Sun. The dust tail becomes curved because the particles of dust orbit the Sun.

As comets pass through the inner solar system they can be broken into pieces by Jupiter's gravity. Comet Shoemaker-Levy 9 was broken into 20 separate pieces, each of which collided with Jupiter in one of the most spectacular examples of interplanetary impacts in recorded history.

The Solar System

GIOTTO SPACECRAFT

The *Giotto* mission was designed to study Halley's Comet, and also explored comet P/Grigg-Skjellerup on its extended trip. The spacecraft itself was named after the artist Giotto, who included the comet in a painting on the wall of a chapel in Padua, Italy, in 1303. He had seen the comet two years earlier.

The spacecraft encountered Halley on March 13, 1986, and the goal was to come within 500 km (310 miles) of Halley's Comet. The actual closest approach was measured at 596 km (370 miles). The *Giotto* spacecraft had a dust shield consisting of a front sheet of 1 mm (0.039 in.) thick aluminium and a 12 mm (0.4 in.) Kelvar near sheet, which could withstand impacts of particles up to 0.1 g. The spacecraft's cameras worked perfectly until 14 seconds before it passed closest to the comet nucleus. Then *Giotto* was hit by a large dust particle which put the camera out of action, and cut off all contact for a short while. Scientific data was transmitted intermittently for the next 32 minutes, but although the experiment sensors had been damaged during the impact, most of its instruments remained operational.

This was the first time that images of a comet nucleus had been studied with any real detail. The nucleus of Halley's Comet was larger then expected, and was described as a 'dirty snowball' or even as an 'icy dirt ball'. During the extended mission, the *Giotto* spacecraft successfully

Giotto spacecraft

encountered comet P/Grigg-Skjellerup on July 10, 1992. The closest approach to this comet was approximately 200 km (124 miles). The *Giotto* mission ended on July 23, 1992 and was considered to be a resounding success.

Comet Shoemaker-Levy 9

In July 1994, over 20 fragments of comet Shoemaker-Levy 9 collided with the planet Jupiter. The comet, discovered the previous year by astronomers Carolyn and Eugene Shoemaker and David Levy, was observed by astronomers at hundreds of observatories around the world as it crashed into Jupiter's Southern hemisphere. The impact caused hot flashes in Jupiter's atmosphere and left huge dark clouds that lasted for several months.

The Solar System

METEORS AND METEORITES

A meteor is a bright streak of light in the sky, usually called a 'shooting star'. This trail of light is not made by a star, it is produced by the entry of a small particle of cosmic matter as it burns up in Earth's atmosphere. It is called a meteor and on a dark, clear night you will probably be able to see these particles of space debris as they speed towards Earth making a meteor shower. An unusually bright meteor is called a 'fireball'. Some of these particles are usually the size of grains of sand, while others are much larger. Sometimes these larger chunks of material enter our atmosphere and survive their journey to the ground, and natural rocks from space that land on Earth are called meteorites.

The average weight of an object producing a faint shooting star is only a small fraction of an ounce. Even a bright fireball may not weigh more than 2 or 3 pounds. Of course the smaller objects are worn to dust by their passage through the atmosphere; it is only the large ones that reach the ground, and many thousands of meteorites may fall to Earth each year.

WHERE DO THEY COME FROM?

Between the planets, space is littered with pieces of rocky material, ranging from microscopic dust particles to large boulders and stray asteroids. There is also evidence suggesting that some meteors we observe originate from beyond our solar system. Such meteors are from other parts of the galaxy and have attained sufficient speed to escape the gravitational pull of their neighbouring large-mass bodies. Meteors from beyond our solar system are termed 'hyperbolic meteors', since their paths are hyperbolic in shape.

LEFT: 49,000 years ago a large meteor created Barringer Meteor Crater in Arizona. Barringer is over a kilometre across. In 1920, it was the first feature on Earth to be recognized as an impact crater. Today, over 100 terrestrial impact craters have been identified.

The Solar System

WHAT ARE METEORITES MADE OF?

Meteorites are exceptionally old, some maybe as old as the solar system itself. They are considerably older than any rocks on Earth, and studying them can tell us things about the early solar system and how the planets formed.

Meteorites are generally classed into three categories: stony, iron and stony-iron. Stony are the most common and make up about 93 percent of all meteorites. Iron meteorites only account for about 6 percent, and stony-iron are the rarest of all.

iron meteorite

The majority of meteorites are recovered in Antarctica, where the constant snow covers the native rocks and makes the meteorites much easier to see.

Most stony meteorites are of a type called chondrites, named because they contain small spherical inclusions called chondrules. The rock in which the chondrules are embedded is extremely old, but it does not contain volatiles. This means that they have been heated enough to rid themselves of any volatiles, but not hot enough to melt the chondrules.

Chondrites formed in the early solar system when the very first solid material condensed.

Carbonaceous chondrites contain both chondrules and volatiles. Even the slightest heat would have destroyed the volatiles, so these meteorites have never been heated and at the least altered.

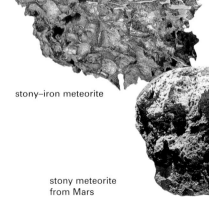

stony–iron meteorite

stony meteorite
from Mars

The Solar System

One fascinating discovery made from the study of chondrites is that in at least one case, amino acids, the building blocks of life, were found in a sample. This indicates that some of the ingredients for life on Earth may have come from outer space.

Iron meteorites have varying amounts of nickel in them. Some show a crystalline structure called Widmanstatten Lines which indicates a very slow cooling process, perhaps only a few degrees every million years.

WHEN METEORITES HIT EARTH

No one in recent history has been killed or seriously hurt by a meteorite, but there is evidence that some large meteorites fell to Earth in the distant past. Impact craters on our planet soon get worn away by wind and rain, but about 70 have now been discovered. The best preserved and the most famous is in Arizona (*pictured on page 157*).

When a meteorite comes in at high speed, there is an enormous explosion, which gouges out a crater and destroys most of the meteorite. A very large meteorite could have a devastating effect around the world, raising dust in the atmosphere and starting huge fires.

Some scientists believe that a giant meteorite hitting what is now Mexico, caused the dinosaurs and many other animal species to die out on Earth about 65 million years ago.

Finding meteorites is not easy, unless of course someone happens to see one fall. Since 1969, the most important place in the world for meteorite hunters has been Antarctica. Thousands of meteorites have been collected there – more than the whole of the rest of the world. They are carried along by the slowly moving ice so that many meteorites that fell long ago have accumulated in particular places, where they stand out against the white of the snow.

Major Meteor Showers

name	main dates
Quadrantids (Boötes)	Jan 1–6
April Lyrids	Apr 19–24
Eta Aquarids	May 4–6
Delta Aquarids	July 29–Aug 6
Perseids	Aug 12
Orionids	Oct 21
Taurids	Oct 20–Nov 30
Leonids	Nov 15–20
Geminids	Dec 13–14

World's Largest Meteorite

The world's largest known meteorite is still where it was found in Namibia, Africa, in 1920. It has become a national monument. The weight of this iron meteorite is 55,000 kg (120,000 lb.).

WATCHING THE SKY

You really don't need fancy telescopes or binoculars to watch the sky, but of course they will enhance what you see. Discovering stars and planets for yourself can be a very rewarding experience and it is not hard to get started. The chances are you have already seen one of the planets in our solar system without even realizing it. Bright planets actually look like bright stars, except that stars twinkle, while planets generally shine with a steady light.

FINDING YOUR WAY AROUND THE SKY

To really see the stars well, you need to be away from bright lights, because you can see so much more from somewhere dark. Ensure you have everything you need so that you don't have to keep going back inside after your eyes have become adjusted to the dark. When you first go out in the dark it is difficult to see anything but the brightest stars, however, after about 20 minutes your eyes become adjusted and you will be able to see even more. Take suitable clothing, something to sit on, some food and drink, as well as binoculars, star maps and notebooks.

Outside, in the dark, your star maps will be difficult to read, so ensure you use a torch covered with red cellophane to localize and soften the light so that your eyes remain dark adapted.

You can start exploring the sky when you have found just one well-known pattern of bright stars, such as Orion (the Hunter). Lines of bright stars, like those in Orion's belt, make helpful 'signposts'

to the constellations. Use your eyes to trace the path from one bright star to another to discover other beautiful constellations. It won't be long before you are able to recognize them all.

Binoculars are probably the most useful optical aid for beginners and experienced observers alike. They are easy to use, portable, as well as being very good value for money. They allow you to see the image the right way up and to use both eyes for viewing, whereas a telescope is used with one eye and shows an object upside down. Binoculars have a low magnification and wide field of view, and this makes them ideal for studying the surface features of the Moon, scanning the Milky Way and observing open and globular star structures.

Before you rush out and buy a telescope for yourself, it is a good idea to find a friend who owns an astronomical telescope, and ask if you may look through it several times. Some clubs own telescopes that they will loan out to their members, so try before you buy.

Watching the Sky

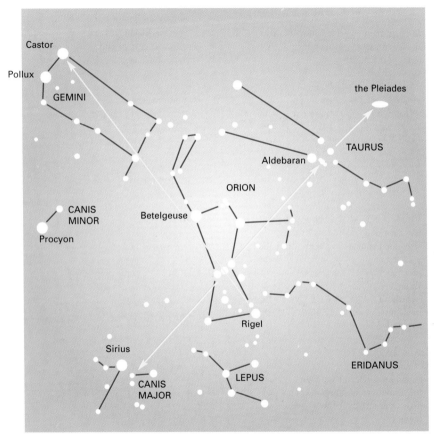

Perhaps second only to the Big Dipper in Ursa Major, the constellation of Orion is one of the most recognizable patterns of stars in the northern sky. Orion, the Hunter, stands by the river Eridanus and is accompanied by his faithful dogs, Canis Major and Canis Minor. Together they hunt various celestial animals, including Lepus, the Rabbit, and Taurus, the Bull.

Watching the Sky

THE NIGHT SKY

On any clear night it is possible to see the most fantastic sights. To find out which stars you can expect to see at a particular time, look at the star maps on pages 189–279. As you start to observe the stars you will notice that they appear to twinkle, and this is because a star is simply a point of light, so its beam is easily disturbed by moving currents of air in our atmosphere. The best nights for observing with a telescope are when the air is fairly still, so that the stars do not appear to twinkle too much.

Planets are all much nearer to Earth than any star, so the beam of light reaching us from a planet's disc is wider than the beam from a star and it flickers far less. This steady light helps you to pick the planets out from the stars. Venus, Mars, Jupiter and Saturn all appear very bright in the night sky at certain times of the year, and they are good objects to observe through a small telescope.

Every other year Mars becomes particularly bright for a few weeks. Mars takes a little over two years to complete its orbit, and for half that time it is too far away to be easily seen.

Jupiter and Saturn change their positions very slowly, but they do appear for several months each year.

If you are just starting to use binoculars, then one of the best things to observe is the Moon. It is very easy to pick out the largest craters and the dark seas. Try looking at the boundary between the bright and dark parts of the Moon – called the 'terminator' – because here the mountains and craters look very dramatic. They cast long, dark shadows because the Sun's light is striking them at a low angle.

A few meteors can be seen most nights, but it is best to watch on a night when a meteor shower is due (*see page 159*). Meteor showers are visible with the naked eye, so you will have no need of a telescope or binoculars to observe this fascinating sight.

Ensure that your binoculars are properly set for your eyes before you start observing. First, move the eyepieces so that they are the right distance apart for you. Turn the centre wheel to focus on an object using your left eye only. Finally, turn the right eyepiece to focus on the same object.

Watching the Sky

PATTERNS IN THE SKY

At first glance all stars appear to be very much the same and distinguishing one star from another initially seems almost impossible. However, if you look closer you will notice that some stars are brighter than others, and if you were to join these together, certain shapes would emerge. These patterns, or constellations, have been used for thousands of years and still provide the best way of learning your way around the sky. A constellation consists of a star pattern and the sky immediately around it.

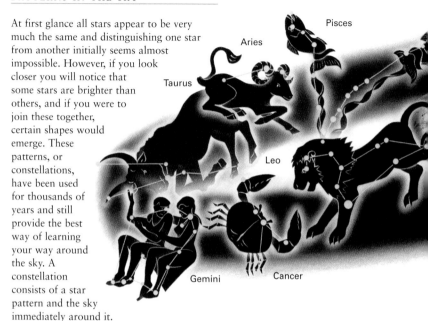

The main constellations and what their names mean

Andromeda	Andromeda*	Capricornus	Sea Goat
Aquarius	The Water-Bringer	Carina	Keel
Aquila	Eagle	Cassiopeia	Cassiopeia*
Ara	Altar	Centaurus	Centaur
Aries	Ram	Cepheus	Cepheus*
Auriga	Charioteer	Cetus	Whale
Boötes	Herdsman	Corona Borealis	Northern Crown
Cancer	Crab	Corvus	Crow
Canis Major	Great Dog	Crux	Cross
Canis Minor	Small Dog	Cygnus	Swan

Watching the Sky

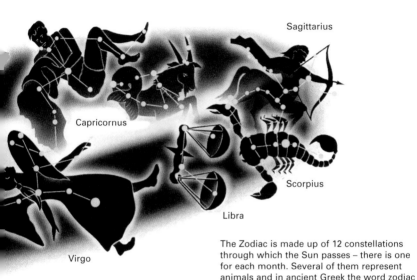

Sagittarius

Capricornus

Scorpius

Libra

Virgo

The Zodiac is made up of 12 constellations through which the Sun passes – there is one for each month. Several of them represent animals and in ancient Greek the word zodiac means 'animals'.

Delphinus	Dolphin	Orion	Hunter
Dorado	Swordfish	Pegasus	Winged Horse*
Draco	Dragon	Perseus	Perseus*
Eridanus	River Eridanus	Phoenix	Phoenix
Gemini	Twins	Pisces	Fish
Grus	Crane	Sagittarius	Archer
Hercules	Hercules*	Scorpius	Scorpion
Hydra	Water Snake	Scutum	Shield
Indus	Indian	Taurus	Bull
Leo	Lion	Tucana	Toucan
Lepus	Hare	Ursa Major	Great Bear
Libra	Scales	Ursa Minor	Small Bear	*names from
Lyra	Lyre	Vela	Sails	ancient
Ophiuchus	Serpent-Bearer	Virgo	Virgin	mythology

Watching the Sky

PATTERNS IN THE SKY

At first glance all stars appear to be very much the same and distinguishing one star from another initially seems almost impossible. However, if you look closer you will notice that some stars are brighter than others, and if you were to join these together, certain shapes would emerge. These patterns, or constellations, have been used for thousands of years and still provide the best way of learning your way around the sky. A constellation consists of a star pattern and the sky immediately around it.

The earliest known efforts to catalogue the stars, dates back to cuneiform texts dating back roughly 6,000 years. These remnants, found in the valley of the Euphrates river, suggest that the people of this period observed the heavens as animals, for example, the Lion, the Bull and the Scorpion. The earliest reference to the mythological significance of the Greek constellations can be found in the works of Homer, which probably date back to the seventh century BC.

There are 88 constellations that can be found in the night sky, and they can be found in several different areas. The amateur observer can find them by simply looking for a cluster of stars, especially the really bright ones, and then try to form a pattern or picture of them.

At one time the constellations consisted of curved lines which outlined the pictures that the constellations represented. However, in the year 1928,

This drawing of Orion is 1,000 years old, and was drawn by Arabic astronomer Al-Sufi. It shows Orion holding a curved sword. Al-Sufi wrote a list of 1,018 bright stars, and also made illustrations like this one to show their positions.

astronomers changed the curved lines to straight ones, so that each constellation consisted of lines that ran from north to south or east to west.

The 12 zodiac constellations are the ones that are most commonly recognized. They can be seen from both the Northern and Southern hemispheres and are called: Cancer, Aquarius, Gemini, Sagittarius, Taurus, Virgo, Pisces, Libra, Leo,

Watching the Sky

Capricorn, Aries and Scorpio. The two most common ones are Sagittarius and Taurus.

Sagittarius is Latin for the word 'Archer', and its picture shows a centaur which is the top of a man's body on a horse's lower body. Within the stars that comprise the Sagittarius constellation, lies the centre of the galaxy known as the Milky Way. This means that when you are viewing this constellation, you are actually looking at the centre of the galaxy. It also contains the Lagoon, Horseshoe and Trifid nebulae. This constellation reaches its highest point in the evening sky in August.

The Taurus constellation which is known as the 'Bull', shows up first in the month of September. This is one of the easiest constellations to see and it is just northwest of the Orion constellation. In Greek mythology, it represents the legendary animal who carried the princess Europa to the island of Crete. It is home to many star clusters such as the Pleiades (M45) and the Hyades (Mel25), and it is also possible to find the Crab Nebula M1 within its borders. This constellation is also home to important stellar formation regions. To the naked eye or with binoculars, we are treated to a wonderful show featuring the Pleiades and the Hyades.

Cancer, the Crab, is small and dim, and lies between Gemini to the west and Leo to the east, Lynx to the north and Canis Minor and Hydra to the south. The brightest star to be found within this constellation is β Cancri which is considered to be the end of the crab's leg. Cancer is best-known among stargazers as the home of Praesepe (M440), an open cluster also called the Beehive Cluster or the Gate of Men, which contains the star β Cancri. In Greek mythology, Cancer was a brave little crab who tried to stop Hercules from defeating the Lernaean Hydra and was squashed for his efforts.

There are so many beautiful and interesting sights to be found in the night sky, and the constellations are just some of the bright sights.

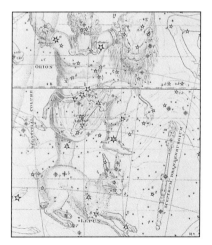

This picture of Orion is taken from a star atlas of 1822. In the centre, three bright stars make up Orion's belt, with the sword below. Several of the stars have the Arabic names given them by Al-Sufi.

Watching the Sky

MOVEMENT OF THE STARS

If you look up at the stars for long enough you will notice that they move across the sky. They do not move relative to one another, but as a whole. Stars are continually moving with respect to our solar system. Some are moving away from us while others are moving towards us. This movement affects the wavelengths of light that we receive from them, and this phenomenon is called the Doppler effect. Measuring the amount of Doppler shift tells us how fast the star is moving relative to us.

In most parts of the world, if you were to follow a particular star throughout the night, you would find that it first appears over the eastern horizon as darkness falls. Next it arcs up through the sky, reaching its highest point in the south. It then arcs down again, eventually disappearing over the western horizon when daylight returns. Most of the stars arc through the night sky in a similar way, travelling from east to west, as the Sun does.

The celestial sphere then appears to be rotating from east to west around the Earth. In fact, it is the reverse. It is the Earth that is moving relative to the stars. It spins around once a day on its axis, an imaginary line passing through the North and South Poles.

It is because of the rotation of the Earth that we must specify on a star map a particular time of night when the stars will appear in the sky in the positions shown on the map. At other times, the

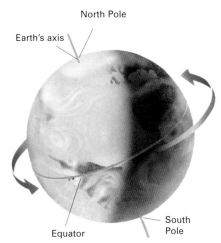

The reason why the stars wheel overhead is because the Earth spins on its own axis, making one revolution each day. We show the axis tilted to reflect the fact that it is tilted in relation to the direction it travels through space.

stars will appear in different positions in the sky.

CHANGING WITH THE SEASONS

If you are a regular watcher of the heavens you will notice that over a period of months some constellations are always present. Others, however, come and go. This is because of Earth's motion in space – its orbit around the Sun once a year.

There are two major motions affecting

Watching the Sky

the Earth: its rotation around its axis, and its rotation around the Sun (its revolution). While the rotation of the Earth on its axis causes the nightly movement of the stars across the sky, the revolution is responsible for the fact that we can see different parts of the sky at different parts of the year.

Take a look at the image below. On a given day you would only be able to see the stars that are in the opposite direction to the Sun. All the stars that are 'behind' the Sun won't be visible during that day, because they are above the horizon during the day, and it is only possible to see stars during the night. However, if you waited six months, the Earth would be at the opposite on its orbit, and you would then be able to see those stars that you couldn't see six months earlier because they were blocked by the Sun. This is why over the course of one year, we end up being able to see all the stars that are possible to observe from our latitude on Earth.

SEASONAL STAR MAPS

The maps that follow show views of the night sky as it appears in late evening in mid-latitudes in the Northern and Southern hemispheres in midwinter and midsummer and at the time of the March and September equinoxes. Using these maps will help you identify the constellations and get your celestial bearings season by season.

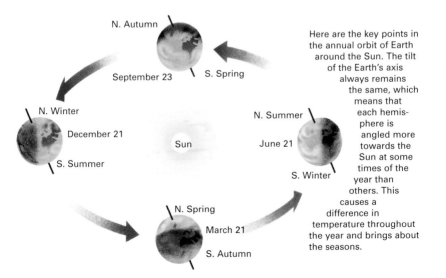

N. Autumn

September 23   S. Spring

N. Winter

December 21

S. Summer

Sun

N. Summer

June 21

S. Winter

N. Spring

March 21

S. Autumn

Here are the key points in the annual orbit of Earth around the Sun. The tilt of the Earth's axis always remains the same, which means that each hemisphere is angled more towards the Sun at some times of the year than others. This causes a difference in temperature throughout the year and brings about the seasons.

Watching the Sky

NORTHERN HEMISPHERE WINTER

In the Northern hemisphere, the Winter Solstice occurs either December 21 or 22, when the Sun shines directly over the Tropic of Capricorn. Winter brings some of the most splendid constellations to northern skies, and they are seen at their best during the long, dark evenings.

DECEMBER 21

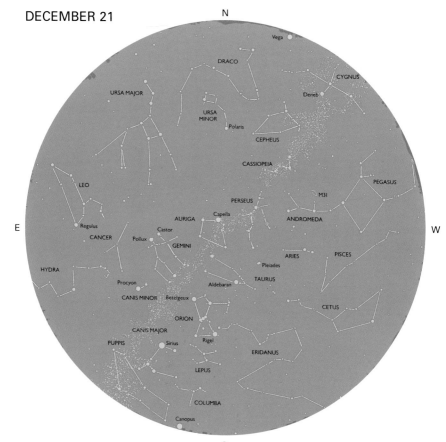

Watching the Sky

USING THIS MAP

★ This map represents the dome of the heavens at 11 p.m. local time on the date of the Winter Solstice, December 21.

★ Because the stars rise about four minutes earlier each night, you will see a similar view of the heavens on December 14 at 11.30 p.m. and on December 28 at 10.30 p.m.

★ The centre of the map is your zenith. The edge of the map is your horizon. You may be able to see a little more or a little less north or south than the map shows, because your horizon depends on your latitude.

Looking south: To locate the constellations in the southern part of the sky, face south. The Sun will have to set on your right. Hold the map in front of you with SOUTH at the bottom. The lower half of the map now represents the part of the sky in front of you.

Looking north: To locate the constellations in the northern part of the sky, face north. The Sun will have set on your left. Turn the map upside down so that NORTH is at the bottom. The lower half of the map now represents the part of the sky in front of you.

Key to star types and phenomena

●	Star
◯	0
◯	0.7
◯	1.3 Apparent
◯	2.0 Visual
•	2.7 Magnitude
·	3.3
·	4.0
◉	
◯	Variable stars
⬭	Galaxy
✦	Globular cluster

Most magnificent of all the constellations is Orion, depicting the mighty hunter facing up to the charging bull Taurus. This constellation dominates the southern aspect of the sky, with its two brightest, first-magnitude stars Betelgeux and Rigel contrasting nicely in colour, the one noticeably red, the other pure white.

The three bright stars in Orion's 'belt' act as pointers for locating two other celestial beacons, Aldebaran, which is higher in the sky; and Syrius, the Dog Star, which is lower. Aldebaran marks the angry red eye of Taurus, while Sirius (Canis Major), is the brightest star in the whole heavens.

Also visible is the pearly white arch of the Milky Way, separating Orion and Canis Major from Gemini and Canis Minor. Gemini boasts two bright stars Castor and Pollux, while Canis Minor has just one, Procyon.

Overhead, at the zenith, on the edge of the Milky Way, is another beacon star Capella (Auriga). The northern aspect of the sky shows Pegasus in the west, Leo in the east, and Cygnus in between, with the ever-brilliant Cassiopeia above it and also embedded in the Milky Way. The two stars at the cup end of the Big Dipper, as always, point to the Pole Star, Polaris.

Watching the Sky

NORTHERN HEMISPHERE SPRING

March 20 or 21 is significant for astronomical reasons, because the Sun will cross directly over the Earth's equator. With the coming of spring, Orion is setting by the late evening, although there is still plenty of time after sunset to view it.

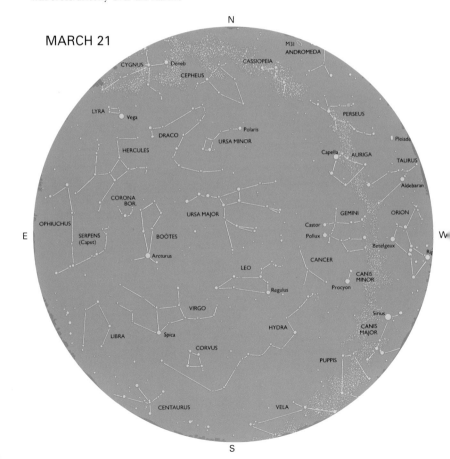

MARCH 21

Watching the Sky

USING THIS MAP

★ This map represents the dome of the heavens at 11 p.m. local time on the date of the Spring, or Vernal Equinox, March 21.

★ Because the stars rise about four minutes earlier each night, you will see a similar view of the heavens on March 14 at 11.30 p.m. and on March 28 at 10.30 p.m.

★ The centre of the map is your zenith. The edge of the map is your horizon. You may be able to see a little more or a little less north or south than the map shows, because your horizon depends on your latitude.

Key to star types and phenomena	
●	Star
●	0
●	0.7
●	1.3 Apparent
●	2.0 Visual
●	2.7 Magnitude
●	3.3
·	4.0
◎	Variable stars
○	
◢	Galaxy
✛	Globular cluster

The central five stars of The Big Dipper, plus Alcor and several other stars, constitute a physical group, the Ursa Major Cluster.

The southern aspect of the sky in late evening belongs to Leo, distinctive back-to-front question mark star pattern (the Sickle) traces the Lion's head and mane.

Arcing southwest towards Orion, the twins Castor and Pollux (Gemini) are still prominent. Between Leo and Gemini, Cancer contains one of the top three star clusters in the northern heavens, Praesepe (Beehive).

Castor and Pollux are approximate pointers, aiming southwest to the brighter Procyon (Canis Minor). Further south, Canis Major and its prime star Sirius are close to setting.

In the east, the only two really bright stars are Spica (Virgo) and Arcturus (Boötes). Arcturus is a warm orange colour and the brightest star in the Northern hemisphere.

The northern aspect of the sky reveals the Big Dipper high up. Cassiopeia is fairly low in the northwest, pointing to the brilliant Capella (Auriga). Seemingly linked with Auriga is Taurus, whose chief star is Aldebaran. Its reddish hue contrasts noticeably with Capella's pure bluish-white. Taurus' other main naked-eye attractions are its two prominent star clusters, the Hyades, surrounding Aldebaran, and the Pleiades, or Seven Sisters.

In the east Deneb (Cygnus) and Vega (Lyra) appear close to the horizon. The distinctive crescent of the Northern Crown (Corona Borealis) appears higher up.

Watching the Sky

NORTHERN HEMISPHERE
SUMMER

In June the Northern hemisphere is tilted
towards the Sun and experiences summer.

With summer come the warmer nights,
which makes stargazing a pleasure.
However, there is also a drawback
because the skies are never really dark.

JUNE 21

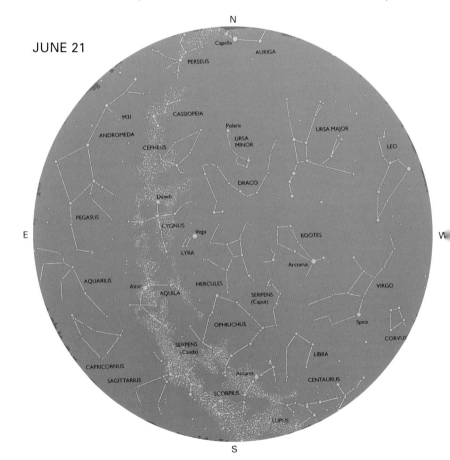

Watching the Sky

USING THIS MAP

★ This map represents the dome of the heavens at 11 p.m. local time on the date of the Summer Solstice, June 21.

★ Because the stars rise about four minutes earlier each night, you will see a similar view of the heavens on June 14 at 11.30 p.m. and on June 28 at 10.30 p.m.

★ The centre of the map is your zenith. The edge of the map is your horizon. You may be able to see a little more or a little less north or south than the map shows, because your horizon depends on your latitude.

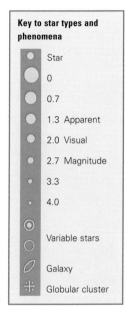

Key to star types and phenomena

Star	
0	
0.7	
1.3	Apparent
2.0	Visual
2.7	Magnitude
3.3	
4.0	
Variable stars	
Galaxy	
Globular cluster	

High in the sky at this time of the summer solstice are three first-magnitude stars, Deneb (Cygnus), Vega (Lyra) and Altair (Aquila). They form the celebrated Summer Triangle. It overlays a rich region of the Milky Way, although it is difficult to appreciate it fully because of the light skies.

One of the truly great stars of our galaxy, Deneb serves a three-fold role among the constellations. Deneb, in the tail of the flying Swan, is the dimmest of the summer trio, at least to the eye. In reality, it is thousands of times more luminous, appearing dimmer only because it is more than 60 to 100 times further away respectively than Vega and Altair.

Deneb shines high in the northeast, while above the eastern horizon is Andromeda and part of the Square of Pegasus, which will become prominent in autumnal skies. Leo, meanwhile, is about to set in the far west.

The other two stars of the Summer Triangle, Vega, and Altair, appear in southeastern skies, the one high up, the other midway to the horizon. Rising just above the horizon here are portions of two of the splendid Southern hemisphere constellations that northern astronomers drool over. They are Sagittarius and, nearly due south, Scorpius, whose pulsating red supergiant star Antares ('Rival of Mars') marks the Scorpion's heart. The easiest way to find Scorpius is to look for his red heart, the star Antares. Antares is a red giant, a very old star that has swollen very large and therefore appears very bright to us. Antares forms one corner of a more widely separated 'summer triangle' with Spica (Virgo), at about the same elevation, and Arcturus (Boötes) further north.

Watching the Sky

NORTHERN HEMISPHERE AUTUMN

On September 22 our planet's 'subsolar point' crosses the equator heading south. With it, spring begins in the Southern hemisphere and autumn in the north. With evening skies darkening perceptibly, the Milky Way can now be better appreciated as it cuts across the sky from northeast to southwest.

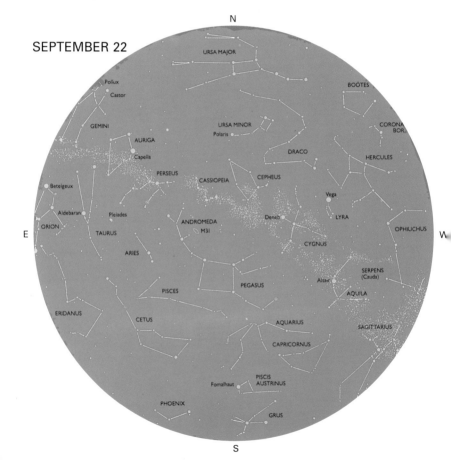

Watching the Sky

USING THIS MAP

★ This map represents the dome of the heavens at 11 p.m. local time on the date of the Autumn Equinox, September 22.

★ Because the stars rise about four minutes earlier each night, you will see a similar view of the heavens on September 16 at 11.30 p.m. and on September 30 at 10.30 p.m.

★ The centre of the map is your zenith. The edge of the map is your horizon. You may be able to see a little more or a little less north or south than the map shows, because your horizon depends on your latitude.

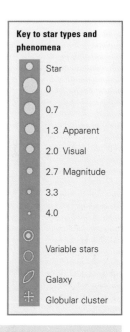

Key to star types and phenomena

●	Star
●	0
●	0.7
●	1.3 Apparent
●	2.0 Visual
●	2.7 Magnitude
•	3.3
·	4.0
◎	Variable stars
○	
⬭	Galaxy
✢	Globular cluster

Looking south, this silvery arch carries with it Cygnus high overhead, and Aquila lower down. The Summer Triangle, formed by their two main stars, Deneb and Altair, together with Vega (Lyra), is still conspicuous, though not for long.

The late evening sky is now graced by Pegasus with its unmistakable Square. The two stars in the westernmost side of the Square act as pointers to Fomalhaut (Piscis Austrinus), just visible above the southern horizon.

The line of stars running east from the northern side of the Square belong to Andromeda. This constellation's main claim to fame is the fuzzy patch of light we can see just to the north of the line of stars. This patch, once thought to be a nebula in our own galaxy, turns out to be a quite separate galaxy, much bigger than our own, but incredibly distant (some 22 million million million kilometres, 13.5 million million million miles).

Looking north, the Big Dipper is near its lowest point, while on the other side of Polaris, Cassiopeia is near its highest.

Pegasus the Flying Horse is an autumnal constellation, not resembling a horse as much as it does a flying brick.

While much of Boötes is visible in the northwest, its bright star Arcturus is below the horizon. Close by is the distinctive curve of the Northern Crown (Corona Borealis).

There is more interest, however, in the east where Auriga and Taurus have now risen, with their two brilliant main stars, Capella and Aldebaran, set for prominence in the winter skies.

Watching the Sky

SOUTHERN HEMISPHERE SUMMER

While astronomers in the Northern Hemisphere shiver in midwinter, their colleagues 'down under' in the Southern hemisphere enjoy the balmy nights of midsummer. The Summer Solstice is the longest day of the year, respectively, in the sense that the length of time elapsed between sunrise and sunset on this day is a maximum for the year.

DECEMBER 21

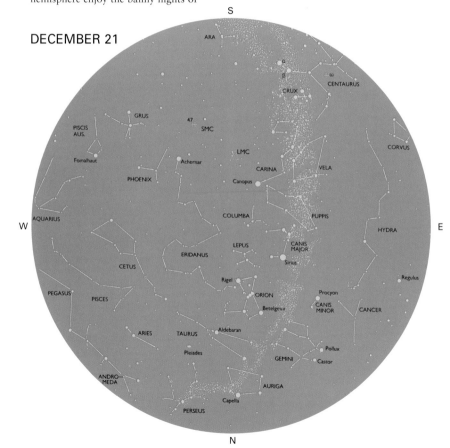

Watching the Sky

USING THIS MAP

★ This map represents the dome of the heavens at 11 p.m. local time on the date of the Summer Solstice, December 21.

★ Because the stars rise about four minutes earlier each night, you will see a similar view of the heavens on December 14 at 11.30 p.m. and on December 28 at 10.30 p.m.

★ The centre of the map is your zenith. The edge of the map is your horizon. You may be able to see a little more or a little less north or south than the map shows, because your horizon depends on your latitude.

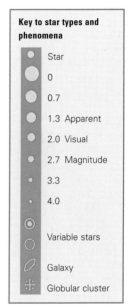

Key to star types and phenomena

- Star
- 0
- 0.7
- 1.3 Apparent
- 2.0 Visual
- 2.7 Magnitude
- 3.3
- 4.0
- Variable stars
- Galaxy
- Globular cluster

As in the Northern hemisphere, Orion is a dominant constellation, seen by southern astronomers in the northern aspect of the sky. These see it with white Rigel in the upper left of the main pattern, and the reddish Betelgeux in the bottom right.

Following a line through the three stars of Orion's 'belt' leads higher up to the brightest star in the heavens, Sirius (Canis Major) and lower down to the reddish Aldebaran (Taurus). Continuing the same line through Aldebaran leads to the Pleiasdes, or Seven Sisters, star cluster. And near the horizon beneath Aldebaran is the brighter Capella (Auriga).

East of Capella are the twins, Castor and Pollux (Gemini), with the brilliant Procyon (Canis Minor) higher up. The brilliant stars in this corner of the sky together form a prominent hexagonal pattern.

The southern aspect of the sky, as always in the Southern hemisphere, is spectacular. The second brightest star in the heavens, Canopus (Carina), sits high in the sky, as does Achernar (Eridanus)

further west. Further west still and lower is Fomalhaut (Piscis Austrinus).

The Southern Cross (Crux) and its two pointers, Alpha and Beta Centauri (Centaurus), are stunning as always, and seen relatively close to the horizon. Beta Centauri is a blue-white supergiant and in about 4,000 years, the proper motion of Alpha Centauri will carry it close enough to Beta Centauri that they will appear to be a magnificent double star. The fuzzy patches we see southwest of Canopus are neighbouring galaxies, the Large (Doradus) and Small Magellanic Cloud (Tucana).

Watching the Sky

SOUTHERN HEMISPHERE AUTUMN

The bright starscapes of winter no longer dominate the northern aspect of the sky in the late evening. Orion, Gemini, Canis Major and Canis Minor are fast slipping away in the west. In the Southern hemisphere, the Autumnal Equinox corresponds to the centre of the Sun crossing the celestial equator moving northwards and occurs on the date of the Northern Vernal Equinox.

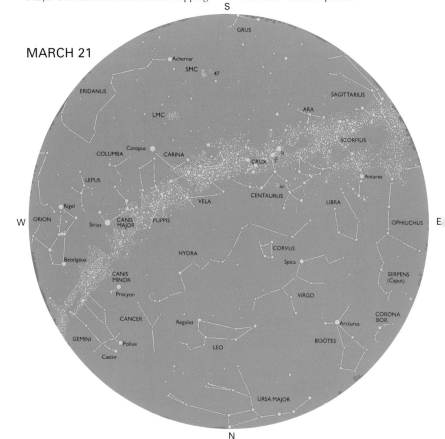

Watching the Sky

USING THIS MAP

★ This map represents the dome of the heavens at 11 p.m. local time on the date of the March equinox, March 21.

★ Because the stars rise about four minutes earlier each night, you will see a similar view of the heavens on March 14 at 11.30 p.m. and on March 28 at 10.30 p.m.

★ The centre of the map is your zenith. The edge of the map is your horizon. You may be able to see a little more or a little less north or south than the map shows, because your horizon depends on your latitude.

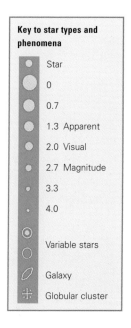

Key to star types and phenomena

Star

0

0.7

1.3 Apparent

2.0 Visual

2.7 Magnitude

3.3

4.0

Variable stars

Galaxy

Globular cluster

It is Leo that now occupies centre stage, with its hook-like pattern of stars 'hanging' from the first-magnitude Regulus. Two other bright stars lie to the east. Spica (Virgo) at about the same elevation as Regulus (Leo) and Arcturus (Boötes) lower down. The remainder of the sky is relatively barren, because of the sprawling constellation Hydra near the zenith, which has no bright stars at all.

Turning to the southern aspect, this is occupied by a great swathe of the Milky Way, with more than its fair share of stellar delights. These range from the Southern Cross (Crux) and Alpha and Beta Centauri (Centaurus) high up, to the wickedly curved tail of Scorpius, the Scorpion, which is just appearing over the eastern horizon and will become one of winter's great pleasures.

The longer arm of the Southern Cross points almost to the celestial South Pole. But there is no convenient bright star to mark the pole's position as there is in the Northern hemisphere (Polaris, the Pole Star).

But the Cross does point more or less in the direction of the Small Magellanic Cloud (Tucana), located on the other side of the pole. The Large Megallanic Cloud (Dorado) is located higher up, in the direction of the brilliant Canopus (Carina). Carina is home to Canopus (Alpha Carinae), the second brightest star in the heavens. The two clouds form a triangle with Achernar, the only bright star in Eridanus, recently risen above the horizon.

Watching the Sky

SOUTHERN HEMISPHERE WINTER

The winter skies in the Southern hemisphere are the stamping ground of the Scorpion (Scorpius), whose curved tail is poised ready to deal a deadly sting. The constellation is high overhead, instantly recognizable and breathtaking in its beauty. The brightest star, the red Antares, lies near the zenith.

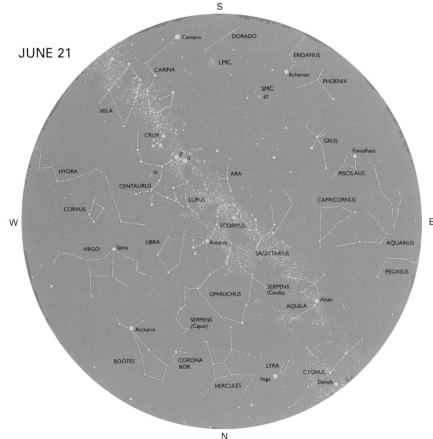

Watching the Sky

USING THIS MAP

★ This map represents the dome of the heavens at 11 p.m. local time on the date of the Winter Solstice, June 21.

★ Because the stars rise about four minutes earlier each night, you will see a similar view of the heavens on June 14 at 11.30 p.m. and on June 28 at 10.30 p.m.

★ The centre of the map is your zenith. The edge of the map is your horizon. You may be able to see a little more or a little less north or south than the map shows, because your horizon depends on your latitude.

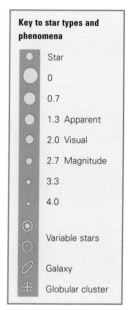

Key to star types and phenomena

●	Star
●	0
●	0.7
●	1.3 Apparent
●	2.0 Visual
●	2.7 Magnitude
·	3.3
·	4.0
◎	Variable stars
○	
⬭	Galaxy
✻	Globular cluster

Cheek-by-jowl with the Scorpion in what is the richest part of the Milky Way is Sagittarius. This constellation overflows with astronomical delights, which binoculars show to perfection. There are dense and brilliant star clouds, swirling nebulae and scattered star clusters. The reason why the Milky Way appears so dense here is because the centre of our galaxy lies in this direction.

The northern aspect of the sky shows, south of Sagittarius and also in the Milky Way, the bright Altair (Aquila), Vega (Lyra) further south and east rises later, while Deneb (Cygnus) rises later still. These three stars form a prominent winter triangle, which northern astronomers call the Summer Triangle to match their own season.

The higher of the only two prominent stars in the northwest is Spica (Virgo); the lower is Arcturus (Boötes). Close by is the half-circle of stars known as the Northern Crown (Corona Borealis), which is so much easier to place than its southern equivalent. The southern aspect of the winter sky reveals the Southern Cross (Crux) and its bright pointers Alpha and Beta Centauri (Centaurus) descending. Alpha Centauri is the nearest bright star to us, around 4.3 light years, or some 40 million million kilometres (25 million million miles) away. The Southern Cross also contains several deep sky objects. The best-known of these are the Jewel Box (NGC 4755), also known as the Kappa Crucis, which is a star cluster composed of over a hundred stars. About 50 of these stars are a mixture of colourful supergiants – reds and blues intermingled with yellows and whites in a profusion of sparkling light. The Coal Sack is a large dark nebula just to the south of the Jewel Box, and this is visible to the naked eye.

Watching the Sky

SOUTHERN HEMISPHERE SPRING

The great delights of winter skies, Sagittarius and Scorpius, are now seen in the southwest. They are still well placed for viewing, but in the next few weeks they will disappear from the late evening skies.

SEPTEMBER 23

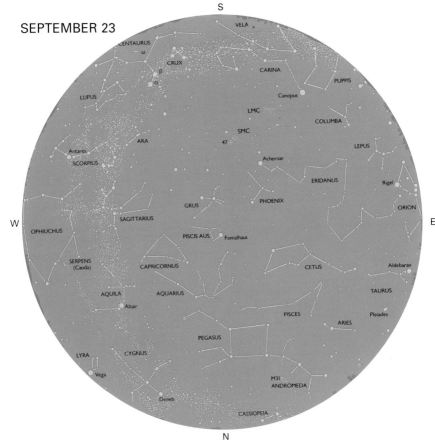

Watching the Sky

USING THIS MAP

★ This map represents the dome of the heavens at 11 p.m. local time on the date of the September Equinox, September 23.

★ Because the stars rise about four minutes earlier each night, you will see a similar view of the heavens on September 16 at 11.30 p.m. and on September 30 at 10.30 p.m.

★ The centre of the map is your zenith. The edge of the map is your horizon. You may be able to see a little more or a little less north or south than the map shows, because your horizon depends on your latitude.

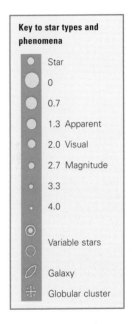

Key to star types and phenomena

Star	
0	
0.7	
1.3	Apparent
2.0	Visual
2.7	Magnitude
3.3	
4.0	
	Variable stars
	Galaxy
	Globular cluster

Still looking south, the Southern Cross (Crux) and its pointers, Alpha and Beta Centauri (Centaurus), are now low down on the horizon. So is the 'False Cross', formed by a pair of stars in Vela and a pair in Carina.

The Magellanic Clouds are particularly well placed for observation, the Small Cloud appearing nearly due south and the Large Cloud (Dorado) more to the east and lower down.

The two Clouds are more or less in line with the brilliant Canopus (Carina), a star only exceeded in brightness by Sirius (Canis Major), which is just rising (or about to rise, depending on the observer's latitude) above the eastern horizon.

The northern aspect of the spring sky shows the Square of Pegasus prominent. The showpiece constellations of summer, Taurus and Orion, are about to rise in the east. The Pleiades, or Seven Sisters, star cluster may well be already above the horizon.

High overhead, near the zenith, Fomalhaut (Piscis Austranus) is conspicuous, not because it is outstandingly bright but because it appears in a relatively barren part of the heavens.

In the northwest, two or even three stars of the 'winter triangle' may still be visible. Altair (Aquila) is relatively high in the sky, while Deneb (Cygnus) is close to setting, and Vega (Lyra) may have set already. Altair, the 12th brightest star in the sky, is one of the stars nearest Earth at only 16.5 light years away and one of the smaller super stars in that it averages only 48.9 million kilometres (30.36 million miles) in diameter.

Watching the Sky

SEASONS ON OTHER PLANETS

Planet	*e* orbital eccentricity	spin axis tilt (degree)	Vernal Equinox Spring begins	Summer Solstice Summer begins	Autumnal Equinox Autumn begins	Winter Solstice Winter begins
Mercury	0.21	<28	n/a	n/a	n/a	n/a
Venus	0.01	3	Sept 17, 2000	Nov 12, 2000	Jan 8, 2001	Mar 4, 2001
Earth	0.02	23.5	Mar 21 0146 UT	June 21 1949 UT	Sept 23 1131 UT	Dec 22 0744 UT
Mars	0.09	24	Jun 1, 2000	Dec 16, 2000	Jun 18, 2001	Nov 11, 2001
Jupiter	0.05	3	Aug 1997	May 2000	Mar 2003	Mar 2006
Saturn	0.06	26.75	1980	1987	1995	2002
Uranus	0.05	82	1922	1943	1964	1985
Neptune	0.01	28.5	1880	1921	1962	2003

SEASONS ON THE PLANETS

With the arrival of autumn in Earth's Northern hemisphere, our planet joins two other worlds where it is also northern autumn – Saturn and Neptune. Autumn on those planets isn't much like Earth – there are no golden leaves that fall to the ground or gently chilled breezes that hint at the onset of winter. Saturn and Neptune don't even have any firm surface for leaves to fall on because they are both giant balls of gas.

Although it may seem strange to us that there are actually seasons on other planets, they are in fact just as defined as they are on Earth. When the Sun shines directly over a planet's equator, that is an equinox. When one of the poles is tilted towards the Sun to its maximum extent, it is a solstice. The equinoxes and solstices for eight of the nine planets are shown in the table above. Pluto has been omitted because so little is known about this distant planet.

Let us use Mars as an example of how the seasons change. Mars has the highest orbital eccentricity of any other planet, with the exception of Mercury and Pluto. Its distance from the Sun varies between 1.64 and 1.36 AU over the Martian year. This large variation, combined with an axial tilt greater than Earth's, produces a very strange seasonal change on this planet. When Mars is closest to the Sun,

Watching the Sky

it is wintertime in the planet's North Pole. Icy temperatures at that end of the planet plunge so low that carbon dioxide, the main constituent of Mar's atmosphere, actually freezes and falls to the ground. So much of the red planet's atmosphere turns to ice, that the global atmospheric pressure drops by 25 percent. This means that Mar's atmosphere is considerably thinner during the northern winter.

The season changes on Uranus are even stranger than those on Mars. Like Earth, Uranus follows an orbit that is nearly circular, which means it keeps the same distance from the Sun throughout its long year. However, Uranus' spin axis is tilted by an amazing 82 degrees. This gives rise to extreme 20-year-long seasons and very unusual weather. For nearly a quarter of the year on Uranus (equal to 84 Earth years), the Sun shines directly over each pole, leaving the other half of the planet in complete darkness. The Northern hemisphere of Uranus is only just coming out of the grip of its decades-long winter. Sunlight, reaching some latitudes for the first time in years, warms the atmosphere and triggers off gigantic springtime storms which are comparable in size to North America. The temperatures during these storms can drop as low as 300° below zero. Bright clouds form which are probably made up of crystals of methane, and these condense as warm bubbles of gas move upwards through the atmosphere.

The seasons on the planet of Mercury are probably the most remarkable of all.

Mercury rotates three times on its spin axis for each two orbits it completes around the Sun. Mercury's strange rotation, together with the high eccentricity of its orbit, help to produce some very strange effects. If you were able to observe the Sun from the surface of Mercury, you would see the Sun rise and gradually increase in apparent size as it slowly moved towards the solstice. At that point the Sun would stop, briefly reverse its course, and then stop again before resuming its path towards the horizon, all the while appearing to decrease in size. Observers on other parts of Mercury would see equally bizarre sights.

The temperatures on Mercury vary drastically, ranging from −200°C (−328°F) at night in the winter to 400°C (752°F) during the day in summer, and they are the most extreme of any world that we know. Summer on Mercury is exceptionally hot, but it is still not the hottest spot in the solar system. The surface of Venus is warmed by a runaway greenhouse effect in its carbon dioxide atmosphere, and it can reach temperatures of 470°C (878°F). Because of the thick clouds that cover Venus and its circular orbit, seasonal changes in temperature are likely to be very small, and it is probably the only planet with a truly endless summer.

Neptune too has been shown to exhibit seasonal changes. Like Saturn, it is sliding into a winter season, from which Neptune will not emerge for another twenty Earth years.

Watching the Sky

THE MONTHLY STAR MAPS

Fourteen star maps appear in this section of the book – one for each month of the year. As with all maps, there is a certain amount of distortion because they are representing a curved surface on flat paper.

The maps are drawn with a grid of celestial latitude and longitude, or 'declination' and 'right ascension'. Declination is measured in degrees north (+) or south (–) of the celestial equator; right ascension is measured in hours and minutes of sidereal time. This grid provides a reference for locating stars on the celestial sphere. It can be used to locate other stars that are not included on these maps.

These maps feature stars down to the fifth magnitude, slightly above naked-eye visibility. Stars fainter than this are shown if they are of particular interest.

The stars are labelled according to the Bayer system with letters of the Greek alphabet, in which α (alpha) is the brightest in the constellation, β (beta) the next brightest and so on. On these maps, usually only the stars featured in the text are labelled, making them easier to locate. In the text the letters are spelled out, as in Alpha Centauri, but to help you the letters of the Greek alphabet are listed on the opposite page.

Many of the brightest stars also have a proper name, such as Sirius for Alpha Canis Majoris. Proper names are given for the best known of these.

Some variable stars are identified by their Bayer letter, but others are identified according to a different system. The first variable discovered in a constellation is denoted R, the next S and so on. After Z, the variables become RR, RS and so on. On the maps, two symbols are used for variables: ◉ for variables that remain visible to the naked eye at minimum, and ◯ for variables that fall below naked-eye visibility.

DEEP-SKY OBJECTS

By deep-sky objects we mean nebulae, open clusters, globular clusters and galaxies. These are marked on the maps with their own symbols, and are usually identified either by an M number or just by a number.

The M number is the Messier number, or the number assigned to the particular object in a catalogue of more than 100 nebulous objects drawn up by the French astronomer Charles Messier in the eighteenth century. M42 in Orion is the Orion Nebula. Messier was an ardent comet-hunter and drew up his catalogue pinpointing nebulae and clusters that might be confused with new comets.

A number by itself next to a deep-sky object symbol denotes the NGC number of the object. This is the number in the New General Catalog of Nebulae and Clusters of Stars compiled by the Danish astronomer Johann Dreyer, and first published in 1888. Some nebulae listed in the NGC are also listed in the Messier catalogue, e.g., the Andromeda Galaxy is listed both as NGC 224 and as M31.

Watching the Sky

This diagram shows how the monthly star maps that follow relate to the celestial sphere. The celestial sphere is shown 'exploded' into 12 segments – one for each month of the year. Each segment covers two hours of Right Ascension. It forms the central part of one of the monthly maps. The stars, of course, appear on the inner surface of the segment. The north polar and south polar star maps are derived from the northern and southern 'caps' of the celestial sphere, centred on the celestial poles.

The Greek Alphabet	
α	Alpha
β	Beta
γ	Gamma
δ	Delta
ε	Epsilon
ζ	Zeta
η	Eta
θ	Theta
ι	Iota
κ	Kappa
λ	Lambda
μ	Mu
ν	Nu
ξ	Xi
ο	Omicron
π	Pi
ρ	Rho
σ	Sigma
τ	Tau
υ	Upsilon
φ	Phi
χ	Chi
ψ	Psi
ω	Omega

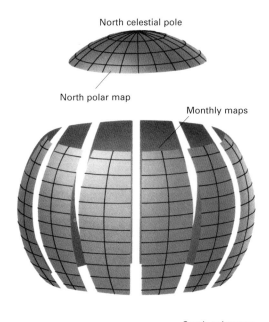

North celestial pole

North polar map

Monthly maps

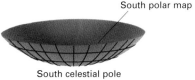

South polar map

South celestial pole

Watching the Sky

JANUARY SKIES

The constellation of Orion is one of the great sights of the winter sky. High in the sky in the early evening, Orion can be easily found by looking to the south around midnight. On a clear night, the brilliant stars of Orion almost seem to blaze in the crisp winter sky.

Orion rises around 8.30 p.m. in the southeast and then climbs higher in the southerly sky, setting in the west at sunrise. With such bright stars (Sirius – just away to the left and below is the brightest of all the night stars), Orion has been noted by astronomers since earliest times. To the ancients, the pattern of stars gave the impression of a giant hunter, holding up a club and shield against the charging bull of Taurus – the constellation to the right. The bright red star of Aldebaran appears to be the eye of the bull.

Across the centre of the constellation, three stars appear to form the belt of the hunter. Below the belt hangs the hunter's sword. Here is found the Orion Nebula (catalogue number M42), a great interstellar gas cloud where new stars are formed. The Orion Nebula contains over 700 young stars in various stages of formation and is visible as a fuzzy object at the lower end of Orion's sword, hanging below the hunter's belt. With binoculars on a clear night, the fuzzy outline of the Nebula will distinguish it from other stars.

Betelgeuse, at the hunter's shoulder, is a red giant and one of the largest stars in the night sky. Diagonally opposite lies Rigel a blue-white supergiant that burns some six times hotter than our own Sun. Both stars appear at approximately magnitude 0.8 (a measure of their brilliance). Brighter still is Sirius, at magnitude −1.0 the brightest star in the night sky, which lies to the left and below Orion in the constellation of Canis Minor (the little dog). Sirius is now known to be a double star with a small and dim white dwarf orbiting around its much brighter twin. The two stars take 50 years to complete an orbit about each other.

Procyon

Procyon is the 'little dog' star because it's in the constellation Canis Minor, which is the constellation of the Little Dog. So Sirius is the Big Dog constellation, and Procyon is a little bit smaller star in the Little Dog constellation.

TOP RIGHT (*opposite*): Northern hemisphere view of the night sky in mid-latitudes looking south at about 11 p.m. local time on about January 7. Orion in mid-sky acts as a signpost to super-bright Sirius in the southeast and to the noticeably orange Aldebaran in the northwest.

BOTTOM RIGHT (*opposite*): Southern hemisphere view of the night sky in Australia and southern Africa looking north at about 11 p.m. local time on about January 7. In this aspect, the hexagon of stars appears a perfect shape and right in the centre of the sky. It is very spectacular.

Watching the Sky

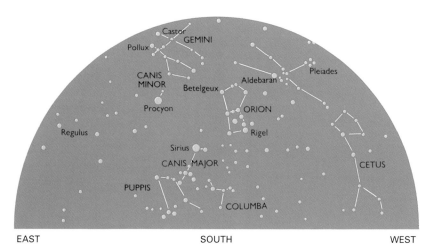

EAST   SOUTH   WEST

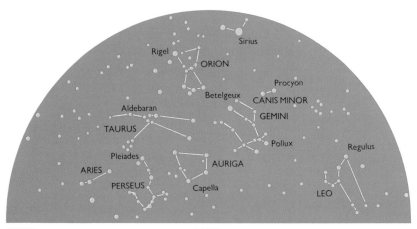

WEST   NORTH   EAST

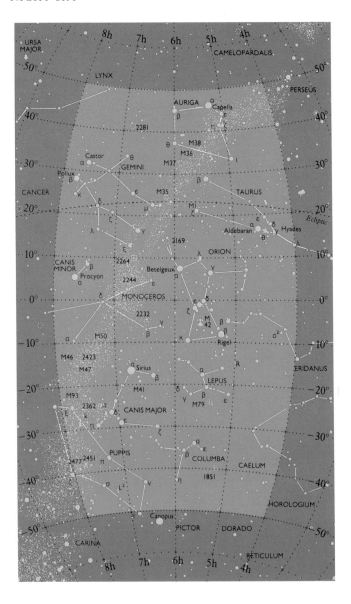

Watching the Sky

THE STARS

Auriga (the Charioteer)

This conspicuous kite-shaped constellation lies astride the Milky Way. It can be quickly located by its leading star, Capella, the sixth brightest star in the sky. Close to Capella is a triangle of fainter stars, known as the Haedi, or the Kids. Of the three, Epsilon and Zeta are the most interesting: they are both eclipsing binaries.

The Epsilon system consists of a yellow supergiant and a huge dark companion star we cannot see. Usually at about magnitude 3, it dims to magnitude 4 every 27 years when the dark companion eclipses the bright star. In the more colourful Zeta system, the components are an orange supergiant and a smaller blue star. The change in brightness, every two years eight months, is not easy to detect.

Auriga also contains three bright open clusters, M36, M37 and M38, easily seen in binoculars. They lie in a more or less straight line at the edge of the Milky Way between Theta Aurigae and Beta Tauri in the adjoining constellation.

Canis Major (the Great Dog)

Although only a small constellation, Canis Major boasts the brightest star in the sky, Sirius (magnitude −1.5), also called the Dog Star. As stars go, pure white Sirius is not truly very bright. It appears so bright because it is relatively close to Earth, less than nine light years away. This is scarcely

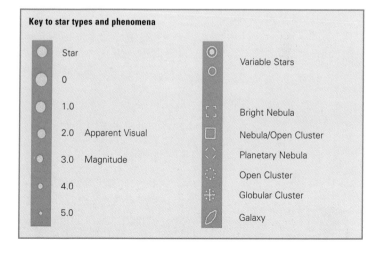

Key to star types and phenomena

○ Star	◉ Variable Stars
○ 0	○
○ 1.0	⸢⸣ Bright Nebula
○ 2.0 Apparent Visual	□ Nebula/Open Cluster
○ 3.0 Magnitude	⟨⟩ Planetary Nebula
○ 4.0	∴ Open Cluster
· 5.0	✛ Globular Cluster
	⬭ Galaxy

Watching the Sky

a stone's throw as far as distances in the Universe are concerned.

Sirius is a binary star with a small but dense companion. This Companion of Sirius (nicknamed appropriately the Pup) is a white dwarf, and indeed the first of this type of star to be discovered, in 1862. Although it is magnitude 8, the Pup is difficult to see because it orbits close to Sirius and tends to be obscured by that star's glare.

Of the other bright stars in Canis Major, the brightest is Epsilon. It is actually tens of thousands of times more luminous than Sirius, but lies a hundred times further away.

Among several open clusters in Canis Major, M41 is the brightest. Located just south of Sirius, it may in good viewing conditions be visible to the naked eye as a misty glow. Small telescopes show up to two dozen bright stars from the total of about 100.

Another striking open cluster is NGC2362, gathered around the fourth-magnitude Tau. It contains about 40 very young stars. In binoculars, the whole of this southern part of the constellation makes spectacular sweeping since it lies in the Milky Way.

Canis Minor (the Little Dog) see page 197.

Carina (the Keel) see page 276.

Columba (the Dove)
This constellation has relatively faint stars, but is easily found because it lies in a usually bare region of the southern

skies. It contains a number of globular clusters and galaxies, but only the cluster NGC1851 is visible in small telescopes.

Eridanus see page 247.

Gemini (the Twins) see page 197.

Lepus (the Hare)
This constellation lies immediately south of Orion and is thus easy to locate. It is small, but contains some interesting objects. They include R Leporis, found by continuing a line through Alpha and Mu. It is a Mira variable star with a wide variation in brightness, between about magnitudes 5 and 10 over a period of about 14 months. It is one of the reddest stars we know and is sometimes called the Crimson Star.

Gamma is an interesting double star, with orange and yellow components. Equidistant from Gamma and Epsilon and in line with Alpha and Beta is the globular cluster M79. It is small but bright.

Lynx (the Lynx) see page 204.

Monoceros (the Unicorn) see page 199.

Orion see page 260.

Perseus see page 249.

Puppis (the Poop) see page 199.

Taurus (the Bull) see page 266.

Watching the Sky

FEBRUARY SKIES

The panoply of brilliant stars astride and to the west of the Milky Way have now moved from centre stage, but are still stunning in the west. However, east of the Milky Way the skies appear rather dull by comparison.

In February, the constellation Taurus is rising in the eastern sky after sunset and can be seen in the south around 10 p.m. Taurus is one of the most beautiful constellations and you can almost imagine the Bull charging down to the left towards Orion. His face is delineated by the 'V' shaped cluster of stars called the Hyades, his eye is the red giant star Aldebaran, and the tips of his horns are shown by the stars Beta and Zeta Tauri. Although Alpha Tauri, Aldebaran, appears to lie amongst the stars of the Hyades cluster, it is, in fact, less than half their distance lying 68 light years away from us. It is around 40 times the diameter of our Sun and 100 times as bright.

To the upper right of Taurus lies the open cluster, M45, the Pleiades. Often called the Seven Sisters, it is one of the brightest and closest open clusters. The Pleiades cluster lies at a distance of 400 light years and contains over 3,000 stars. The cluster, which is about 13 light years across, is moving towards the star Betelgeuse in Orion. Surrounding the brightest stars are seen blue reflection nebulae caused by reflected light from many small carbon grains. These reflection nebulae look blue as the dust grains scatter blue light more efficiently than red. The grains form part of a molecular cloud through which the cluster is currently passing.

Close to the tip of the left hand horn lies the Crab Nebula, also called M1 as it is the first entry of Charles Messier's catalogue of nebulous objects. Lying 6,500 light years from the Sun, it is the remains of a giant star that was seen to explode as a supernova in the year 1056. It may just be glimpsed with binoculars on a very clear dark night and a telescope will show it as a misty blur of light.

Orion can be seen in the south at around 11–12 p.m. during February. The three stars of Orion's belt lie at a distance of around 1,500 light years. Just below the lower left hand star lies a strip of nebulosity against which can be seen a pillar of dust in the shape of the chessboard knight, and is called the Horsehead Nebula. It shows up very well photographically but is exceedingly difficult to see visually – even with a relatively large telescope.

Pollux

Pollux is the sky's 17th brightest star. From its distance of 34 light years, it is calculated that the visual luminosity for Pollux is 32 times that of the Sun, with a 4500°K temperature. Pollux emits X-rays and an outer magnetically supported corona similar to the Sun.

Watching the Sky

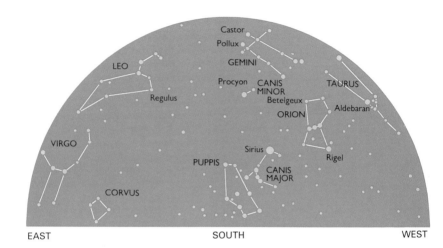

EAST   SOUTH   WEST

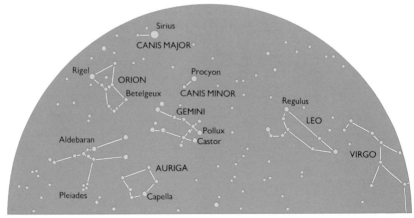

WEST   NORTH   EAST

Watching the Sky

THE STARS

Auriga (the Charioteer) see page 193.

Cancer (the Crab)
Sandwiched between Leo and Gemini, Cancer is one of the constellations of the zodiac. Though relatively faint, it contains much of interest. In the middle of the constellation is the beautiful open cluster M44, called Praesepe, or the Beehive. It is one of the most prominent clusters, easily visible to the naked eye. Binoculars show up dozens of its stars; while large telescopes reveal hundreds.

Close to Alpha is another open cluster, M67, visible in binoculars, but needing a telescope to bring out individual stars. Cancer also features two lovely double stars, Iota and Zeta. Both have yellow and blue components.

TOP LEFT: Northern hemisphere view of the night sky in mid-latitudes looking south at about 11 p.m. local time on about February 7. The bright stars in mid-sky line up more or less parallel with the horizon. From the east, they are Regulus, Procyon, Betelgeux and Aldebaran.

BOTTOM LEFT: Southern hemisphere view of the night sky in Australia and southern Africa looking north at about 11 p.m. local time on about February 7. The hexagonal arrangement of bright stars has slipped west, with Capella barely visible. In the east, Leo is ascending.

Canis Major (the Great Dog) see page 193.

Canis Minor (the Little Dog)
Little by name and little in size, this constellation is notable for its one bright star, Procyon. At a distance of about 11 light-years, Procyon is the third closest bright star to Earth, after Alpha Centauri and Sirius. And like Sirius, it has a faint white dwarf companion.

Carina (the Keel) see page 276.

Columbia (the Dove) see page 194.

Gemini (the Twins)
This splendid constellation of the zodiac is well named, for it boasts twin first-magnitude stars, Castor and Pollux. Pollux is the brighter of the two and is more colourful, being a rich yellow-orange.

Castor, however, is the more interesting twin because it is a multiple star system. A small telescope resolves Castor into two components and brings a fainter third into view. The spectra of the three stars reveal that each is a spectroscopic binary, with a close companion, making a six-star system in all.

Among Gemini's double stars is Zeta. Its brightest component is a Cepheid variable, which fluctuates in brightness over a period of ten days. The change in brightness can be seen by comparison with the steady shining Delta, which a small telescope will reveal to be a double.

A good binocular subject in the constellation is M35, a large and bright

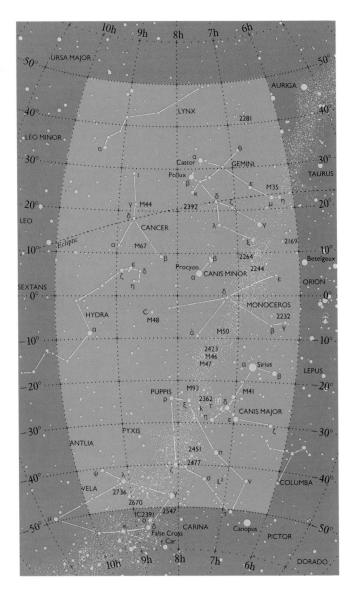

Watching the Sky

open cluster just north of Mu and Eta. Telescopes will reveal close to Delta the greenish disc of NGC2392, a fine planetary nebula.

Hydra (the Water Snake) see pages 203 and 207.

Leo (the Lion) see page 203.

Lepus (the Hare) see page 194.

Lynx (the Lynx) see page 204.

Monoceros (the Unicorn)
A faint constellation, Monoceros is located between the two 'Dogs', Canis Minor and Major. It has no bright stars, but spans a particularly rich area of the Milky Way.

Beta is one of the most interesting stars. It is a multiple star, whose three components can be seen as a neat triangle even in small telescopes.

Close by Epsilon is a striking open cluster, NGC2244. Large telescopes show it to be surrounded by one of the most beautiful nebulae in the heavens, the flower-like Rosette Nebula (NGC2237). Another nebula, the Cone Nebula, surrounds the open cluster NGC2264, just south of Chi Geminorum. Midway between Alpha and Beta is another open cluster, M50.

Puppis (the Poop)
Puppis is a fine southern constellation nestling in the Milky Way. It abounds in rich star fields and clusters. The second-magnitude Zeta is the brightest star. Electric blue in colour, it is one of the hottest stars known, with a surface temperature of tens of thousands of degrees.

Numerous doubles dotted around the constellation include Kappa and Sigma. Pi is one of a quartet of stars, well seen in a small telescope. Close to Sigma is L2, a long-period variable that changes noticeably in brightness from magnitudes 3 to 6 over a period of about five months.

Among the many open clusters are the naked-eye M47 and the fainter M46, which are located side by side and close to NGC2423. M93 is further south, near Xi. Close to Zeta is NGC2477, containing hundreds of faint stars so densely packed that it almost looks like a globular cluster.

Ursa Major (the Great Bear) see page 268.

Vela (the Sails) see page 204.

Regulus
As the brightest star in Leo, Regulus almost always has been universally associated in ancient cultures with the concept of royalty or kingly power, and the name comes from the Latin *rex*, or king. Regulus is the twenty-first brightest star in the sky, and lies at the base of the Sickle of Leo, resembling a reversed question mark.

Watching the Sky

MARCH SKIES

While Orion takes its curtain call in the west, the majestic Leo, with its distinctive 'Sickle' head, occupies the mid-sky. Its presence heralds the onset of spring in the Northern hemisphere and of autumn in the Southern.

March skies are well worth looking at. The evenings are warmer, skies tend to be clearer and some of the best-known constellations are high in the sky.

The constellation of Orion is easy to find lying in the southern sky. But below it and to the left is Canis Major easily identified by the brilliant Sirius. Sirius, the Dog Star, is the brightest star in the night sky. This is partly due to the fact that it is only 8.7 light years away but also it is twice the size of the Sun and it shines 23 times brighter. Although not visible without a fairly powerful telescope Sirius is accompanied by Sirius B or the Pup.

Sirius B is a white dwarf star which has burnt up all of its hydrogen fuel and which has consequently collapsed on itself. One teaspoonful of material from the Pup would weigh about 2.5 tons.

With a pair of binoculars mounted on a tripod it should be possible to identify the bright open cluster M41, where several clumps of bright stars can be seen immersed in a misty patch.

Two planets feature prominently in the evening sky. Jupiter appears at sunset rising in Cancer and the slightly fainter Saturn should be visible in the constellation Taurus around the same time.

Mars rises in the southeastern sky at around 3.30 a.m. This is followed by Venus, the brightest object in the morning sky, with a magnitude of –4.0.

The much fainter Mercury (magnitude –0.3) may just be visible at the very end of the night although its rising begins to coincide with that of the Sun.

As the planets all orbit the Sun in the same plane it should be possible to draw an imaginary line through Mars and Venus towards Mercury on the horizon.

Spica

Spica is the brightest star in the constellation of Virgo. Its name is Latin for 'ear of grain', referring to an ear of grain held by the figure traditionally associated with the constellation Virgo. Spica is at a distance of about 200 light years away.

TOP RIGHT (*opposite*): Northern hemisphere view of the night sky in mid-latitudes looking south at about 11 p.m. local time on about March 7. Rigel is close to setting in the west. Sirius is also low down and about to make its exit. In the east, Spica is making its entrance.

BOTTOM RIGHT (*opposite*): Southern hemisphere view of the night sky in Australia and southern Africa looking north at about 11 p.m. local time on about March 7. Regulus appears due north in the mid-sky. Spica and Arcturus appear in the east, the one vertically above the other.

Watching the Sky

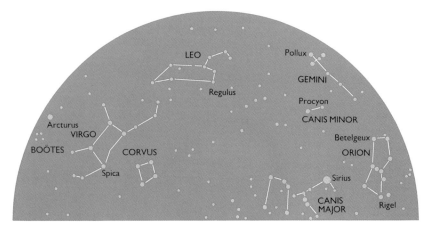

EAST   SOUTH   WEST

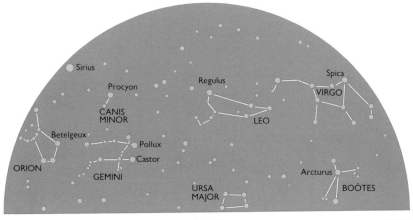

WEST   NORTH   EAST

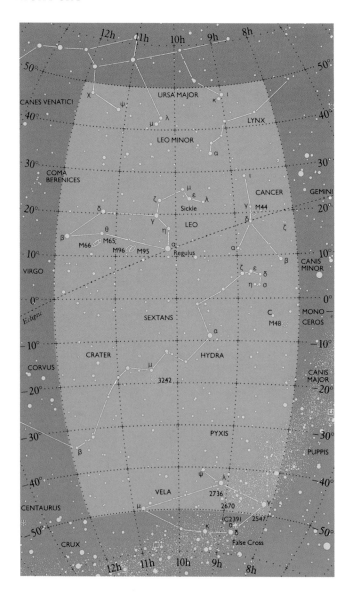

Watching the Sky

THE STARS

Cancer (the Crab) see page 197.

Gemini (the Twins) see page 197.

Hydra (the Water Snake) (head)
Hydra winds its way, serpent-like, more
than a quarter of the way around the
celestial sphere. Indeed, it is the largest of
all the constellations. It rears its head near

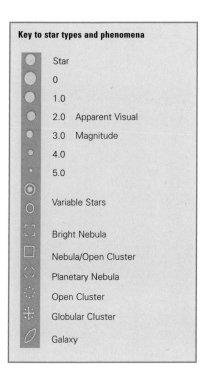

Key to star types and phenomena

●	Star
●	0
●	1.0
●	2.0 Apparent Visual
●	3.0 Magnitude
•	4.0
·	5.0
◉	
○	Variable Stars
::	Bright Nebula
□	Nebula/Open Cluster
◇	Planetary Nebula
∴	Open Cluster
✛	Globular Cluster
⬭	Galaxy

Canis Minor, just north of the celestial
equator, while its tail extends as far as
Libra.

The only bright star in Hydra, the
second-magnitude Alpha, is called
Alphard, meaning the 'Solitary One'
because it is the only reasonably bright
star in a barren region of the heavens. It
is also known as Cor Hydrae, or the
Hydra's Heart.

The stars in the Hydra's head make an
attractive group in low-powered
binoculars. One of them, Epsilon, is a
colourful double, separated in larger
telescopes. M48 is a bright cluster
approaching naked-eye visibility, found by
moving southwards from the head past
the close trio of stars, c.

The brightest planetary nebula in the
heavens, NGC3242, lies in Hydra, just
south of Mu. Small telescopes show this
magnitude 9 object as a faint bluish-green
disc. Sometimes called the Ghost of
Jupiter Nebula, its central star is clearly
seen. (For Hydra's tail, see page 207.)

Leo (the Lion)
This constellation of the zodiac is one
that looks passably like the animal it is
supposed to represent. The most
recognizable shape in Leo is the Sickle,
the sickle-like arrangement of stars that
forms the lion's head and mane.

In the Sickle, Gamma, Mu and Lambda
are all orange in colour. Gamma, often
called Algeiba, the Lion's Mane, is a
double, which can be resolved in a
telescope into a pair of golden yellow stars.

Watching the Sky

Brighter than the Sickle stars in the first-magnitude Regulus, also called Cor Leonis, or the Lion's Heart. It is a double, with the fainter star of the eighth-magnitude.

The other prominent shape in Leo is at the tail end, where there is a triangle of bright stars. Of this trio Beta, also called Denebola, is the brightest at about magnitude 2.

Beginning just south of Delta is a region rich in galaxies. The brightest ones lie south of a line joining Beta and Regulus. South of Theta are M65 and M66, both about magnitude 9 and both visible in binoculars in good seeing conditions. Like our own galaxy, they are spirals, although large telescopes are needed to bring out their spiral form.

About halfway between them and Regulus is another pair of spiral galaxies, M95 and M96. All four galaxies lie about the same distance away from Earth, some 30 million light years.

Lynx (the Lynx)
Said to be so named because you have to be lynx-eyed to spot it, this is a faint constellation in a relatively empty part of the northern heavens. The third-magnitude Alpha is distinctly red.

Monoceros (the Unicorn) see page 199.

Puppis (the Poop) see page 199.

Ursa Major (the Great Bear) see page 268.

Vela (the Sails)
Vela spans the Milky Way in the southern skies and, like the adjacent constellations Centaurus, Puppis and Carina, is rich in star fields and clusters. In the constellation, the Milky Way splits up because of distant obscuring dust clouds.

Kappa and Delta are second-magnitude stars which, along with Iota and Epsilon in Carina, form a noticeable cross-shape, the so-called False Cross. The False Cross has much the same orientation as the true cross of Crux close by, but is larger.

Immediately north of Delta is Omicron, which forms part of the cluster IC 2391. Delta, Omicron and the rest of the cluster look great through binoculars. Another good binocular subject is NGC2547, just south of Gamma.

Gamma is easy to spot as a double, and its blue-white brighter component is particularly hot and luminous. It is a type known as a Wolf-Rayet star, an unstable body thought to be on the brink of becoming a supernova and blasting itself apart.

South of Lambda, long-exposure photographs reveal wisps of an extensive nebula, known as the Gum Nebula (NGC2736). It is a supernova remnant, the gaseous remains of a supernova explosion that took place about 11,000 years ago.

Watching the Sky

April Skies

Leo is still prominent, but as a whole the sky looks bare because of the presence of the sprawling Hydra and Virgo. These, the two largest constellations in the heavens, have no very bright stars, with the exception of Spica.

Crater is an April constellation and is a companion to Corvus the Crow on the back of Hydra the Water Snake. To find Crater look north in the evening to find the bright stars Regulus and Spica. Find the distinctive quadrilateral of Corvus, and look west to find the upside-down cup or sundae dish shape.

It is a sure indicator that spring is here when Orion begins to disappear from the evening sky. At the start of the month it appears low in the western sky but by late April it has all but disappeared from view, leaving some of the less familiar constellations, such as Virgo, Hydra and Boötes to dominate the northern portion of the night sky.

Mercury begins to appear low on the western horizon at the start of the month. If you have a very clear view towards the horizon you may be able to spot it close to the New Moon at the beginning of the month. Mercury will be ascending during the month placing increasing distance between itself and the setting Sun.

Although Jupiter and Saturn appear bright in the evening sky they now set earlier in the night, around 5 a.m. and 2 a.m. respectively at the start of the month.

Venus rises in the east shortly before sunrise and is the brightest object in the night sky, with a magnitude of –3.9.

The Lyrid meteor shower is the first significant shower of the year. The Lyrid meteor shower is normally a very fine shower and will be appearing in 2004 from the 16 to the 25 of April and will peak around April 22.

April also seems to have quite a large number of sporadic fireballs. A fireball is a really bright shooting star that streaks across the sky and leaves a trail that can last for 30 seconds or longer, before it fades from view. Even if there is a full moon, a fireball is an exciting object, which will shine through moonlight or even street lights.

Castor

To the naked eye, Castor shines down to us as a seemingly ordinary hydrogen-fusing 'class A' star, being fairly hot, with temperatures between 7000–10,000°K.

TOP RIGHT (*page 206*): Northern hemisphere view of the night sky in mid-latitudes looking south at about 11 p.m. local time on about April 7. High in the east, Arcturus is the brightest star, forming an expansive triangle with Regulus and Spica. Procyon lies in the west.

BOTTOM RIGHT (*page 206*): Southern hemisphere view of the night sky in Australia and southern Africa looking north at about 11 p.m. local time on about April 7. This is a good month to experience the extragalactic delights of the 'empty' region between Leo and Boötes.

Watching the Sky

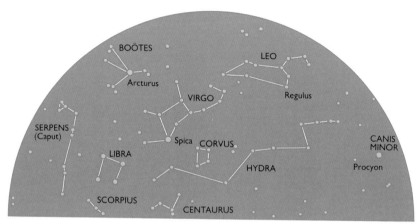

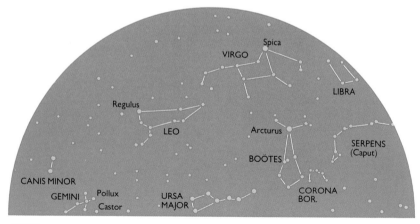

Watching the Sky

THE STARS

Canes Venatici (the Hunting Dogs)

Overall, this is a faint constellation, located underneath the handle of the Big Dipper. However, it boasts one of the finest globular clusters in northern skies and one of the most distinctive galaxies.

Even its leading star, Alpha, is only slightly brighter than the third magnitude. It is also called *Cor Caroli*, meaning Charles's Heart, a name given to it by Britain's second Astronomer Royal, Edmond Halley. The heart in question is that of the executed Charles I of England. Alpha is a double, which a small telescope will resolve.

The first of the telescopic highlights of Canes Venatici is the M3 globular cluster. It is located about halfway between Cor Caroli and the bright Arcturus in the neighbouring constellation Boötes. At about magnitude 6, it is on the limit of naked-eye visibility, and binoculars show it as a fuzzy patch. Telescopes will resolve it into an enormous globe of closely packed stars.

The other telescopic highlight of the constellation is M51, the famous Whirlpool Galaxy. Small telescopes show it as a pair of hazy spots. Larger instruments bring out its classic face-on spiral shape. The two spots in fact turn out to be the centres of two connected galaxies. Historically, the Whirlpool is important because it was the first galaxy to have its spiral structure resolved.

Like the neighbouring constellation Coma Berenices, Canes Venatici is richly endowed with galaxies. Among the brighter ones worth looking for are M63, M94 and M106. M63 is located just north of 20 Canes Venatici; M94, just over halfway from 20 to Beta; and M106, from Beta about halfway to Gamma Ursa Majoris. Larger telescopes will reveal a string of fainter galaxies going south from M106.

Centaurus (the Centaur) see page 256.

Coma Berenices (Berenice's Hair) see page 213.

Corvus (the Crow)

Corvus the crow is a small constellation situated beside Crater the cup and Hydra the water snake. One legend connects them all and, according to this story, Apollo sent the crow to fetch water for a sacrifice to Jupiter. The crow flew off but got waylaid by a fig tree waiting for the fruit to ripen. Much later, the crow returned to Apollo with a water snake in his claws, claiming it was the snake's fault for the delay. Apollo knew better and for punishment placed the bird in the sky, beside the cup of water. Then Apollo placed the water snake beside them with the task of preventing the crow from drinking.

A tiny constellation on Hydra's back, easy to spot because of its quartet of leading stars, all of (or slightly below) third magnitude. They make a nice group for watching through binoculars. Delta is

Watching the Sky

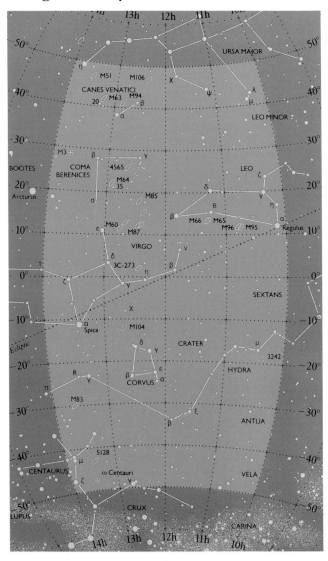

Watching the Sky

an easy double, with components of contrasting colours.

Hydra (the Water Snake) (tail)

Hydra continues to wind through this segment of the celestial sphere. Among viewable objects in this, the tail end of the Water Snake, is the star R, located near Gamma. It is a Mira variable star, distinctly red. It varies markedly in brightness between magnitudes 4 and 11 over a period of just over a year.

Due south of R, on the edge of the constellation is one of the brightest face-on spiral galaxies in the heavens, M83. Larger instruments reveal it is a barrel spiral galaxy, with a distinct bar across the middle.

Leo (the Lion) see page 203.

Arcturus

In 1635, Arcturus became the first star ever seen through a telescope in the daytime. Arcturus takes its name from its nearness to the sky bears, Big and Little, otherwise known as Ursa Major and Ursa Minor. 'Arcturus' in Greek means 'bear watcher' or 'guardian of the bears'.

Observers rank this star as the brightest star in the northern sky.

Ursa Major (the Great Bear) see page 268.

Vela (the Sails) see page 204.

Virgo (the Virgin) see page 270.

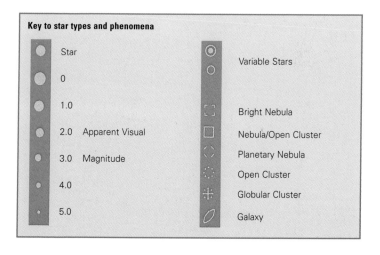

Key to star types and phenomena

Star	
0	
1.0	
2.0	Apparent Visual
3.0	Magnitude
4.0	
5.0	

	Variable Stars
	Bright Nebula
	Nebula/Open Cluster
	Planetary Nebula
	Open Cluster
	Globular Cluster
	Galaxy

Watching the Sky

MAY SKIES

Arcturus and Spica are close to the meridian this month and provide a pleasing colour contrast. Arcturus is a lovely orange, while Spica is pure white. Both are giants, the one cool, the other very hot.

The planets of our solar system dominate the evening sky early in May. Venus is by far the brightest object in the night sky, and it lies low in the northwestern sky at sunset. Mercury is also visible sitting almost on the horizon, but you will need a really clear night for a good sighting.

In ascending order above Venus lie Mars (very faint), Saturn and Jupiter. Early in the month Mars and Venus form an alignment, appearing to us as a single bright point.

Whilst looking at the cluster of planets in the northwestern sky, look out for the bright star Capella which appears just above the planets. It forms part of a roughly circular group of stars which make up the constellation Auriga.

If you have a clear view of the southwestern horizon then you might look out for the constellation Hydra which stretches across much of the sky between southeast and west.

The head of the 'Water Snake' lies just to the left of Canis Major which, in turn, can be found just below Gemini.

If you are up and about in the early morning at the start of the month the constellation Sagittarius can be observed in the southwestern sky, lying behind the waning gibbous moon.

The Eta Aquarids meteor shower should be visible early in May. Not one of the most spectacular of meteor showers, the radiant (the point from which meteors appear to originate) never reaches very high in the night sky before morning twilight. So try facing towards the east and look high above your head. Expect to see no more than ten meteors per hour.

Antares

The name Antares means 'rival to Mars' or 'anti-Mars', probably because the star's vivid reddish hue reminded ancient astronomers of the Red Planet. Antares is 700 times larger, 9000 times more luminous, and about 15 times more massive than the Sun.

TOP RIGHT (*opposite*): Northern hemisphere view of the night sky in mid-latitudes looking south at about 11 p.m. local time on about May 7. Coloured Arcturus has a rival appearing over the horizon, red Antares. The whole of Serpens – Caput and Cauda – is now visible in the east.

BOTTOM RIGHT (*opposite*): Southern hemisphere view of the night sky in Australia and southern Africa looking north at about 11 p.m. local time on about May 7. Leo is slipping towards the horizon. At lower latitudes, the Big Dipper may just be glimpsed on the horizon.

Watching the Sky

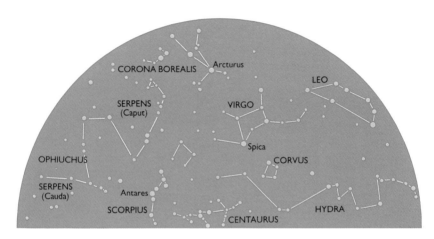

EAST   SOUTH   WEST

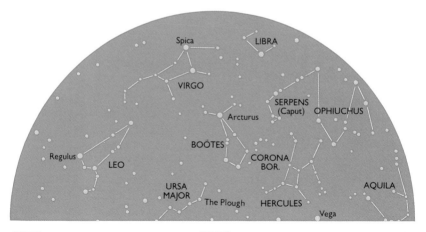

WEST   NORTH   EAST

Watching the Sky

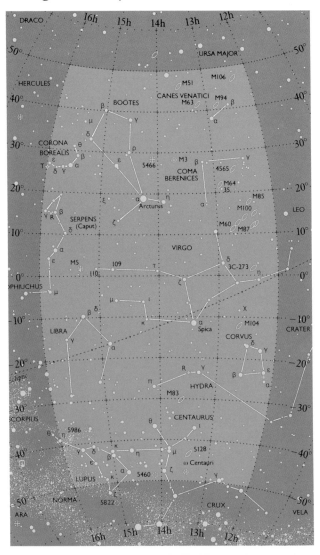

Watching the Sky

THE STARS

Boötes (the Herdsman)

This fine kite-shaped constellation boasts the brightest star in northern skies and the fourth brightest star in the whole heavens. This star is Arcturus ('Bear-keeper'). It is a red giant, which explains its noticeable orange colour. It can perhaps best be found by following around the curve of the handle of the Big Dipper.

There are several doubles of note in Boötes, none finer than Epsilon. The star appears only slightly coloured in binoculars, but a telescope separates it into beautiful yellowish-orange and bluish-green components, making it one of the most attractive doubles in the heavens.

Xi is another colourful double, which even small telescopes should be able to separate into a yellow and orange pair. The third fine double in the constellation is Mu. Binoculars will separate it into two yellow stars. A telescope will split the fainter of the two into a further yellow pair.

Boötes has few interesting deep-sky objects, such as galaxies and clusters. There is, however, one reasonable globular cluster, NGC5466, which forms one corner of a parallelogram with Rho, Alpha and Eta.

Canes Venatici (the Hunting Dogs) see

page 207.

Centaurus (the Centaur) see page 256.

Coma Berenices (Berenice's Hair)

Like Canes Venatici to the north, Coma Berenices is faint and inconspicuous at first sight, but look at it in binoculars, small, and large telescopes, and it becomes increasingly richer with every increase in magnification.

Essentially, it is a constellation dominated by galaxies. Literally hundreds of them lie in this region of the heavens, forming the so-called Coma Cluster. At a distance of some 450 million light years, these galaxies are mostly beyond the range of amateur telescopes. However, there are quite a few much closer galaxies, which are visible in small telescopes. M64 is one of them. It is located on a line joining Alpha and Gamma, near star 35. Large telescopes show it as an ellipse, with a distinctive dark spot. For this reason, it is known as the Black-Eye Galaxy.

Further along the Alpha-to-Gamma line is the slightly fainter NGC4565, known as the Needle Galaxy. It appears needle-like because we are looking at it edge-on. The galaxies M85 and M100, both of the ninth magnitude, form part of a dense grouping of galaxies at the southern edge of the constellation, which continues into Virgo. This whole region is a fascinating one for the telescopic browser.

Corona Borealis (the Northern Crown)

see page 217.

Corvus (the Crow) see page 207.

Watching the Sky

Hydra (the Water Snake) see pages 203 and 207.

Libra (the Scales)
Libra is a faint constellation of the zodiac, which lacks any really bright stars. It perhaps suffers from being cheek-by-jowl with the bright stars in the head of Scorpius.

Indeed, originally, the stars in Libra formed the claws of the Scorpion. Its leading star Alpha (magnitude 2.7) is named Zubenelgenubi, meaning the 'southern claw'. It is slightly less bright than Beta, the 'northern claw' Zubenelchemale.

Alpha is a fine wide double star, which binoculars separate easily. If the dim component (fifth magnitude) were somewhat brighter, Alpha would just be separable with the naked eye.

Beta has an unusual greenish colour. Delta is an eclipsing binary, similar to Algol. Every 56 hours, the dim component passes in front of the bright one, and the brightness of the system dips briefly from the fourth to the sixth magnitude.

Lupus (the Wolf)
This constellation is sandwiched between Scorpius and Centaurus on the edge of the Milky Way. It is therefore a rewarding region of sweeping with binoculars. There are several doubles worth looking at in the constellation, including Pi, Kappa and Eta. The figured part of the constellation, the stars that make up the wolf shape,

contains several bright single, double and multiple stars. Alpha, Beta, Gamma, Delta, Epsilon and Zeta Lupi form a rough oblong representing the body and front legs of the animal.

As for clusters, there are many that can be found in larger telescopes. More modest instruments will be able to pick up the globular cluster NGC5986, close to Eta, and the open cluster NGC5822, close to Zeta.

Scorpius (the Scorpion) see page 264.

Serpens Caput (the Serpent's Head) see page 219.

Ursa Major (the Great Bear) see page 268.

Virgo (the Virgin) see page 270.

Vega
One of the most famed stars of the sky, Vega is the luminary of the dim but exquisite constellation Lyra, the Lyre, which represents the harp of the great mythical musician Orpheus. Vega is one of three brilliant stars that divide the northern heavens into thirds, the others Arcturus and Capella, and with Altair and Deneb forms the great Summer Triangle. Because it is 2.5 times as massive as the Sun, it uses its internal fuel much faster and will burn out in less than a billion years, less than 10 percent of the solar lifetime.

Watching the Sky

JUNE SKIES

In this month and July, Scorpius is a constellation to watch, low in northern skies and near the zenith in southern. Its brightest star, Antares, joins Arcturus, Vega, Deneb, Altair and Spica in the night sky starscape.

Virgo the Virgin is the second largest constellation in the sky and is a constellation that is visible in June. Virgo contains a rich cluster of galaxies which is the nearest major galaxy cluster to us. The Virgo Galaxy Cluster lies about 65 million light years away and contains about 3,000 members. Virgo also contains the brightest quasar 3C 273. In an 8-inch telescope or bigger 3C 273 appears as a 13th magnitude star. It is estimated to lie 2,000 million light years away. To find Virgo look north early evening and find Spica.

Also visible in the June night sky are the constellations Triangulum Australe, Norma and Circinus. To find these constellations look south to find the pointers to the Southern Cross. Circinus and Triangulum Australe are below and slightly to the left of the pointers, with Norma to the left of the pointers and at the same level.

June is the month in which we say goodbye to Jupiter as a bright evening planet. For several months it has been the brightest planet in the evening sky, tracking the constellation Gemini across the heavens.

Its place in the evening sky will be more than filled by Venus at the beginning of the month. The two planets will appear to meet as Jupiter descends and Venus ascends.

The only other fairly bright planet in the evening sky is Mars, which sets by 11 p.m.

The Space Shuttle *Endeavour* is due to dock with the International Space Station (ISS) on June 1, 2004. The ISS is visible during the late evening, and will appear just 15 minutes before the *Envisat*. The two should not be confused however, as the ISS passes from east to west, whereas the *Envisat* crosses from south to north.

Altair

Altair is the 12th brightest star in the sky and the Alpha star of Aquila the Eagle, and is also the southern anchor of the famed Summer Triangle, which it makes with Vega and Deneb.

TOP RIGHT (*page 216*): Northern hemisphere view of the night sky in mid-latitudes looking south at about 11 p.m. local time on about June 7. The heads of the Serpent and the Scorpion lie due south. Compare the colours of Antares low down and Arcturus high up.

BOTTOM RIGHT (*page 216*): Southern hemisphere view of the night sky in Australia and southern Africa looking north at about 11 p.m. local time on about June 7. This month provides a good opportunity for observing the northern constellations Boötes and Hercules.

Watching the Sky

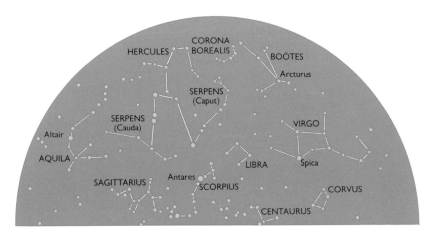

EAST   SOUTH   WEST

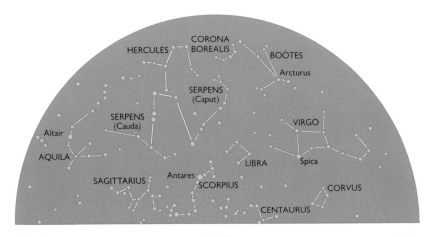

WEST   NORTH   EAST

Watching the Sky

THE STARS

Ara (the Altar)

Ara is one of the most northern of the southern constellations. Not visible from high northern latitudes, the constellation of Ara lies just south of Scorpius, and begins to peek over the horizon for observers in the southern United States. However, it fails to draw much attention due to the lack of any major deep sky objects, as well as its position low on the southern horizon.

Since Ara is located near the galactic centre in Sagittarius, the globular clusters can be counted as part of the galactic halo. The open clusters are part of the rich area of the Milky Way spilling off from Sagittarius and Scorpius.

This constellation is one of the original Greek Constellations, and represents the altar the Greek gods erected in recognition of their victory over the Titans.

Boötes (the Herdsman) see page 213.

Centaurus (the Centaur) see page 256.

Corona Boralis (the Northern Crown)

This is a tiny, but easily recognizable constellation, a neat semicircle, of stars with the second-magnitude Alpha in the middle of the arc. It contains a number of doubles, including Zeta and Nu, but is particularly notable for two remarkable variable stars.

One is R, located north of Delta in the 'bowl'. For most of the time, R is about

magnitude 6 and readily visible in binoculars, but from time to time it suddenly dims to about magnitude 12 or even lower. It may recover its brightness in a matter of months, but sometimes takes years. Astronomers think one explanation of the sudden dimming might be that the star periodically ejects clouds of sooty material, which blocks its light.

The other fascinating variable is T, located south of Epsilon. This star is usually only about magnitude 10, but sometimes flares up to brighter than 6 and becomes visible to the naked eye. Indeed, in 1866 and 1946, T became as bright as the second magnitude. Aptly called the Blaze Star, T periodically flares up in this way, over a matter of hours, because it is a type called a recurrent nova. No one knows when it may flare up again, so it is always worth watching.

Underneath the 'bowl', beyond Beta, large telescopes will show one of the densest clusters of galaxies known, called Abell 2065. Over 400 galaxies are clustered closely together about 1,000 million light years away.

Draco (the Dragon) see page 273.

Hercules

Hercules is a large constellation, in fact, the fifth largest in the heavens. It is not overly impressive to the naked eye, but is richly endowed to the binocular and telescopic observer.

Its *pièce de résistance* is M13, the finest globular cluster in the northern skies, just

Watching the Sky

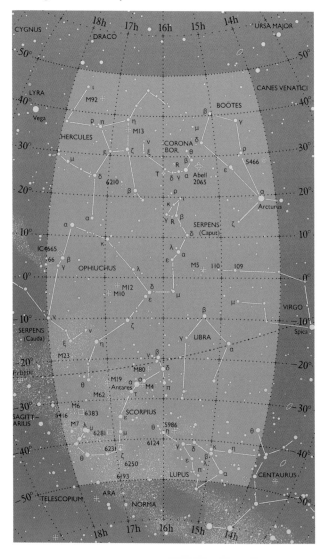

Watching the Sky

about visible to the naked eye on a really dark night. M13 is found on a line joining Zeta and Eta. Binoculars show it as a fuzzy blob, but telescopes resolve it into a conglomeration of countless stars.

M92 is another fine globular cluster, slightly fainter than M13, found on a line joining Eta with Iota. In large telescopes NGC6210 is well worth observing. It is a small, bright planetary nebula with a brilliant blue central star.

Among the stars in Hercules, Alpha is noticeably red and varies over a period of months between the third and fourth magnitudes. It is also a double star with reddish and greenish components. Delta, Rho and Mu are also doubles worth investigating.

Hydra (the Water Snake) (tail) see page 207.

Libra (the Scales) see page 214.

Lupus (the Wolf) see page 214.

Ophiuchus (the Serpent-Bearer) see page 224.

Sagattarius see page 262.

Scorpius (the Scorpion) see page 264.

Serpens Caput (the Serpent's Head)
This is the head part of Serpens, the Serpent, a constellation that is split into two by Ophiuchus, the Serpent-Bearer. The tail part is Serpens Cauda (see page 224). The triangle of stars in the Head look attractive in the same field in

binoculars. Its period is slightly less than a year. Delta and the orange Alpha are visible as doubles in a telescope.

However, the Head's most impressive object is the globular cluster M5, one of the finest of its type in northern skies. You can find it, close to the dim star 5, by continuing a line through Lambda and Alpha. It is also in line with the stars 110 and 109 Virginis in the neighbouring constellation Virgo.

Virgo (the Virgin) see page 270.

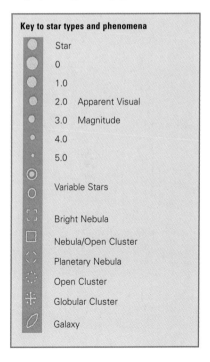

Key to star types and phenomena

●	Star
●	0
●	1.0
●	2.0 Apparent Visual
●	3.0 Magnitude
·	4.0
·	5.0
◎	
○	Variable Stars
⌣⌣	Bright Nebula
▢	Nebula/Open Cluster
⟨⟩	Planetary Nebula
⁖	Open Cluster
�֎	Globular Cluster
⬭	Galaxy

Watching the Sky

JULY SKIES

Vega is high in the northern skies and low in the southern. With Altair and Deneb, it makes up the Summer Triangle. The Milky Way, particularly the Sagittarius region, is now well placed for viewing in both hemispheres.

Jupiter is at its closest point to the Earth on July 4. Because it is so close to our planet it is very easy to see the four Galilean moons with a good pair of binoculars. These big moons of Jupiter are called Ganymede, Callisto, Io and Europa.

July also provides a good view of Saturn. For this you will need a small scope to see the rings, but you can see Saturn with the naked eye in the mid-evening towards the end of the month. It is possible to see Saturn in the southeast about 10 p.m. during the last week in July, in more or less the same place that Jupiter was early in the month. Once again, look for a very bright star. Saturn won't be as bright as Jupiter, but it will be one of the brightest objects in the sky anyway.

July is also the month when the Milky Way is highest in the sky. When you look into the smoky cloud of stars you are really looking towards the centre of our galaxy. Look into the thick part of the Milky Way with binoculars and you will be able to see the rich field of stars.

This month's constellation is Scorpius. This huge scorpion crawls along the southern horizon. During July it marches across the sky leading the planet Jupiter. Look for an arrangement of stars that looks like a sideways T.

Hercules is best seen during the summer in the Northern hemisphere. It is the fifth largest constellation in the sky, but can be difficult to locate because of its dim stars. You can find it by looking between Draco and Ophiuchus. Hercules is visible in the Southern hemisphere from May until August. This constellation contains two Messier objects, both of which are globular star clusters, as well as a large number of binary stars.

Deneb

'Deneb' is from an Arabic word meaning 'tail', as this first magnitude star, the 19th brightest as it appears in our sky, represents the tail of Cygnus the Swan, a classical figure seen flying perpetually to the south along the route of the Milky Way.

TOP RIGHT (*opposite*): Northern hemisphere view of the night sky in mid-latitudes looking south at about 11 p.m. local time on about July 7. Sagittarius joins Scorpius near the southern horizon, offering northern observers a tantalizing glimpse of the delights of southern skies.

BOTTOM RIGHT (*opposite*): Southern hemisphere view of the night sky in Australia and southern Africa looking north at about 11 p.m. local time on about July 7. The Swan and the Eagle take wing along the Milky Way. The stars Deneb and Altair lie on a near-vertical line.

Watching the Sky

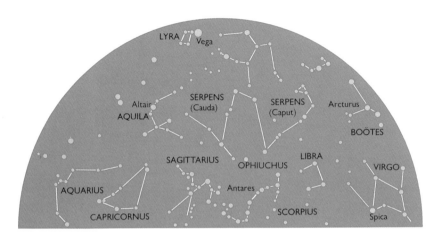

EAST   SOUTH   WEST

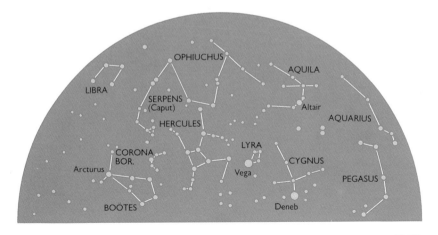

WEST   NORTH   EAST

Watching the Sky

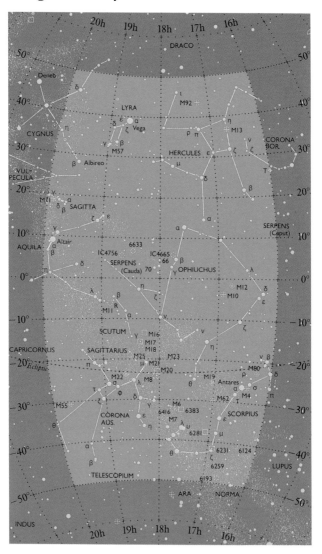

222222222111

Watching the Sky

THE STARS

Aquila (the Eagle) see page 227.

Cygnus (the Swan) see page 258.

Hercules see page 217.

Lyra (the Lyre)
Although this is only a small constellation, it is packed with interesting objects, particularly a surfeit of fine double stars.

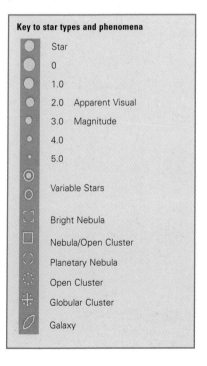

Key to star types and phenomena

	Star
	0
	1.0
	2.0 Apparent Visual
	3.0 Magnitude
	4.0
	5.0
	Variable Stars
	Bright Nebula
	Nebula/Open Cluster
	Planetary Nebula
	Open Cluster
	Globular Cluster
	Galaxy

The only really bright star in Lyra is the first-magnitude Vega, sometimes called the Harp Star. The fifth brightest star in the heavens, it shines brilliantly in summer skies in the Northern hemisphere and is one of the trio of stars (along with Deneb in Cygnus and Altair in Aquila) that make up the Summer Triangle.

Close to Vega lies Epsilon, the well-known 'double-double' star. It is so-called because it is a double star easily visible in binoculars. And when its two components are observed in a small telescope, they are also seen to be double.

Immediately south of Vega, four stars form a parallelogram. Astronomically, the most interesting of them is Beta. First, Beta is a double star, with yellowish and bluish components. In addition, the brighter yellowish star is an eclipsing binary system. Its two stars are very close together, probably less than 35,000,000 kilometres (22,000,000 miles). Because of this, they are almost certainly egg-shaped, with gas streaming between them.

Beta changes from the third to the fourth magnitude every 13 days. And its variation can readily be followed using Delta or Zeta (both a steady magnitude 4.3) for comparison. Both these stars are also doubles, the Delta system easily being visible in binoculars.

Sandwiched between Beta and Gamma is one of the most striking of all heavenly objects, M57, the Ring Nebula, a colourful 'smoke ring' puffed out by a dying star. It is not especially impressive in small telescopes and requires long exposures in

Watching the Sky

larger instruments to show its true splendour.

Ophiuchus (the Serpent-Bearer)

This is a large constellation, which splits Serpens, the Serpent, into two – Caput (Head) and Cauda (Tail). In the south, it enters a particularly rich region of the Milky Way, where globular clusters abound.

Among these southern clusters is M19, found midway between Theta and Antares in the adjacent constellation Scorpius. Just north of Antares, on the Ophiuchus/Scorpius boundary, is the faint star Rho. It is worth scanning this region because it is occupied by extensive clouds of gas and dust. Even in binoculars you may be able to make out the dust lanes.

Two bright globular clusters, M10 and M12, lie in the relatively barren interior of Ophiuchus. M12 makes a triangle with Lambda and Delta, and M10 is close by.

Among the stars, 70 is a colourful orange and yellow double visible in telescopes. Close to star 66 is a faint (magnitude 9) red star called Barnard's Star. It is interesting for two related reasons. First, it is the nearest star to Earth after Proxima and Alpha Centauri, only 5.9 light years away. Second, it is the star with the largest proper motion, or visible motion across the sky: over ten seconds of arc per year.

Sagitta (the Arrow) see page 227.

Sagittarius (the Archer) see page 262.
Scorpius (the Scorpion) see page 264.

Scutum (the Shield)

Although it is a small constellation with no really bright stars, Scutum lies on the edge of a rich part of the Milky Way. It abounds in star clouds and dark nebulous regions.

The constellation's two highlights lie close together. Just south of Beta is R, a variable star that changes brightness irregularly between about the sixth and ninth magnitudes. Close by is a beautiful open cluster, M11, called the Wild Duck because its fan of stars is said to look like a duck in flight.

Serpens Cauda (the Serpent's Tail)

This constellation is unique among all others as it is the only one, which consists of two parts: Serpens Caput (the Head of the Serpent) and Serpens Cauda (the Tail of the Serpent). Between both parts lies the constellation of Ophiuchus, the Serpent Holder. The stars of Serpens form the shape of a long writhing snake that starts near the Northern Crown, passes southwards through Serpens Caput, then through the body of Ophiuchus. When the shape emerges into Serpens Cauda, it turns northwards again, and carries on to reach its end into the Milky Way.

Perhaps the most interesting object in Serpens Cauda is M16, a scattered cluster of stars visible with binoculars quite close to Gamma Scuti in the adjacent constellation. Telescopes show the stars embedded in a glowing nebula, called the Eagle Nebula.

Watching the Sky

AUGUST SKIES

The Summer Triangle of the brilliant white Deneb, Vega and Altair spans the meridian, high in the sky in the Northern hemisphere, low in the Southern. The appearance of Pegasus in the east, however, hints at a changing season.

Mercury is at its observing best in the evening sky in August. Mars, the red planet, will come within 55.76 million km (34.64 million miles) of Earth, closer than it has been for thousands of years. It will not be this close again until 2208 AD. Mars remains in Aquarius for August, and is in retrograde motion until the beginning of October.

Jupiter is seen in Leo low in the western evening sky in August.

The Southern Cross can be found to the right of the South Celestial Pole in the southern sky during August. Around mid-month and mid-evening, the Cross is south-southwest at an altitude of about 35 degrees. Just above the southern horizon is the sparkling bright blue giant star Canopus. This is the second brightest star in the night sky, about 1,100 light years away. To the southeast we find another bright blue star, Achernar at a distance of 85 light years. We find the star Altair at around 35 degrees altitude near mid-evening and mid-month, in the northeastern sky. It lies at a distance of 16.6 light years. Due east around the same time of the evening and mid-month, the star Fomalhaut can be seen at an altitude of about 35°. Fomalhaut is the brightest star in the constellation of Piscis Austrinus (The Southern Fish) at a distance of 23 light years from us. During August the centre of our Milky Way Galaxy is almost directly overhead. On any clear night when you look straight up, you can see a dust concentration or cloud of stars. This can be found by first locating the constellation of Scorpius and then east of Scorpius we find Sagittarius and within it the dusty cloud of stars. This cloud outlines the central bulge of our home galaxy.

Fomalhaut

Fomalhaut means 'mouth of the fish' and is the brightest star in the constellation Piscis Austrinus, the Southern Fish. Fomalhaut is 22 light years away, is twice as large as the Sun and about 14 times more luminous.

TOP RIGHT (*page 226*): Northern hemisphere view of the night sky in mid-latitudes looking south at about 11 p.m. local time on about August 7. Part of Sagittarius is still visible this month; so, at lower latitudes, is Antares. But at higher latitudes, this star is just below the horizon.

BOTTOM RIGHT (*page 226*): Southern hemisphere view of the night sky in Australia and southern Africa looking north at about 11 p.m. local time on about August 7. Vega and Deneb are bright and prominent low down in the south, while Altair appears higher up.

Watching the Sky

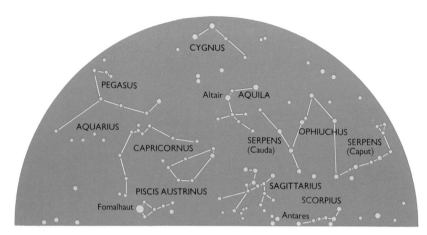

EAST   SOUTH   WEST

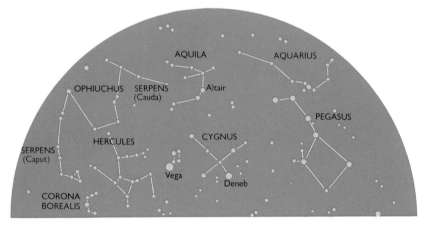

WEST   NORTH   EAST

Watching the Sky

THE STARS

Aquarius (the Water-Bearer) see page 233.

Aquila (the Eagle)
This is a fine constellation, whose curve of bright stars does rather resemble the wings of a bird in flight. Aquila straddles the Milky Way and the celestial equator, and contains rich star fields that are a delight to sweep with binoculars.

The brightest star, Altair, is one of the trio that form the prominent Summer Triangle. (The others are Deneb in Cygnus and Vega in Lyra.) Altair is a brilliant pure white star, contrasting nicely with one of its neighbours, the fainter Gamma, which is distinctly orange.

South of Altair is a noticeable line of three stars. Theta and Delta flank the central Eta, which is a Cepheid variable. It varies between the third and fourth magnitudes over about a week. Its progress can be followed by reference to the third-magnitude Theta and Delta, and the fourth-magnitude Iota.

The curve of stars around Lambda acts as a good pointer to the Wild Duck cluster M11, in the neighbouring constellation Scutum.

Capricornus (the Sea Goat)
Capricornus is one of the constellations of the zodiac, but is fairly inconspicuous. Its brightest stars, of about the third magnitude, form a pattern rather like a crooked triangle.

Alpha is a naked-eye double, but the two stars are not physically associated: the fainter one is more than ten times further away than the brighter one. Both stars are themselves doubles. Beta is also double and is a true binary star, whose components travel through space together.

The only noteworthy cluster in the constellation is M30, just outside the 'crooked triangle' near Zeta. It is a globular cluster, visible in small telescopes, but needing larger ones to resolve the stars properly.

Cygnus (the Swan) see page 258.

Delphinus (the Dolphin)
You can easily imagine this tiny constellation to be a leaping dolphin. Its bright stars form a group so compact that they almost look like an open cluster. In binoculars they all appear in the same field. In the main quadrilateral of stars, Gamma is a fine double, separated in small telescopes into golden yellow components.

Grus (the Crane) see page 233.

Lacerta (the Lizard) see page 234.

Lyra (the Lyre) see page 223.

Sagitta (the Arrow)
This is one of the smallest constellations in the heavens, but it has quite a distinctive, arrow-like shape. It lies within the Milky Way, almost due north of the bright stars in Aquila.

Watching the Sky

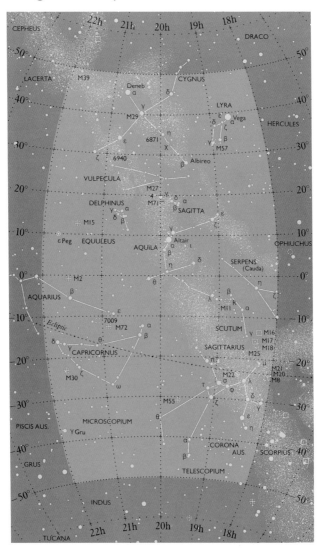

Watching the Sky

To the naked eye, Sagitta appears a rather bland region of the sky, but in binoculars it is well worth viewing for the beautiful star fields it contains. The four main stars are also an attractive sight in binoculars. About midway between Delta and Gamma, small telescopes will show a bright, dense grouping of stars, M71, which is almost certainly a globular rather than an open cluster.

Sagittarius (the Archer) see page 262.

Scutum (the Shield) see page 224.

Serpens Cauda (the Serpent's Tail) see page 224.

Vulpecula (the Fox)
Vulpecula is a dim constellation containing no stars brighter than 4th magnitude. It can be found nestled between the more obvious patterns of Cygnus and Sagitta. It is worth trying to identify this constellation because it contains a couple of very interesting sights for binoculars and telescopes. The Milky Way flows through Vulpecula and it is rich with fainter stars. This constellation can be seen from late spring to late autumn but is best seen during the summer months.

Perhaps the finest object in Vulpecula is the Dumbbell Nebula, M27, one of the brightest planetary nebulae in the heavens. It is located due north of Gamma Sagittae in the neighbouring constellation and is best found by reference to that star. Through binoculars,

M27 appears as a misty patch, but most telescopes will reveal its characteristic dumbbell shape.

Close to the border with Sagitta, and west of the arrow's 'flight', is 4, which lies in a curve of faint stars that form part of a loose open cluster. In binoculars, this curve and a straight line of six stars nearby have the appearance of a coat hanger, and the cluster is often referred to as the 'Coathanger'.

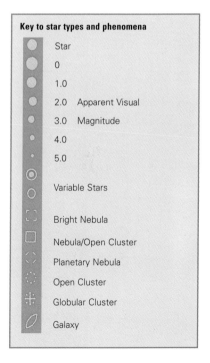

Key to star types and phenomena	
●	Star
●	0
●	1.0
●	2.0 Apparent Visual
●	3.0 Magnitude
●	4.0
·	5.0
◉	
○	Variable Stars
⌂	Bright Nebula
▢	Nebula/Open Cluster
⟨⟩	Planetary Nebula
⋮	Open Cluster
✛	Globular Cluster
⬭	Galaxy

Watching the Sky

SEPTEMBER SKIES

As September progresses Pegasus, the Winged Horse, continues chasing the stars of the Summer Triangle towards the western horizon. This signals the approach of autumn in the Northern hemisphere, and of spring in the Southern.

September is noticeable by the lack of planets appearing in the night sky. Venus sets soon after sunset and Jupiter and Saturn do not rise until after midnight.

Around mid-month and mid-evening, the Southern Cross is south-southwest at an altitude of about 25 degrees. Just above the southeast horizon is the sparkling bright blue giant star Canopus. This is the second brightest star in the night sky, about 1,100 light years away. High in the southeast we find another bright blue star, Achernar at a distance of 85 light years. To the left and above Canopus, we see two dusty regions that look like clouds. These are in fact companion galaxies to our home Milky Way Galaxy. They are the Small and Large Magellanic Cloud Galaxies. They lie at distances of 260,000 and 165,000 light years respectively. We find the star Altair at around 40 degrees altitude near mid-evening and mid-month, in the northern sky. Altair is an optical double star, which is the brightest star in the constellation Aquila (The Eagle). It lies at a distance of 16.6 light years. Low on the northern horizon is the star Vega, at a distance of 24 light years. During

September the centre of our Milky Way Galaxy is almost directly overhead. On any clear night at this time of year, when you look straight up, you can see a dust concentration or cloud of stars. This can be found by first locating the constellation of Scorpius and then east of Scorpius we find Sagittarius and within it the dusty cloud of stars. This cloud outlines the central bulge of our home galaxy. Study it with binoculars and you will be amazed.

Rigel

Rigel is 900 light years away, but if it were as close to us as Sirius is, it would be a blazing point of light as bright as a crescent moon. Rigel is almost 60,000 times as bright as the Sun, and is as big as the orbit of Mercury.

TOP RIGHT (*opposite*): Northern hemisphere view of the night sky in mid-latitudes looking south at about 11 p.m. local time on about September 7. This sky view reveals Altair fairly high in the west and Fomalhaut low in the south. Much of the sky is occupied by rather barren constellations.

BOTTOM RIGHT (*opposite*): Southern hemisphere view of the night sky in Australia and southern Africa looking north at about 11 p.m. local time on about September 7. Vega and Deneb are now close to the horizon. Pegasus is the most prominent of the rising constellations.

Watching the Sky

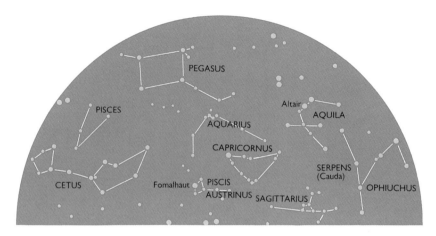

EAST   SOUTH   WEST

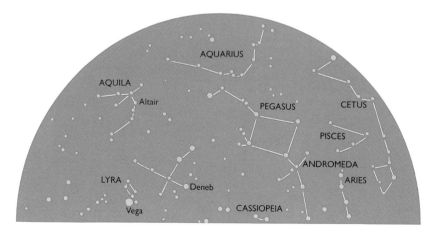

WEST   NORTH   EAST

Watching the Sky

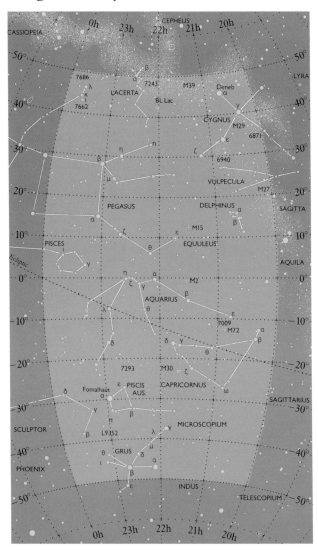

Watching the Sky

THE STARS

Aquarius (the Water-Bearer)

This is a sprawling zodiacal constellation, but a faint one, with leading stars of only about the third magnitude. It adjoins other 'watery' constellations, Pisces, Cetus, Piscis Austrinus and Capricornus (Fishes, Whale, Southern Fish and Sea Goat).

The brightest star, Alpha, can perhaps best be found by extending a diagonal of the Square of Pegasus from Alpha Andromedae through Alpha Pegasi. Once Alpha is found, the adjacent stars Gamma, Zeta and Eta are easy to spot. The pattern of these four stars represents the mouth of the water jar.

Beta is found just off the extended diagonal through Pegasus. Due north of Beta, and forming a right-angled triangle with Alpha and Beta, is M2. This globular cluster is one of the brightest in the heavens, visible as a misty patch in binoculars and resolved into stars in larger telescopes.

Also worth searching for in Aquarius are two fine planetary nebulae. The brighter of the two is NGC7009, which lies south of a line through Beta and Epsilon, forming a right-angled triangle with them. Seen through larger telescopes, NGC7009 appears to have a ring around it rather like the planet Saturn, and it is called the Saturn Nebula. In the same binocular field of view as the Saturn Nebula is M72, another fairly bright globular cluster.

The other planetary nebula, NGC7293, is called the Helix Nebula because of its spiral appearance in long-exposure photographs. In small telescopes, it looks like a faint smoke ring.

Capricornus (the Sea Goat) see page 227.

Cygnus (the Swan) see page 258.

Delphinus (the Dolphin) see page 227.

Grus (the Crane)

This is one of the 'southern birds', with outstretched wings and a long neck. The long, slightly curving line of stars that marks the neck and body line are readily spotted looking south from the bright Fomalhaut, in the neighbouring Piscis Austrinus.

The leading star Alpha has a magnitude of 1.7, slightly brighter than the second-magnitude Beta. These two stars provide a nice colour contrast, Alpha being bluish white, Eta being distinctly orange.

Lambda and Iota also have an orange tinge. Delta and Mu are naked-eye doubles, but their pairs of stars are, in reality, far apart.

The area between Theta and the border with the neighbouring constellation Phoenix is well worth exploring in telescopes because it contains a veritable cluster of galaxies.

Lacerta (the Lizard)

Watching the Sky

This northern constellation is small and faint, with only its leading star Alpha above the fourth magnitude. Its zigzag of stars, however, overlaps a section of the Milky Way between Cassiopeia and Cygnus, and so it contains glittering starscapes that make fine sweeping with binoculars.

One or two fairly bright open clusters are visible in small telescopes, including NGC7243. This one forms an equilateral triangle with Alpha and Beta.

Of great astronomical interest in the constellation, but far too faint to be seen in ordinary amateur instruments, is the object BL Lacertae. It is a variable galaxy, which changes noticeably in brightness in a relatively short time. Astronomers now think it is a quasar.

Pegasus (the Flying Horse) see page 237.

Phoenix (the Phoenix) see page 237.

Pisces (the Fishes) see page 239.

Piscis Austrinus (the Southern Fish)
Piscis Austrinus is one of the original 48 constellations that appeared in the works of Ptolemy, and so it is a truly ancient constellation. The southern fish are thought to be drinking from the Urn of water being poured out by the nearby Aquarius. This small constellation is dominated by a single bright star, the first-magnitude Fomalhaut. The name Formalhaut derives from the Arabic word *Fum al Hut*, meaning Fish Mouth. No

other stars are above the fourth magnitude in this constellation. Although pure white, Fomalhaut rates as only the 18th brightest star in the heavens, but it is easy to spot because it occurs in a region devoid of any other really bright stars.

Perhaps the most interesting star in this otherwise undistinguished constellation is one called Lacaille 9352. Of the eighth magnitude, it is found south of Pi. At a distance of some 11.7 light years, it lies relatively close to Earth and shows a substantial proper motion. It moves noticeably across the background of the other stars over a relatively short period.

Vulpecula (the Fox) see page 229.

Aldebaran

Aldebaran is a red giant star, with a diameter about forty times that of the Sun. Aldebaran is by far the brightest star of the constellation Taurus. It is 60 light years away, but if placed at the position of the Sun, Aldebaran would extend halfway to the planet Mercury and would appear 20 degrees across in our sky, making life on Earth quite impossible.

The ancient name, from Arabic, means 'the Follower', as the star seems to follow the Pleiades, or Seven Sisters star cluster, across the sky.

Watching the Sky

OCTOBER SKIES

The October skies are dominated by the unmistakable Pegasus. With few bright stars, the other constellations are harder to trace. This month is good for observing our galactic neighbour, the Great Spiral in Andromeda.

The skies are now getting darker much earlier and by the end of the month the clocks will have changed bringing us even more hours of darkness to view the night sky. At this time of year three constellations fill the southern sky: Capricornus, Aquarius and Pegasus. These all lie outside the Milky Way and so we are beginning to see globular clusters again. Of course we should not forget that rising east of Pegasus is Andromeda with its famous galaxy, but that does not come due south for the next month to get a good sighting.

The month of October dawns with Jupiter gracing our morning sky. Mars continues to be an evening star, while Saturn continues to be the nighttime star throughout the entire month. Venus will make a spectacular debut as an evening star as she climbs out of the western sky in October.

Also watch out for the Orionid Meteor Shower that peaks this month. Meteor showers occur when the Earth passes through debris left behind by comets. The Orionids are compliments of Halley's comet, and are active between October 15 and 29, with peak activity occurring on the 21 and 22. The radiants of this shower stem from the constellation Orion, which is located beneath Taurus and Gemini along the Ecliptic.

This month Mars is rising in the east before the sun sets in the west, and will therefore be well above the horizon as the evening twilight encroaches. Mars will lose over a magnitude of brightness in October, and appear to shrink in size as well. We find Mars amidst the stars of the constellation Aquarius. If you look further north, or higher than the Ecliptic and slightly east, you can spot the Great Square of Pegasus.

Pleiades

The Pleiades, known as the Seven Sisters, are a compact cluster of stars, high in the sky about 10 degrees from Aldebaran.

TOP RIGHT (*page 236*): Northern hemisphere view of the night sky in mid-latitudes looking south at about 11 p.m. local time on about October 7. The Square of Pegasus occupies centre stage, while Orion is just rising in the east. Aldebaran and Altair are at a similar altitude.

BOTTOM RIGHT (*page 236*): Southern hemisphere view of the night sky in Australia and southern Africa looking north at about 11 p.m. local time on about October 7. Pegasus sits in the mid-sky, and Orion is appearing over the eastern horizon. Fomalhaut is prominent near the zenith.

Watching the Sky

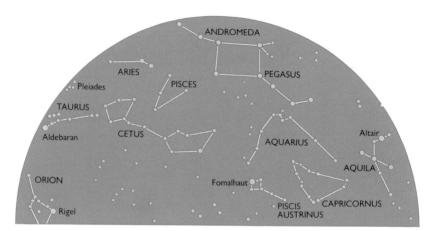

EAST   SOUTH   WEST

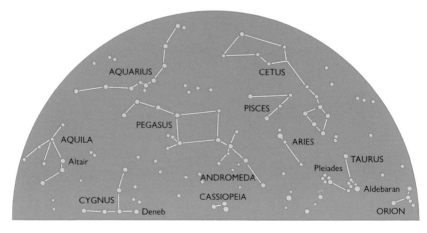

WEST   NORTH   EAST

Watching the Sky

THE STARS

Andromeda see page 252.

Aquarius (the Water-Bearer) see page 233.

Aries (the Ram) see page 243.

Cassiopeia see page 254.

Cetus (the Whale) see page 243.

Eridanus see page 247.

Grus (the Crane) see page 233.

Lacerta (the Lizard) see page 234.

Pegasus (the Flying Horse)
This is a large and distinctive constellation, which dominates autumnal skies in the Northern hemisphere. Its four leading stars form one of the most recognizable patterns in the heavens – the Great Square of Pegasus.

Once located, the Square serves as a useful signpost to other constellations. To the naked eye, the area enclosed by the Square is remarkably empty of stars. You would be hard-pressed to see more than a dozen.

Pegasus shares one of the stars in the Square with the neighbouring constellation Andromeda – Alpha Andromedae. (Its Arab name is Alpheratz.) Going clockwise around the Square, the three other stars are Beta (Scheat), Alpha (Markab) and Gamma (Algenib).

All of these stars are of the second magnitude, with Alpha Andromedae being the brightest. Beta is a variable star, although its variation in brightness is not easy to follow. It is a red giant star, and its reddish tinge, apparent even to the naked eye, contrasts with the pure white of Alpha.

The noticeably yellow Epsilon (Enif) lies some distance from the Square, roughly in line with Gamma and Alpha. It is fractionally brighter than Alpha and is a double, whose fainter component can be spotted in binoculars.

Among deep-sky objects in Pegasus, the globular cluster M15 is outstanding. It lies in line with Theta and Epsilon, a fraction too faint to be seen with the naked eye, but readily visible in binoculars and small telescopes. Larger instruments will resolve the outer regions into individual stars.

Phoenix (the Phoenix)
Phoenix is one of the Southern hemisphere constellations introduced by Johann Bayer in 1603. The constellation is in fact rather like a large bird, rising into the air. The second-magnitude Alpha marks the eye of this 'southern bird', which in mythology was reincarnated from its own ashes. It is a fairly large, but rather barren constellation. Beta is a double; both components are yellow and equally bright. Zeta is another double; the brightness of the brighter component varies slightly, and instruments show that it is a close eclipsing binary.

Watching the Sky

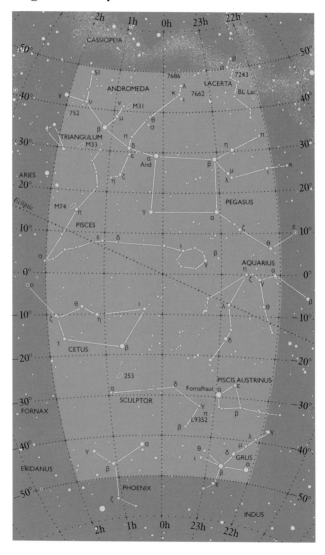

Watching the Sky

Pisces (the Fishes)

This is a large but rather uninteresting constellation of the zodiac, formed of a string of faint stars little brighter than about the fourth magnitude.

One of the two fishes the constellation depicts is marked by a circle of stars south of the Great Square of Pegasus. This is the easiest part of the constellation to identify. The curved line of stars from there to the leading star Alpha is not so easy to follow; nor is the line from Alpha to Eta and Alpha is a close double star, separated in larger telescopes into bluish-white components. Zeta is a much wider double, with twin pale yellow stars. Among several galaxies in Pisces, M74 is the brightest. Located close to Eta, it can just be picked up by small telescopes.

Piscis Austrinus (the Southern Fish) see page 234.

Sculptor (the Sculptor)

Sculptor is one of those obscure constellations invented by Nicolas Louis de Lacaille to help fill in part of the southern sky. The full name was *L'Atelier du Sculpteur*, the Sculptor's Studio. With Phoenix and Fornax, this constellation appears in a relatively barren region of the mid-southern skies. It is best found by reference to the bright Fomalhaut in the neighbouring Piscis Austrinus.

Sculptor is notable mainly for its galaxies, several of which (if you can find them!) can be glimpsed in binoculars. Larger telescopes will pick up many more.

Definitely in binocular range is NGC253, visible as an elongated misty patch about a third of the way along a line from Alpha towards Beta Ceti to the north. Larger telescopes reveal NGC253 to be a spiral galaxy, much like our own but smaller.

NGC253 is the brightest member of a cluster of galaxies in the region, known as the Sculptor group. They lie about 10 million light years away.

Triangulum (the Triangle) see page 244.

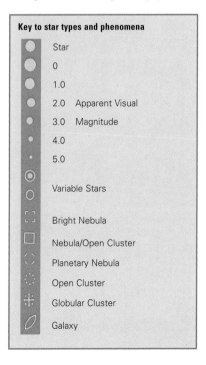

Key to star types and phenomena	
Star	
0	
1.0	
2.0	Apparent Visual
3.0	Magnitude
4.0	
5.0	
Variable Stars	
Bright Nebula	
Nebula/Open Cluster	
Planetary Nebula	
Open Cluster	
Globular Cluster	
Galaxy	

Watching the Sky

NOVEMBER SKIES

As Pegasus begins its slow descent in the west, Taurus and Orion begin climbing to prominence in the east. Orange Aldebaran, the Hyades and the Pleiades clusters are becoming well placed for observations in both hemispheres.

Pisces is visible in the sky between October and December in the Northern hemisphere. Pisces is an ancient constellation representing a pair of fishes tied by their tails, the knot being marked by the star α (alpha) Piscium. To find Pisces, look towards the middle of the north evening sky to find α (alpha) Piscium above and to the right of the great square of Pegasus.

Andromeda is visible in the Southern hemisphere in November. It represents the daughter of Cepheus and Cassiopeia, the king and queen of Ethiopia. Andromeda was chained to a rock as a sacrifice to the sea monster Cetus. She was saved by Perseus when he turned Cetus to stone by using the dismembered head of the Medusa.

Venus and Mars are both still visible in November skies. Currently, Venus is visible low in the western sky just after sunset and, as the month progresses, will get higher.

Mars, which has had lots of attention over the past few months, is now much less prominent in the sky as it moves further away from us. It can still be seen as a red 'star' in the constellation of Aquarius.

Jupiter, the largest of the planets, is becoming more visible as it moves through the constellation of Leo. To see Jupiter means an early start as it doesn't rise until around 1.30 a.m. for most of the month. Those of you with small telescopes may want to see if you can find Jupiter and see four of its moons.

Saturn is the last of the planets visible this month. It is found lying in the constellation of Gemini and throughout most of the month rises around 10 p.m. The two bright stars in Gemini, Castor and Pollux serve as useful pointers to Saturn.

Algol

Algol comes from the Arabic name of the star 'Ra's al Ghul', the Demon's Head. Algol is a three star system containing an eclipsing binary pair.

TOP RIGHT (*opposite*): Northern hemisphere view of the night sky in mid-latitudes looking south at about 11 p.m. local time on about November 7. Faint constellations such as Eridanus and Cetus cover much of the sky. The interest lies in the east, in sparkling Orion and Taurus.

BOTTOM RIGHT (*opposite*): Southern hemisphere view of the night sky in Australia and southern Africa looking north at about 11 p.m. local time on about November 7. Pegasus and Andromeda are about to set in the west. In the east, Aldebaran, Betelgeux and Rigel form a nice triangle.

Watching the Sky

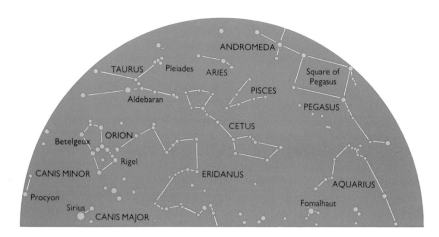

EAST   SOUTH   WEST

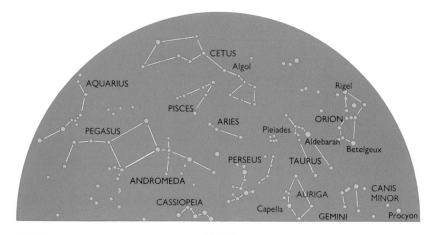

WEST   NORTH   EAST

Watching the Sky

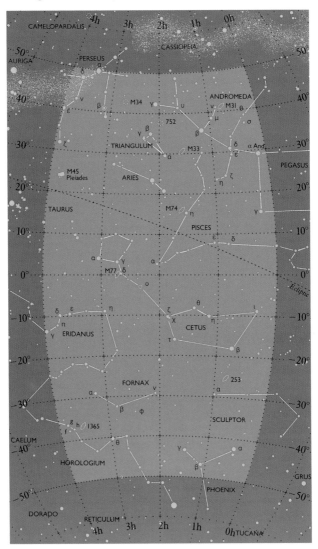

Watching the Sky

THE STARS

Andromeda see page 252.

Aries (the Ram)

This small constellation of the zodiac has just two noticeably bright stars, the second-magnitude Alpha and the somewhat less bright Beta. This pair can probably best be found by reference to the Great Square of Pegasus. Alpha is also at the same declination as the Pleiades cluster in the neighbouring Taurus. Gamma, due south of Beta, is a fine double, visible in small telescopes as a pair of equally bright bluish-white stars.

Cetus (the Whale)

Although it is one of the largest constellations in the heavens, Cetus is not easy to trace because of its lack of bright stars. Only Alpha in the Whale's head and Beta in its tail are above the third magnitude.

However, both these and the other main stars lie more or less on a line between Aldebaran in Taurus and Fomalhaut in Piscis Austrinus.

In the Whale's head, Alpha is a wide binocular double. It is a red giant, whose orange tinge is discernible to the naked eye and very obvious through binoculars. A telescope is needed to split the adjacent bright double star, Gamma, into its two components, which provide a marked colour contrast of bluish-white and yellow.

In the tail region of Cetus, Tau is interesting in that it is a star of a similar type to the Sun. Some 12 light years away, it is one of the closest stars that

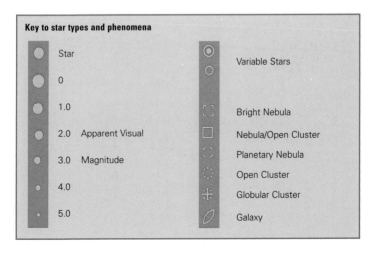

Key to star types and phenomena

Star	
0	
1.0	
2.0 Apparent Visual	
3.0 Magnitude	
4.0	
5.0	

Variable Stars	
Bright Nebula	
Nebula/Open Cluster	
Planetary Nebula	
Open Cluster	
Globular Cluster	
Galaxy	

Watching the Sky

astronomers think could have a planetary system like the Sun's. It is a favourite target for SETI (Searches for Extraterrestrial Intelligence) projects.

Historically, the most important star in the constellation is Omicron, also called Mira, meaning 'wonderful'. It is the prototype long-period variable star, a huge red giant that varies widely in brightness over a period of several months or a year or more.

Mira Ceti varies between magnitudes of about 3 and 10 every 11 months or so. It is found midway between Gamma and the distinctive pair Zeta and Chi, and is easily seen when it is near maximum, but difficult to find when it is near minimum.

A number of galaxies lie near Delta, the brightest of which, M77, can be sighted in binoculars as a hazy patch. A telescope will show it is a face-on spiral with bright, widely spaced arms. It is one of the most remote Messier objects, lying at a distance of over 50 million light years.

Eridanus see page 247.

Fornax (the Furnace) see page 247.

Pegasus (the Flying Horse) see page 237.

Perseus see page 249.
Phoenix (the Phoenix) see page 237.

Pisces (the Fishes) see page 237.

Sculptor (the Sculptor) see page 239.

Triangulum (the Triangle)

Triangulum is a small, compact constellation which, unlike many others in the night sky, looks exactly like the object it is supposed to depict. Triangulum is situated east of the Square of Pegasus and south of Andromeda. This constellation can be seen from late summer to early spring but is best seen during the autumn and winter. With its three main stars arranged in a neat triangle, this constellation is well named. However, it is far from bright, with just two stars, Alpha and Beta, of about the third magnitude. The third main star, Gamma, makes up the third corner of the triangle, along with two close fainter companions.

Triangulum's main claim to fame is the beautiful face-on spiral galaxy M33, which lies about halfway between Alpha Trianguli, and Beta Andromedae in the neighbouring constellation. It is just about visible to the naked eye on a really dark night and can readily be seen as a hazy patch in binoculars. Larger telescopes, however, are needed to bring out its wide-open spiral arms.

Capella

Capella is a brilliant yellowish star rising in the north-northeast after sunset. Of the ten brightest stars from mid-northern latitudes, Capella is the one closest to the North Celestial Pole. Capella is 16 times as large as the Sun in diameter and 174 times as luminous

Watching the Sky

DECEMBER SKIES

A hexagonal arrangement of bright stars – Sirius, Rigel, Aldebaran, Capella, Pollux and Procyon – in Canis Major, Orion, Auriga, Gemini and Canis Minor make spectacular stargazing in this month and next.

The highlight of the month for astronomers is the appearance of the Geminid Meteor Shower. The Geminids, one of the most prominent meteor showers in the heavens radiates from Gemini (the region around Castor), reaching its peak during mid-December. The appearance of this meteor shower was first noted in 1862. The meteor shower Rho Geminids is usually visible from the end of December to the end of January. It was first detected in 1872.

Aries can be seen in the Northern hemisphere during December, and it is a small constellation bounded by Taurus, Pisces and Cetus. To find Aries, look to the north, find Orion, then the bright star Aldebaran, look further to the west to find the Pleiades star cluster (the Seven Sisters) and look between the Pleiades and the Great Square of Pegasus.

Saturn is the first planet visible in the evening (eastern) sky at sunset. Saturn is followed by the brighter Jupiter at around 9 p.m. After 4 a.m. Jupiter and Saturn are joined by Mars and Venus. Venus is unmistakable, outshining all other objects in the night sky, with the exception of the Moon, of course.

Orion is the most prominent and familiar of the constellations visible in the evening sky. The stars of the Great Square of Pegasus and of Andromeda can still be seen low in the north, with the Andromeda Galaxy visible as a faint fuzzy spot below the star Beta Andromedae. The bright stars of the Crane and the Southern Fish are in the west on December evenings, while Achemar is a bit south of the zenith and somewhat north of the dim glow of the Small Magellanic Cloud.

Betelgeuse
This star marks the eastern shoulder of mighty Orion, the Hunter, and derives its name from an Arabic phrase meaning 'the armpit of the central one'.

TOP RIGHT (*page 246*): Northern hemisphere view of the night sky in mid-latitudes looking south at about 11 p.m. local time on about December 7. The meridian neatly splits the sky into two. The eastern half sparkles with bright stars and provides a marked contrast to the lacklustre western half.

BOTTOM RIGHT (*page 246*): Southern hemisphere view of the night sky in Australia and southern Africa looking north at about 11 p.m. local time on about December 7. The December hexagon of bright stars is stunning in the east. The Pleiades cluster is in an ideal viewing position.

Watching the Sky

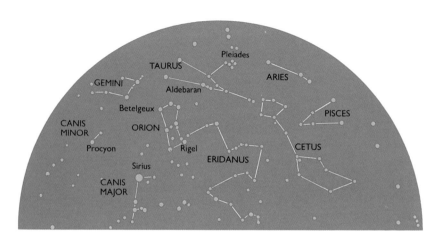

EAST   SOUTH   WEST

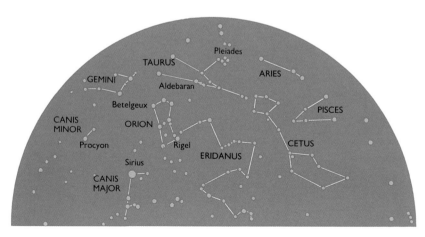

WEST   NORTH   EAST

Watching the Sky

THE STARS

A hexagonal arrangement of bright stars – Sirius, Rigel, Aldebaran, Capella, Pollux and Procyon – in Canis Major, Orion, Auriga, Gemini and Canis Minor make spectacular stargazing in this month and the next.

Aries (the Ram) see page 243.

Auriga (the Charioteer) see page 193.

Carina (the Keel) see page 276.

Cetus (the Whale) see page 243.

Columba (the Dove) see page 194.

Eridanus

One of the largest of the constellations, Eridanus represents a river. The ancient Middle Eastern astronomers associated it with their life-giving rivers, the Euphrates and the Nile.

With broad meanders, Eridanus winds itself through the heavens. It 'rises' at Beta, near the bright Rigel in Orion, and works its way towards the brilliant Alpha far south. The Arab name for Alpha, Achernar, means 'end of the river'. Achernar, of magnitude 0.5, is the ninth brightest star in the sky.

Heading 'upstream' from Achernar, Theta is perhaps the first interesting star. It is a fine double, which small telescopes will separate as a bluish-white pair. The other interesting stars lie in the northern reaches of the river. Omicron 2 is a wide and easy double. The fainter of its components is a white dwarf star and is the easiest of its type to see. Larger telescopes reveal that the white dwarf itself has a companion, a red dwarf.

Delta and Pi are both distinctly orange and form an obvious triangle with Epsilon. Epsilon lies relatively close to Earth (10.7 light years) and is a similar type of star to the Sun. Astronomers have long thought that it might have a planetary system like Earth's.

Fornax (the Furnace)

This is one of the faint constellations in mid-southern skies, which, like the neighbouring Sculptor, lacks prominent stars. Only Alpha is brighter, just, than the fourth magnitude. Mostly, Fornax is encircled by one of the broad meanders of Eridanus.

Although binoculars find little of interest, small telescopes begin to reveal the riches Fornax possesses. Zeroing in on the faint twin stars Lambda reveals a dense star cluster nearby. Larger instruments show it to be an irregular galaxy, called the Fornax System. It is a dwarf galaxy, like the Magellanic Clouds.

On the edge of the constellation, close to the triangle of stars, g, f and h Eridani, telescopes reveal the Fornax Cluster of galaxies. Larger instruments show the cluster to have about 18 members, one of which is NGC1365, one of the brightest barred-spiral galaxies in the heavens. At a distance of about 55 million light-years,

Watching the Sky

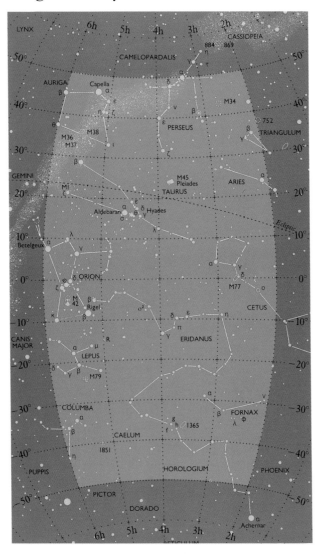

Watching the Sky

the Fornax Cluster is one of the nearest clusters of galaxies.

Lepus (the Hare) see page 194.

Orion see page 260.

Perseus
Perseus is a wishbone-shaped constellation located below Cassiopeia in the northeastern sky and was named after a hero of Greek mythology. This bright northern constellation has some splendid stars and glorious star fields, since it straddles the Milky Way. The brightest star, Alpha (also called by its Arab name Mirfak), is surrounded by a myriad of faint stars, and the group prettily fills the whole field in binoculars.

Binoculars will also reveal the rare beauty of one of the showpiece features of Perseus, the famous Double Cluster. Also called the Sword Handle, it is easily located midway between Gamma Persei and Delta Cassiopeiae in the neighbouring constellation. It is a pair of glorious open clusters, each of which would be beautiful by itself. The keen-eyed should see them without optical aid on a dark night. On star charts they are usually separately identified as h and Chi Persei, or NGC869 and 884.

The other showpiece feature in Perseus is Beta. Its Arab name Algol, or the Winking Demon, describes it well. For most of the time, it shines steadily at about magnitude 2, but about every $2\frac{1}{2}$ days it fades over a few hours to about magnitude 3.5 before regaining its former brightness. Algol is a classic example of an eclipsing binary and was the first of its type to be recognized.

In the same binocular field as Algol is another open cluster, M34, which is just visible to the naked eye.

Taurus (the Bull) see page 266.

Triangulum (the Triangle) see page 244.

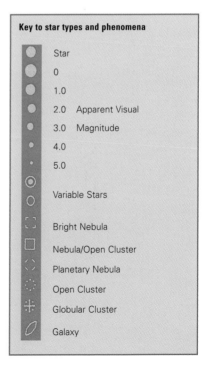

Key to star types and phenomena

⬤	Star	
⬤	0	
⬤	1.0	
⬤	2.0	Apparent Visual
●	3.0	Magnitude
•	4.0	
·	5.0	
◎		
○	Variable Stars	
⸬	Bright Nebula	
▢	Nebula/Open Cluster	
◇	Planetary Nebula	
∴	Open Cluster	
✛	Globular Cluster	
⬭	Galaxy	

Watching the Sky

THE CONSTELLATIONS

Below is a list of the constellations in
alphabetical order:

Andromeda	Delphinus
Antlia	Dorado
Apus	Draco
Aquarius	Equuleus
Aquila	Eridanus
Ara	Fornax
Aries	Gemini
Auriga	Grus
Australe	Hercules
Boötes	Horologium
Caelum	Hydra
Camelopardalis	Hydrus
Cancer	Indus
Canes Venatici	Lacerta
Canis Major	Leo
Canis Minor	Leo Minor
Capricornus	Lepus
Carina	Libra
Cassiopeia	Lupus
Centaurus	Lynx
Cepheus	Lyra
Cetus	Mensa
Chamaeleon	Microscopium
Circinus	Monoceros
Columba	Musca
Coma Berenices	Norma
Corona Austrina	Octans
Corona Borealis	Ophiuchus
Corvus	Orion
Crater	Pavo
Crux	Pegasus
Cygnus	Perseus

Phoenix	Sextans
Pictor	Taurus
Pisces	Telescopium
Piscis Austrinus	Triangulum
Puppis	Triangulum
Pyxis	Tucana
Reticulum	Ursa Major
Sagitta	Ursa Minor
Sagittarius	Vela
Scorpius	Virgo
Sculptor	Volans
Scutum	Vulpecula
Serpens	

Of the 88 constellations that cover the
celestial sphere, a number are truly
outstanding for one reason or another. In
the Southern hemisphere they include
Sagittarius. This constellation is
magnificent not so much for its stars, but
for the abundance of clusters and nebulae
it contains, and for its dense star clouds.
In the Northern hemisphere, Taurus
boasts two exceptional star clusters.
Orion, which spans the celestial equator,
displays fine stars, brilliant nebulae and
acts as a signpost for locating stars in
other constellations.

Sagittarius, Taurus and Orion are
three of the eleven key constellations that
are featured in this section. The others are
Andromeda, Cassiopeia, Centaurus and
Crux, Cygnus, Scorpius, Ursa Major and
Virgo. The descriptive text is prefaced by
the fascinating story behind the
mythological figure which the
constellation purports to resemble.

Watching the Sky

The 11 constellations featured in this chapter are among the most spectacular in the heavens. They are drawn from both the Northern and Southern hemispheres. Each has more than its fair share of coloured stars and variables, doubles and clusters and nebulae and galaxies. Many of them, moreover, are invaluable in guiding astronomers around the sky.

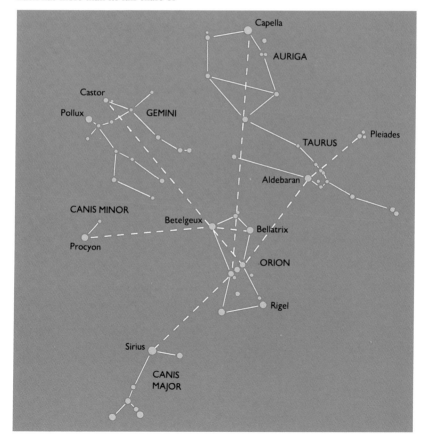

Watching the Sky

ANDROMEDA

Andromeda was the beautiful daughter of King Cepheus and Queen Cassiopeia. By boasting about her own beauty, the Queen upset Poseidon, the sea god, who sent a monster, Cetus, to terrorize the shores of Cepheus's kingdom. To placate Poseidon, the King chained Andromeda to rocks on the shore as a sacrifice. Just as Cetus was about to pounce on her, the hero Perseus happened by and killed her. He later wed Andromeda.

This large constellation is easily found because it is linked to one of the most distinctive constellations in the heavens, Pegasus. The leading star, Alpha Andromedae, or Alpheratz, forms the northeastern corner of the Square of Pegasus.

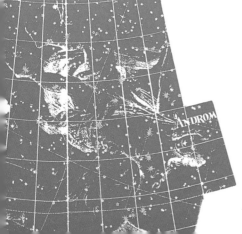

Andromeda has its fair share of doubles, variables and clusters, but it is best known for a fuzzy patch of light that looks like a nebula, but isn't, and is clearly visible to the naked eye. M31 in the Messier catalogue, this fuzzy patch used to be called the Great Nebula in Andromeda. However, we now know that it is a neighbouring galaxy similar to our own, but considerably bigger and containing many more stars.

THE GREAT SPIRAL

The Andromeda Galaxy is one of the showpiece objects of the northern heavens. It is a spiral galaxy like our own, but is much bigger, with a diameter of 150,000 light years. It is in fact the largest galaxy in our Local Group of galaxies, and is well named the Great Spiral.

Of about the fourth magnitude in brightness, the Great Spiral is easily seen near Nu. It lies about 2.3 million light years away, which makes it easily the furthest naked-eye object in the night sky.

In binoculars the Great Spiral shows as a distinct oval, while larger telescopes bring out individual stars and a dark dust lane. M31 also has two companion galaxies, M32 and M110 (NGC205), both visible in binoculars.

INTERESTING COMPANIONS

Among Andromeda's more interesting stars is the second-magnitude Gamma.

Watching the Sky

One of the most beautiful doubles in the night sky, it is readily resolved in small telescopes into a bright golden yellow primary and a bluish-green companion. The companion is also a double, but resolved only in larger telescopes.

An easier double than Gamma is Pi, while a harder one, with yellow components, is 36 Andromedae, located between Eta and Zeta near the border with Pisces.

Among the variable stars in the constellation is the distinctly red Mira-type R Andromedae. It is located close to a trio of fifth-magnitude stars Theta, Rho and Sigma, north of Alpha in the Square of Pegasus. It comes into binocular range at its brightest (about magnitude 7), but fades to magnitude 14. It is a pulsating, red giant star, varying over a period of 409 days.

A GREEN DOUGHNUT

Following an arc through Lambda, Kappa and Iota leads you to NGC7662, one of the brighter planetary nebulae. In small telescopes it looks like a fuzzy, greenish star, but larger instruments reveal the doughnut-shaped disc and the very hot central star.

South of Gamma is a trio of stars, 59, 58 and 56. Close to 56, which is a wide double, is a fairly scattered, open cluster, NGC752. Next to Beta (Mirach) is NGC404, an elliptical galaxy which has a fuzzy appearance similar to that of a developing comet.

East of Gamma, in the direction of Algos in the adjoining constellation, is NGC891, which is a classic edge-on spiral, bisected with a dark dust lane. But only larger telescopes will pick this up.

Collision with the Milky Way

Observations with the Hubble Space Telescope suggest that the Andromeda Galaxy may have two cores. This is thought to be the result of a past merger with another galaxy. Such processes were once common in the Universe and still occur today. Indeed, the galaxy is approaching us at a speed of 68 km (42.25 miles) per second and a collision with the Milky Way is a possibility in the distant future.

Watching the Sky

CASSIOPEIA

Queen Cassiopeia was the vain wife of King Cepheus and the mother of Andromeda. It was a consequence of the Queen's vanity that Andromeda nearly met an untimely end in the jaws of the sea monster Cetus. Cassiopeia boasted that she was fairer than the Nereids, sea nymphs famed for their beauty. The nymphs were offended and asked Poseidon, who was married to one of their number, to punish the vain Queen. He did so by sending Cetus (see page 252).

With its brightest stars aligned in a distinctive W-shape, Cassiopeia is unmistakable. It is a far northern constellation, located on the opposite side of the Pole Star from Ursa Major. From Canada, the northern United States and northern Europe, it is circumpolar and always visible.

Cassiopeia sits in the Milky Way, and the region is rich in clusters and dense star fields, which reward leisurely sweeping with binoculars.

THE 'W' STARS

Alpha (Shedir), Beta and Gamma are almost identical in brightness (about magnitude 2.2). Alpha, the southern-most star of the 'W', has a distinctly orange hue, compared with the pure white of Beta. Telescopes will resolve it into a double star, with the orange of the brilliant primary contrasting with the bluish-white of the fainter companion.

Nearby Eta is another fine double star, with golden yellow and purplish components. The central star of the 'W', Gamma, varies rather unpredictably. It is a very hot blue giant star that periodically throws off shells of luminous gas, causing its brightness to increase. In the 1930s, it rose to a magnitude of 1.6 to be the brightest star in the constellation, but later dipped to below 3.

Extending the 'W' from Delta through Epsilon, you reach Iota. This is an excellent triple star for amateur telescopes.

Watching the Sky

INTERESTING VARIABLES

Continuing the same line through Iota brings you to RZ Cassiopeiae. This is an eclipsing binary variable star within binocular range. Usually of about the sixth magnitude, it falls nearly to the eighth when it is in eclipse, every 29 hours. The dimming can easily be followed because it takes place over just two hours.

On the other side of the constellation, beyond Beta, is a line of three stars, Tau, Rho and Sigma. The central star Rho is an irregular variable of unknown type, which fluctuates between about magnitudes 4 and 6 quite unpredictably. The fifth-magnitude flanking stars Tau and Sigma are useful for comparison.

A regular Mira-type variable, R Cassiopeiae, lies south of Rho, though it is not easy to find because of the dense star fields of the Milky Way. At full brightness it reaches the sixth magnitude, but fades to the thirteenth over a period of 431 days.

FINE CLUSTERS

Rich star fields lie around Epsilon, Delta and Gamma, together with a number of clusters. They include the open clusters NGC663, 654 and M103, the brightest. However, the open cluster NGC457, south of Delta and close to Phi, is a more interesting object. It is a compact group of more than 100 stars. Binoculars show it well, and small telescopes will resolve its stars.

Another open cluster worth observing is M52, found, though with some difficulty, by extending a line through Alpha and Beta. It is a cluster of about 100 hot young stars rather like the Pleiades. It is an excellent subject for the small telescope.

Cassiopeia is a big 'W' in the sky, a well-known and easy to find constellation.

Watching the Sky

CENTAURUS

Centaurus the Centaur was one of the mythical creatures that were half-man, half-horse. Most centaurs were wild creatures, but this particular centaur was different. Named Chiron, he was wise and learned, and became a great teacher, especially of hunting, healing and music. Despite his medical skills, he could not heal himself when he was accidentally hit by one of Hercules' poisoned arrows.

Centaurus is one of the largest constellations in the heavens and one of the most spectacular. It has its 'feet' in the Milky Way and envelops the distinctive Crux, the Southern Cross.

Centaurus boasts the third brightest star in the night sky, the nearest star, a wealth of open and globular clusters and galaxies and it contains one of the most intense radio sources in the sky.

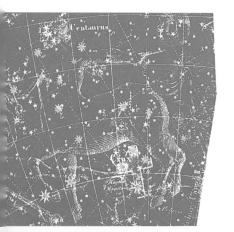

THE ALPHA CENTAURI SYSTEM

The leading star Alpha, sometimes called Rigil Kent, has a magnitude of –0.3 and is outshone in the heavens only by Sirius and Canopus. Alpha Centauri is a double star, separated in small telescopes into yellow components. It lies just 4.3 light years away, less than half the distance of Sirius.

When Alpha is viewed in large telescopes, a third faint star comes into view. It is a red dwarf of the eleventh magnitude, and it is closer even than Alpha. Indeed, it is the nearest star to Earth and is appropriately called Proxima Centauri.

Beta, also called Agena, has a magnitude of 0.6. It forms a prominent pair with Alpha, and the two are called the Pointers because they point to the Southern Cross. Being bluish-white, Beta contrasts with yellow Alpha. Though side by side in the heavens, the two are literally light years apart, more than 450 in fact.

Between the Pointers is the Mira-type variable R. It is an easy binocular subject at its maximum, when it is at the fifth magnitude, but fades to the eleventh at minimum over a period of 547 days.

OUTSTANDING OMEGA

Following a line from Beta through Epsilon to an equal distance beyond brings you to yet another glorious feature of the southern skies. It looks like a fuzzy fourth-magnitude star labelled Omega.

Watching the Sky

However, Omega Centauri is not a star at all, but a grouping of hundreds of thousands of stars, maybe as many as a million! It is in fact the finest example of a globular cluster there is. It is readily visible to the naked eye, and even binoculars will begin to resolve its stars.

Another globular cluster worth investigating in binoculars and a small telescope is NGC5286, just north of Epsilon. One of the finest open clusters in the constellation is NGC3766, near Lambda on the opposite side of the Southern Cross from Alpha and Beta.

CRUX, THE SOUTHERN CROSS

This, the smallest constellation, is circumpolar in New Zealand and much of Australia. Four main stars make up the Cross, Alpha (Acrux), Beta, Gamma and Delta. Warm reddish Gamma makes a nice contrast with the other bluish-white stars. Alpha (magnitude 0.8) is a double, as are Beta and Gamma and the pair Theta.

Near Beta is Crux's finest gem, a beautiful coloured open cluster nicknamed the Jewel Box, but officially termed Kappa Crucis or NGC4755. It is a glittering spectacle as its name implies, featuring a prominent red super-giant that shines like a ruby.

Kappa Crucis lies at the edge of a dark 'hole' in the Milky Way star fields, appropriately named the Coal Sack. It is, in fact, a large dark nebula.

Plumes from the Centaurus galaxy

The Chandra spacecraft (*below*) sent back images of the Centaurus galaxy cluster, which showed a long plume-like feature resembling a twisted sheet. The plume is some 70,000 light years in length and has a temperature of about 10 million°C. It is several million degrees cooler than the hot gas around it.

The plume contains a mass comparable to 1 billion Suns. It may have formed by gas cooling from the cluster on to the moving target of the central galaxy, as seen by Chandra in the Abell 1795 cluster. Other possibilities are that the plume consists of debris stripped from a galaxy which fell into the cluster, or that it is gas pushed out of the centre of the cluster by explosive activity in the central galaxy.

Watching the Sky

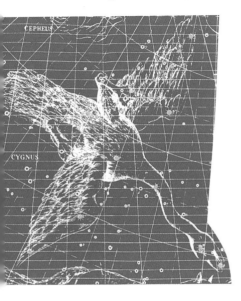

Cygnus is a beautiful northern constellation and one of the few to resemble the figure it is named for. The Swan is depicted flying south along the Milky Way. Cygnus' distinctive cross shape gives it the alternative name of the Northern Cross.

Cygnus provides an astronomical feast. It features many fine doubles and variables. Being largely in the Milky Way, it also abounds in star fields and clusters, which put on a magnificent display in binoculars. Larger telescopes reveal magnificent nebulae and diaphanous wisps of glowing gas.

DAZZLING DENEB

The leading star Alpha, or Deneb, in the Swan's tail, is of the first magnitude. It is exceptionally luminous, with the light output of more than 60,000 Suns. It lies very much further away than all the other bright stars, at a distance of more than 1,800 light years. If the brightest star in the sky, Sirius, were at that distance, we would hardly notice it.

Deneb is one of the three bright stars that make up the Summer Triangle. The others are Altair in Aquila and Vega in Lyra.

CYGNUS

Cygnus the Swan is supposed to be Zeus (Jupiter), king of the gods, in disguise. Zeus assumed this form when visiting one of his many lady loves, Leda, Queen of Sparta. The result of the liaison was an egg, out of which hatched the twins Castor and Pollux and also Helen, who would become the beautiful Helen of Troy, with the 'face that launched a thousand ships'. Pollux and Helen were both Zeus' children, but Castor was not; he was the son of the King of Sparta.

LOVELY DOUBLES

Beta, or Albireo, is at the opposite end of Cygnus from Deneb and is much fainter (third magnitude). But viewed even through a small telescope, it is a gem of a

Watching the Sky

double, probably the loveliest in the sky. Its blue and yellow components always appear clear and bright.

Delta and Gamma are also double, as is 61, under the Swan's right 'wing'. 61 Cygni has a greater claim to fame than just being a double. It was the first star to have its distance measured accurately. The German astronomer Friedrich Bessel worked out the distance, by the parallax method, in 1838. It proved to be over 105 million million km ($65^1/_4$ million million miles). That the stars were so remote caused a sensation.

RED VARIABLES

Cygnus contains several Mira-type variables, visible in binoculars at maximum brightness and worth viewing if only for their intense red colour. One of the most interesting is Chi, located in the Swan's neck. At maximum, Chi Cygni rivals the steady and nearby Eta (magnitude 3.6) in brightness. At minimum, it fades to below magnitude 14 over a period of 407 days, thus displaying one of the greatest changes in brightness known among variables.

Other Mira variables include U and R Cygni which come within binocular range near maximum, but fade way beyond it for much of the time. U is east of the star 32, which is itself north of the pair Omicron 1 and 2 under the Swan's left wing. R is located close to Theta further out.

W. Cygni, on the opposite side of the constellation close to the fourth-magnitude Rho, is a semi-regular variable with a period of about four months. Its change in brightness, from the fifth to the eighth magnitude, keeps it within range of binoculars throughout its cycle.

DEEP-SKY REVELATIONS

In all, there are up to 30 open clusters in the constellation, including two Messier clusters. M29 is located just south of Gamma; and M39 is found in the tail end of the constellation, forming a right-angled triangle with Pi-2 and Rho. M39 is the larger of the two, with more than 20 stars nearby covering half a Moon diameter.

Between Deneb and the much fainter Xi, the Milky Way noticeably brightens. Viewed through binoculars or a telescope, the region is revealed as a large nebula (NGC7000). Long-exposure photographs show a distinctive shape that gives it the name of the North America Nebula.

South of Epsilon in the Swan's right wing is a fourth-magnitude star 52. When the region is viewed in large binoculars or a telescope, filaments of glowing gas show up. And long-exposure photographs reveal a delicate looping tracery known as the Cygnus Loop. It is a supernova remnant, the remains of a supernova explosion that happened maybe 30,000 years ago. We know a bright part of the Loop as the Veil Nebula, sometimes called the Cirrus Nebula.

Watching the Sky

ORION

In mythology, Orion was a mighty hunter. He was the son of the sea god Poseidon, who gave him the power to walk on the sea. Orion features in many tales. In one he fell in love with seven sisters, the Pleiades, and pursued them, as he does still in the heavens. Different stories tell of how Orion died. One tells of Orion's boast that he could kill any creature alive, which caused the Earth to open. Out came a scorpion, which promptly stung him to death.

The celestial equator passes through this magnificent constellation, which is therefore equally familiar to sky-watchers in both hemispheres.

'Magnificent' is certainly the right word to describe the most readily recognizable of all the constellations. Also, its outline really does look like the figure it is meant to represent, the mighty hunter with club upraised and shield at the ready.

TWIN GIANTS

Two stars vie with each other to be the finest in the constellation, Alpha, or Betelgeux (sometimes spelt Betelgeuse and pronounced 'beetle-juice'), and Beta, or Rigel.

Betelgeux is one of the larger stars that can be seen, indeed one of the larger stars to be found anywhere. If it were where the Sun is, its globe would reach beyond the Earth's orbit nearly to Mars. It is obviously red and variable. At maximum brightness, it reaches a magnitude of 0.5, but can fade below 1 over an irregular period of about five to six years. Betelgeux is so large that it is the first star to be directly imaged as a disc from Earth by the Hubble Space Telescope.

Rigel, which is diametrically opposite Betelgeux in the main star pattern, is actually brighter, shining steadily at magnitude 0.1. It too differs in colour, being bluish-white. It is an intensely hot star with the energy output of more than 50,000 Suns. Larger telescopes will show it to be a double.

Watching the Sky

The other bright stars in Orion are also named: Gamma – Bellatrix, Delta – Mintaka, Epsilon – Alnilam, Zeta – Alnitak and Kappa – Saiph.

GREAT NEBULAE

Apart from the main star pattern, the most conspicuous feature of the constellation to the naked eye is a misty patch below the three stars, Delta, Epsilon and Zeta, which form Orion's Belt. Binoculars show it to be a bright nebula, M42, aptly named the Great Nebula in Orion. Long-exposure photographs of the nebula are needed to bring out its staggering beauty, which few other heavenly sights can match.

A much smaller, nearly round nebula, M43, lies close to the Great Nebula. There is a small reddish nebula close to Zeta, identified as NGC2024, and a slightly brighter and more bluish one further north, M78.

South of Zeta is the glowing nebula IC434, which has obscuring dark matter silhouetted against it in the shape of a horse's head. This Horsehead Nebula, also called Barnard 33, is the most distinctive dark nebula in the heavens. Unfortunately, it is beyond the reach of smaller telescopes.

The nebulae highlighted above are really the 'tip of the iceberg' because virtually the whole constellation sits in a tenuous gas cloud. It is this vast reservoir of interstellar matter that spawned hot white stars like Rigel and those in Orion's Belt.

MULTIPLE CHOICE

Orion is rich, too, in double and multiple stars. Pride of place must go to the star Theta Orionis, which is embedded in the Great Nebula. Called the Trapezium after the arrangement of its four components, it can be separated in small telescopes. It is the light from these that illuminates the Nebula. Iota, at the southern edge of the Nebula, is also double.

Going northwards, Sigma appears double in binoculars, but small telescopes reveal it as a triple, with white, bluish and reddish components. Larger instruments separate a fourth component. In Orion's Belt, Zeta and Delta are double. So is Lambda, the third-magnitude star marking Orion's 'eye'.

And Orion has still more to offer, in the way of variables, open clusters and planetary nebulae. Perhaps the easiest variable to find is the very red W, at the southern end of the arc of the six Pi stars that form Orion's Shield. W is a long-period variable of the Mira type, which varies between about the sixth and eighth magnitudes over a period of 212 days and is always within binocular range.

The open cluster NGC2169 is the brightest in the constellation at about the eighth magnitude. It forms an equilateral triangle with Xi and Nu in Orion's upraised right hand. Going further north, NGC2174/5 is an attractive combination open cluster and nebula, in line with Chi 1 and 2.

Watching the Sky

SAGITTARIUS

Sagittarius the Archer is depicted as a half-man, half-horse centaur, but one of the war-like ones (unlike Centaurus on page 256). He has his bow drawn, with the arrow pointing to Antares, the Scorpion's heart. In early times, Sagittarius was thought of rather as a satyr, a two-legged creature that was half-man, half-goat. He was identified with Crotus, the inventor of archery, whose father was the pipe-playing god Pan.

Sagittarius is one of the richest constellations in the heavens, spanning the Milky Way. The Milky Way here is magnificent, studded with clusters and beautiful nebulae and brilliant with dense star clouds. The densest mark the direction of the centre of our galaxy some 30,000 light years away. Swept with binoculars, this part of the night sky takes the breath away.

Alas for most sky-watchers in the Northern hemisphere, Sagittarius never rises high enough to be fully appreciated. How they envy astronomers down under!

A MESSIER FEAST

The constellation has a number of double and variable stars (such as the Cepheid variable W, close to Gamma). However, its chief attraction lies in its deep-sky objects. Charles Messier catalogued more of them in Sagittarius than in any other constellation, including some of the best-known nebulae and many globular clusters.

M8, the Lagoon Nebula, is one of the brightest of the Messier nebulae. Of the fifty magnitude, it can be glimpsed with the naked eye, making a triangle with Lambda and Mu. It is a fine object in binoculars and a small telescope, but as always with nebulae, only long-exposure photographs bring out its full beauty. Such pictures show up dark gas lanes and many tiny black condensations known as Bok globules, which are probably on the way to becoming stars.

Just to the north of M8 is an equally famous nebula, M20, the Trifid. This is visible in binoculars as a small misty patch. Telescopes will reveal its three dark dust lanes, which give the nebula its name.

Watching the Sky

The third major nebula in Sagittarius, M17, is located at the northern border of the constellation on the edge of the Milky Way. It is probably best found by following a line between Gamma Scuti in the neighbouring constellation and Mu. M17 has roughly the shape of the Greek letter omega, and so is usually the Omega Nebula. It has the alternative names of the Swan and the Horseshoe Nebula.

CLUSTER COLLECTION

Immediately south of the Omega Nebula is the open cluster M18 and south of this M24. M24 is neither a nebula nor a cluster, but a general brightening of the Milky Way otherwise known as the Small Sagittarius Star Cloud.

Making a triangle with M24 and Mu is a good binocular open cluster M23, a collection of over 100 stars of up to the ninth magnitude. Further south, near the Trifid Nebula, is a similar object, M21.

GREAT GLOBULARS

Sagittarius boasts more than 20 globular clusters, about one tenth of the number known. That it contains so many is not really surprising, because globulars tend to congregate around the centres of galaxies.

The top globular is undoubtedly M22, which forms a triangle with Lambda and Phi. M22 is a dense grouping of literally millions of stars. It rates the sixth magnitude and is just visible to the naked eye. It looks great in binoculars and small telescopes, which begin to resolve its outer stars.

Other notable globulars include M54 and M55. M54 is located close to Zeta, while M55 is at about the same declination some way to the east. M55 is a much looser condensation of stars, counted in thousands rather than millions like M22.

The End of Sagittarius

Using data from the Two-Micron All Sky Survey – a study of the sky in infrared light – astronomers are showing that our Milky Way is devouring one of its neighbours. The analysis is the first to map the full extent of the nearby Sagittarius Galaxy, showing how it is being stretched out, torn apart and devoured by our own Milky Way. Until now, researchers only knew of a few disrupted and scattered pieces of the Sagittarius Galaxy.

Watching the Sky

SCORPIUS

*Scorpius the Scorpion was the creature
that stung to death the mighty hunter
Orion. Orion and Scorpius were therefore
placed on opposite sides of the heavens,
so that Orion disappears as the Scorpion
rises. In the sky, however, Scorpius itself
is threatened by Sagittarius the Archer,
whose arrow is pointing at the Scorpion's
heart, marked by Antares. The
constellation that is now Libra once
formed the Scorpion's front claws.*

Scorpius is another of those southern
constellations that are the envy of modern
astronomers. It is relatively small, but
brilliant, boasting no less than 11 stars
above the third magnitude. Also,

practically all of the constellation lies
within the Milky Way, and in one of the
richest parts of it, too, where open and
globular clusters abound.

The name given to the constellation is,
for a change, appropriate. Only the
slightest imagination is required to picture
a scorpion poised to strike, with head in
the north of the constellation and its
curved tail in the south.

RIVAL OF MARS

Scorpius' brightest star is Alpha, or Antares,
which marks the heart of the Scorpion. Its
name means 'rival of Mars', alluding to its
resemblance to the Red Planet. It is perhaps
the reddest of the bright stars, more so than
Betelgeux, for example.

Like Betelgeux, Antares is a red
supergiant, but it is even bigger,
probably as much as 700 times
the size of the Sun. If it were
where the Sun is, its surface
would stretch beyond the orbit
of Mars up to the asteroid belt.

Being so large, Antares is
unstable and pulsates, changing
in brightness slightly as it does
so and averaging about
magnitude 1.

THE SCORPION'S 'HEAD'

An arc of four stars, Nu, Beta,
Delta and Pi, mark the
Scorpion's 'head'. In the present

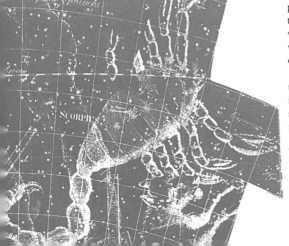

Watching the Sky

constellation, the claws are missing, the claw stars now forming part of the neighbouring constellation Libra.

Of the 'head' stars, Nu appears double in binoculars, and telescopes show each component itself to be double, making Nu a quadruple system. Second-magnitude Beta is also a fine double star with bluish-white components. Nearby Omega is an easy binocular double.

Moving south along the 'backbone' of bright stars, Sigma is double (as, incidentally, is Antares). Mu and Zeta, at the base of the 'tail', are wide, easy doubles. Zeta 1, the brighter component, is a reddish-orange; Zeta 2 is bluish-white. In binoculars or a small telescope, the region around Zeta is fascinating. It includes the third-magnitude open cluster NGC6231 composed, like the Pleiades, of young hot stars and plainly visible to the naked eye.

STING IN THE TAIL

The tail region of Scorpius is also a delight for the naked-eye sky-watcher, binocular viewer or Shaula, at magnitude 1.6, marking the Scorpion's tail. Both can be resolved into stars in binoculars. The third-magnitude M7 is the brighter and larger of the two, covering an area of sky larger than that of the Full Moon. M6 is also known as the Butterfly Cluster, because of the 'open-wing' arrangement of its principal stars.

Other Messier objects in the constellation include the sixth-magnitude M4 right next to Antares, a fine globular cluster for small telescopes. M80 is a somewhat fainter globular roughly midway between Antares and Beta.

FACTS ABOUT ANTARES – RED SUPERGIANT STAR

Origin of Name:
Greek for 'rival of Mars' (Ares is Greek for Mars). Sometimes Antares is mistaken for Mars when they are close together because both are red

Claim to Fame:
Brightest star in the constellation Scorpio, the Scorpion. 16th brightest star in the sky (apparent visual magnitude = 0.9)

Type of Star:
Red Supergiant (M1 Ib Spectral Class)

How Far Away:
325 light years away

How Big:
300 times as big as the Sun (more than twice the diameter of the Earth's orbit)

How Bright:
3000 times the Sun's luminosity (Mv = –4.5)

Where to View:
In the constellation Scorpio, the Scorpion

When to View:
July through August from northern middle latitudes

Watching the Sky

TAURUS

Taurus the Bull was one of the many disguises adopted by king-of-the-gods Zeus on his amorous adventures. Zeus assumed the form of a magnificent snow-white beast with shining horns when he set out to woo the fair Europa. He encouraged her to climb on his back, then carried her off to the island of Crete. There he revealed his true self. One of their children was King Minos, who built the palace of Knossos.

This large constellation adjoins Orion, and as far as stars are concerned, it is faint by comparison, but it boasts a fine leading star which marks the 'eye' of the Bull, two of the brightest open clusters in the heavens and the best-known supernova remnant.

The leading star is Alpha, or Aldebaran, which is easily found by following a line through Orion's Belt towards the northwest. Aldebaran is unmistakable both because of its brightness (magnitude 0.8) and its lovely orange colour. It is similar in brightness and appearance to Betelgeux in Orion, not far away.

Beta, or Al Nath, is the second brightest star (magnitude 1.6), and marks the tip of one of the Bull's horns. Third-magnitude Zeta marks the tip of the other. Both Beta and Zeta lie on the edge of the Milky Way.

Among the other stars, Lambda is worth watching because it is an eclipsing binary of the Algol type. Every four days, its brightness dips momentarily from the third to the fourth magnitude as the dim star of the pair passes in front of the bright one.

THE HYADES

Close to Aldebaran lies a scattered group of stars which form a distinctive V-shape and which are clearly visible to the naked eye. Known as the Hyades, they form one of the finest open clusters in the night sky.

The brightest star in the Hyades is Theta, a naked-eye double consisting of a white primary of magnitude 3.4 and a slightly fainter orange companion.

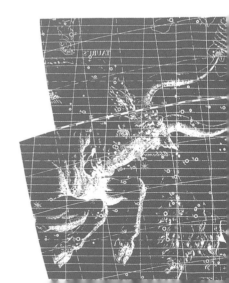

Watching the Sky

Binoculars show the colour difference well. Several of the other stars in the cluster are of similar brightness, including Epsilon, Delta and Gamma. Delta forms a double with a fainter star 64 Tauri. Sigma is another double close to Aldebaran.

Under good viewing conditions, as many as 20 stars can be detected in the Hyades with the naked eye. This is about one tenth of the total number of stars in the cluster. On average, the Hyades lies about 130 light years away, making it one of the nearest open clusters. Aldebaran itself is not part of the group, being only about half the distance away.

SEVEN SISTERS

Northwest of the Hyades lies an even more spectacular cluster, M45 or the Pleiades. It is also called the Seven Sisters, because keen-sighted people should be able to spot at least seven of its brightest stars with the naked eye. Binoculars and telescopes reveal more and more stars, which probably number in total more than 300.

Compared with the Hyades, the Pleiades is much more concentrated and thus more brilliant, shining nearly as brightly as a first-magnitude star. It differs from the Hyades in several other ways. It is much further away, at about 400 light years, and it is much younger. Whereas the Hyades stars are on average about 400 million years old, those in the Pleiades are youngsters of 10–20 million years old. They are hot and white, and surrounded by nebulosity which becomes visible in photographs.

The brightest Pleiades star is Alcyone (magnitude 2.9), and in descending order of brightness come the other six of the 'Seven Sisters': Atlas, Electra, Maia, Erope, Taygete and Pleione.

THE CRAB

Close by Zeta, at the tip of the Bull's southern horn, is another of Taurus' great sights, M1, the Crab Nebula. It is a supernova remnant, an expanding cloud of writhing gas that resulted from supernova explosion. It is one of the few whose precise age we know. The supernova was witnessed in July 1054 by Chinese astronomers, who recorded that it was so bright that it was visible in daylight for several weeks.

The Crab is just visible in powerful binoculars, and in small telescopes appears as an oval glow. Larger telescopes are required for closer study. They bring out bright interlacing filaments which appear red in long-exposure photographs.

The nebula was named, incidentally, in 1844 by the English astronomer, the third Earl of Rosse, but it had been discovered over a century earlier. It was the first sight of the nebula by the French astronomer Charles Messier in 1758 that inspired him to begin his historic catalogue of nebulous objects. This explains why the Crab Nebula is M1.

Watching the Sky

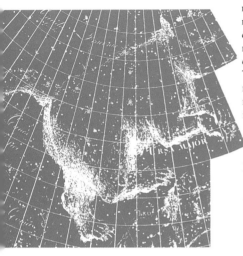

northern Europe, Canada and the northern United States. Even though it does not boast any stars of the first magnitude, it is the best-known constellation in the Northern hemisphere. This is because of the distinctive pattern made by seven bright second- and third-magnitude stars which stands out clearly in an otherwise relatively dark area of sky.

This pattern is known as the Big Dipper because of its resemblance to a ladle. It is called the Plough in Europe because it also resembles the handle and plough blade of an old horse-drawn plough.

It should be emphasized that the Big Dipper itself is not a constellation, but represents just the 'tail' and 'hindquarters' of the Bear. It occupies only a small part of the whole constellation of Ursa Major.

URSA MAJOR

Ursa Major the Great Bear is usually associated with the huntress Callisto, a favourite of Artemis, the goddess of hunting. One day Zeus, cunningly assuming the guise of Artemis, lay with Callisto and made her pregnant. She bore a son, Arcas. Zeus' wife Hera was not amused and turned Callisto into a bear. Later, Zeus placed Callisto in the heavens as the Great Bear, to prevent her from being killed by her son, who came upon her when hunting.

The third largest constellation, Ursa Major occupies a vast region of far northern skies. It is circumpolar for

FOLLOWING THE BIG DIPPER

As might be expected in such a prominent pattern, the stars all have names. Alpha is named Dubhe, Beta is Merak, Gamma is Phad, Delta is Megrez, Epsilon is Alioth, Zeta is Mizar and Eta is Alkaid.

The Alpha-to-Eta designation in this instance does not give the order of brightness of the stars. In fact, Epsilon vies with Alpha to be the brightest star, both having a magnitude of 1.8. Eta runs them a close third, followed by Zeta. Delta is the dimmest of the seven, at magnitude 3.3.

Perhaps the most interesting of the Big

Watching the Sky

Dipper stars is Mizar (Zeta), marking the bend in the ladle's handle. Mizar is a complex multiple star. To begin with, it is a naked-eye double, whose companion is a fourth-magnitude star named Alchor. Seen through a small telescope, Mizar itself is seen to be double, and examination of the spectra of the two components reveals that they are both close binary systems.

POINTING NORTH

Dubhe (Alpha) differs from the other stars in the Big Dipper, which are white, by having a pronounced orange hue. It and Merak (Beta) are known as the Pointers, because a line drawn northwards through them points to Polaris, the Pole Star.

For this reason, the Big Dipper has been a boon to navigators in the Northern hemisphere for centuries, but it will not always be so. Dubhe and Alkaid (Eta) are moving in different directions from the other stars in the Big Dipper. So Merak and Dubhe will end up pointing in quite a different direction.

VARIABLES

Ursa Major has a number of variables that are binocular subjects. They include two long-period variables of the Mira-type: R, north of Dubhe; and T, which makes an equilateral triangle with Epsilon and Delta. They both vary from a respectable magnitude 6.7 down to beyond 13. R has a period of 301 days; T

a period of 265 days.

Z, west of Delta, is a semi-regular variable, which always stays within binocular range, varying between magnitudes 7 and 9 in about 200 days.

A FINE PAIR

Ursa Major is a region of the sky that is well-endowed with galaxies, many of them within reach of amateur telescopes and a few within reach of binoculars. The two brightest are a close pair, M81 and M82, which appear to be physically associated, or 'interacting'. They are perhaps best found from Dubhe and 23, with which they form a right-angled triangle. These two galaxies form part of a small cluster that lies relatively close to Earth, only about 8 million light years away.

M81 is a classic spiral galaxy not dissimilar to our own, and bright at a magnitude of about 7. M82 is somewhat fainter and irregular in shape. It is a powerful radio source, which indicates that some almighty upheaval is occurring inside it.

Another galaxy of interest is the eighth-magnitude M101. It is a large spiral seen face-on, located north of the handle of the Big Dipper, and forms an equilateral triangle with Eta and Mizar. M101 has several extremely luminous star-forming regions in the outer spiral arms, some sporting their own NGC numbers. Large telescopes are needed to identify the spiral arms and to bring out nebulae therein.

Watching the Sky

VIRGO

Virgo the Virgin represents the goddess of justice Astraea in Greek and Roman mythology. Earlier, she was the goddess Ishtar in Babylon and Isis in Egypt. Astraea is depicted with wings, with which she flew into the heavens when she despaired of the human race. In her left hand she holds an ear of wheat marked by Spica.

Virgo spans the celestial equator and covers a vast region of the heavens. It is very nearly the largest constellation, second only to Hydra. It has a discernible Y-shape, but to see any resemblance to a maiden, with or without angel wings, requires considerable imagination.

To the naked eye, Virgo is disappointing, since it has only one really bright star. However, telescopes reveal the constellation to be crammed with deep-sky objects, particularly galaxies. They form part of a huge cluster that extends into Coma Berenices.

Virgo's brightest star is Alpha, or Spica, whose magnitude is exactly 1. It is bluish-white and is actually a binary, although this can only be detected from its spectrum.

Gamma and Epsilon are the next brightest stars, each of magnitude 2.8. Gamma is also a binary, with twin yellowish components (magnitude 3.6), which can be separated by small telescopes. The third-magnitude Delta, between Gamma and Epsilon, is noticeably reddish, as is Nu, north of Beta. Both Delta and Nu are red giants.

THE VIRGO CLUSTER

Extending right through the constellation, from south of Spica to the west of Epsilon, is a broad band of sky containing literally thousands of galaxies. They make up the celebrated Virgo Cluster.

This band of galaxies extends well into the neighbouring constellation, Coma Berenices. The whole system, called the Coma-Virgo Cluster, contains at least 3,000 galaxies. It is one of

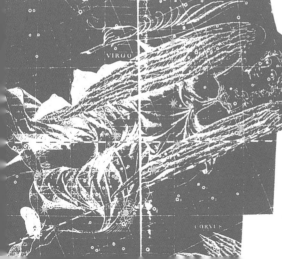

Watching the Sky

the largest of the many groupings of galaxies that populate the Universe and also one of the nearest. The closest galaxies lie about 40 million light years away, the furthest ones about 70 million light years.

A number of the galaxies in the Virgo Cluster are bright enough to be visible in small telescopes, and a few may even be glimpsed with powerful binoculars. Most, however, require large telescopes for detection or for bringing out any structure.

THE MESSIER GALAXIES

The French astronomer Charles Messier catalogued many of the brighter galaxies (averaging about the ninth magnitude) and these are worth pursuing. Several are to be found in the region between Epsilon Virginis and Beta Leonis. In order they are M60, M59, M58, M89, M90, M87, M84 and M86.

M60 and M59 are a close pair of elliptical galaxies due north of the fifth-magnitude Rho. M58, slightly to the west, is a barred-spiral galaxy. The elliptical M89 and spiral M90 lie to the north of M58, and M87 lies to the west. The close pair M84 and M86, both ellipticals, appear in the same telescopic field of view north of M87.

Among these galaxies, M87 is outstanding in more ways than one. It is a giant elliptical galaxy, which is nearly spherical; its diameter is similar to that of our own galaxy, about 120,000 light years, but our galaxy is essentially a disc,

so the near-spherical M87 contains very many more stars. Indeed, it is one of the most massive galaxies known and is a powerful source of radio waves.

Another interesting Messier galaxy, M104, an edge-on spiral, is found right on the border with Corvus, due south of Chi. It is of the eighth magnitude and may just be glimpsed in binoculars. Larger telescopes or long-exposure photographs are needed to bring out the dark dust lane that cuts through the oval image, giving it the vague appearance of a hat. That is why it is known as the Sombrero Galaxy.

QUASAR QUEST

Beyond the range of small telescopes, but detectable with large ones, is an object called 3C273, located at the corner of a right-angled triangle with Gamma and Eta Virginis. It is a quasar, and is of great historical interest and importance.

3C273 was the first quasar to be recognized as such, in 1962. The strange name '3C273' comes from a radio survey that detected many strong radio sources in the sky such as this quasar. A very remote star-like object with an incredible energy output, it shines at about the thirteenth magnitude, yet it is over 3,000 million light years away. No ordinary galaxies would show up at such a distance. 3C273 shows evidence that it may harbour a black hole, with its 150,000 light year long jet which is being expelled at tremendous velocities from the heart of the 'galaxy'.

Watching the Sky

NORTH POLAR SKY

The north polar region is centred on Polaris, the Pole Star, which moves scarcely at all in the sky. Ursa Major is the outstanding constellation and is circumpolar – always visible – to observers north of latitude 40°.

Two bright regions occupy opposite sides of the Pole Star – the Big Dipper and Cassiopeia. As the celestial sphere rotates (or appears to rotate), these constellations also march in circles around the pole. Depending on the hour of the night and the day of the year, one or the other may be low near the horizon where it is barely seen, or even hidden below the horizon. However, when that happens the other constellation will be high in the sky and, weather permitting, it is easy to see.

THE BIG DIPPER

The Big Dipper consists of seven bright stars, forming a dipper, a small pot with a long handle. The Big Dipper isn't a constellation in itself, it is part of the constellation Ursa Major, or Great Bear.

URSA MINOR (LITTLE BEAR)

The constellation Ursa Minor contains a group of stars commonly called the Little Dipper. The handle of the Dipper is the Little Bear's tail and the Dipper's cup is the Bear's flank. The Little Dipper is not a constellation in itself, but an *asterism*, which is a distinctive group of stars. The most famous star in Ursa Minor is Polaris, the North Star. This is the star that is nearest to the North Celestial Pole. If you stood at the North Pole, Polaris would be almost directly overhead. If you can spot Polaris in the sky, you can always tell which way is north. In addition, the angle of Polaris above the horizon tells you your latitude on the Earth. Because of this, Polaris was the most important star for navigating at sea.

URSA MAJOR (GREAT BEAR)

The constellation Ursa Major contains the group of stars commonly called the Big Dipper. Seven bright stars in Ursa Major form the Plough, one of the most familiar shapes in the northern sky. The entire constellation, however, is much bigger, with the Plough marking just the hindquarters and tail of the bear. Mizar in the tail is a multiple star. Among the stars near the bear's head is a pair of galaxies, M81 and M82.

If you live in the Northern hemisphere, you can use the Big Dipper to find all sorts of important stars, for example:

• If you draw an imaginary line from Merak through Dubhe out of the cup of the Dipper and continue five times as far as Dubhe is from Merak, you will arrive at Polaris, the North Star.
• Now draw an imaginary line along the handle of the dipper and continue the arc across the sky. Eventually this will lead you to the very bright star,

Watching the Sky

Arcturus in the constellation Boötes. If you continue the arc further, you will reach Spica in Virgo. You can remember this by saying 'Arc to Arcturus and Speed to Spica'.

- If you follow the other two stars in the cup of the Dipper (Megrez and Phecda) down below the cup, you will get to Regulus, the brightest star in Leo.

CEPHEUS (CEPHEUS)

Cepheus and Cassiopeia, representing the King and Queen of Ethiopia, lie together in the sky. Cepheus contains star clusters and noted stars such as the red Garnet Star (μ) and Delta (δ). Delta was the first Cepheid variable to be discovered, and gave its name to the entire category. The constellation of Cepheus is one of the oldest constellations and plays an important part in Greek Mythology.

Although of a distinctive shape, the main stars in Cepheus are not blazingly bright. Today, Cepheus looks like a crooked house drawn by a child (*see page 274*).

DRACO (THE DRAGON)

Draco is not an easy constellation to make out. It is one of the largest constellations in the sky and winds around Ursa Minor. To find the dragon, start by locating the four stars that mark the dragon's head. Imagination is needed to trace out the rest. This constellation is noted for double stars. Nu (ν), the faintest star in the dragon's head, is a wide double star that can be seen through binoculars.

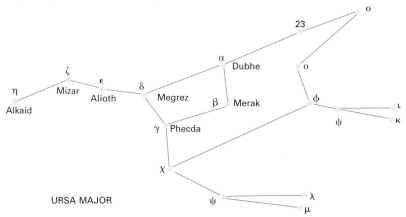

Watching the Sky

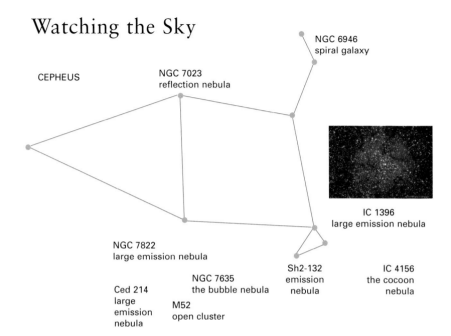

CEPHEUS

NGC 6946
spiral galaxy

NGC 7023
reflection nebula

IC 1396
large emission nebula

NGC 7822
large emission nebula

Ced 214
large
emission
nebula

NGC 7635
the bubble nebula

M52
open cluster

Sh2-132
emission
nebula

IC 4156
the cocoon
nebula

CAMELOPARDALIS (THE GIRAFFE)

Camelopardalis sits between Cassiopeia and Ursa Major, and the best way to begin studying it is to first find your bearings. With the naked eye locate Capella (alpha Aurigae). If you aren't sure which of the bright stars is Capella, start from the Big Dipper. Now instead of moving north to the Pole Star, move across the top part of the Dipper (a line from delta Ursae Majoris drawn through alpha Ursae Majoris) and continue straight into the southern portion of the skies. As you approach the Milky Way, the very bright star you see is Capella.

CASSIOPEIA (CASSIOPEIA)

The bright stars in Cassiopeia make a recognizable shape in the sky. When the stars are below the north celestial pole they form a 'W' and when above it they form an 'M'. The most interesting star is Gamma (γ), a blue giant that alters in brightness as rings of gas are blown off. Cassiopeia also has several notable star clusters, such as open cluster M52 and NGC457, an elongated open cluster. Cassiopeia is associated with the Perseus constellation family, and viewing this area with binoculars is especially rewarding.

Watching the Sky

SOUTH POLAR SKY

The south polar region might lack a convenient pole star, but it is richly endowed with brilliant objects. The Milky Way here is dazzling and contains the unmistakable Southern Cross and its pointers, Alpha and Beta Centauri.

CRUX (THE SOUTHERN CROSS)

This may be the smallest constellation in the sky, but it has a wealth of interesting objects and is very easy to find. Crux, the Southern Cross, is visible from latitudes south of 25° north and completely invisible in latitudes above 35° north.

As the southern hemisphere does not have a bright star near the South Pole, many ancient sailors used Crux (which is some 25° from true south) for their navigation. They would draw a line using the stars in the cross to the South Pole and could then make a determination of their position.

The Southern Cross also contains several deep sky objects. The best known are The Jewel Box (NGC4755) star cluster which is composed of over 100 stars, about 50 of which are a mixture of colourful supergiants: reds and blues intermingled with yellows and whites in a profusion of sparkling light. The Coal Sack is a large dark nebula just to the south of the Jewel Box, and is visible to the naked eye.

CENTAURUS (THE CENTAUR)

Centaurus the Centaur is the most magnificent of the southern constellations and is packed with interesting sights. It is the ninth largest constellation and contains two of the ten brightest stars, Alpha Centauri (Rigel Kentaurus) and Beta Centauri (Hadar). Beta Centauri is a blue-white supergiant and in about 4,000 years, the proper motion of Alpha Centauri will carry it close enough to Beta Centauri that they will appear to be a magnificent double star.

Centaurus also contains Omega Centauri (NGC5139), the largest and richest globular cluster in the sky. It looks like a fourth-magnitude star to those lucky enough to see it, but even through a

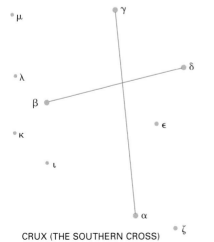

CRUX (THE SOUTHERN CROSS)

Watching the Sky

small telescope the stars resolve into pinpoints of light.

Centaurus also contains 20 open clusters and several galaxies including Centaurus A (NGC5128), one of the brightest radio objects in the sky. It also contains a significant portion of our own galaxy, the Milky Way, and the river of stars through Centaurus is an amazing sight on a dark moonless night. Centaurus contains over 100 visible stars (brighter than 5.5 magnitude). Centaurus is truly a jewel of the southern sky.

CARINA (THE KEEL)

Carina was originally part of a much larger constellation, Argo Navis, which was split into four in 1763 by Nicolas Louis de Lacaille. The other three constellations formed as a result are: Puppis the Stern, Pyxis the Compass and Vela the Sails. The constellation was split up because it originally covered some 75 degrees of the sky, an area which was much too large for astronomical use.

Carina contains a highly unstable star called Eta Carina, which pulls mass from a nearby nebula. The star is so great that it cannot hold all the material it gathers, and so from time to time it puffs off the excess material in a great explosion, or a nova. Eta Carina's last eruption was during the eighteenth and nineteenth centuries in which it brightened by more than 4,000 times. This star is 100 times the mass of the Sun, and is visible with the naked eye.

DORADO (THE GOLDFISH)

Dorado contains the bulk of the Large Magellanic Cloud (LMC), our nearest galaxy. This galaxy can be seen with the naked eye as a light patch. Inside the patch, about the size of the Full Moon, is a fuzzy object, the Tarantula Nebula (NGC2070), which binoculars show as a cloud of gas intertwined with rifts. The constellation lies west of the bright star Canopus in Carina, but unfortunately it is invisible to most of the United States.

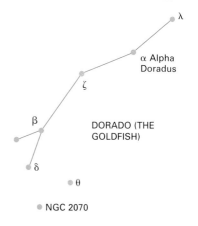

OCTANS (THE OCTANT)

Most stars in Octans are faint, and not easily visible to the naked eye. It is in this constellation that the South Celestial Pole lies. Octans, the Octant, is completely visible in latitudes south of the equator,

Watching the Sky

and is circumpolar. Unlike its northern counterpart, Ursa Minor, Octans does not contain any bright stars. The nearest star to the South Celestial Pole is Sigma (σ), a small open cluster containing about 40 stars. The South Celestial Pole is the point in the sky about which all the stars seen from the Southern hemisphere rotate. Octans also contains Melotte 227, the southern-most visible open star cluster.

TUCANA (THE TOUCAN)

Tucana, the Toucan Bird, is completely visible in latitudes south of 14 degrees north from August to October. Tucana was invented by Pieter Dirksz Keyser and Fredrick de Houtman between 1595 and 1597.

The constellation Tucana contains the Small Magellanic Cloud (SMC), which is a satellite galaxy to the Milky Way, and 47 Tucanae, two fascinating objects lying close together in the corner nearest to the South Celestial Pole. SMC can be seen with the naked eye but binoculars or a telescope will show some of its clusters and nebulae. 47 Tucanae is a globular cluster with tens of thousands of stars.

How Octans got its name

Octans was named by Abbé Nicolas Louis de Lacaille. Octans is the constellation which contains the South Celestial Pole and, unlike Ursa Minor's Polaris, there is no bright star near the South Pole.

The Octant is a navigational tool used to determine the altitude of a star, and thus one's latitude on the Earth. The choice of names for this constellation is significant because the Octant was used to measure the position of Polaris innumerable times in the early years of celestial navigation. In later years, the Octant was replaced by the sextant (which also has a constellation, Sextans, named after it).

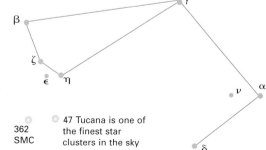

47 Tucana is one of the finest star clusters in the sky

Watching the Sky

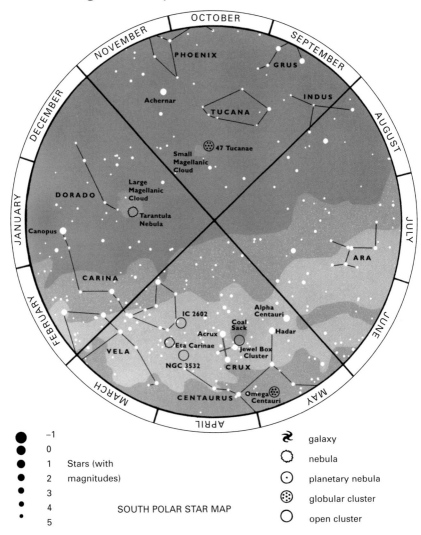

SOUTH POLAR STAR MAP

Stars (with magnitudes)

●	−1
●	0
●	1
●	2
●	3
●	4
●	5

↯ galaxy
⬡ nebula
⊙ planetary nebula
⊛ globular cluster
○ open cluster

Watching the Sky

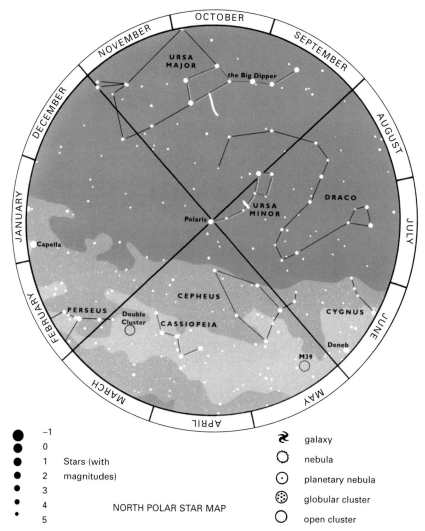

NORTH POLAR STAR MAP

Stars (with magnitudes)

- −1
- 0
- 1
- 2
- 3
- 4
- 5

↩ galaxy
○ nebula
⊙ planetary nebula
⊛ globular cluster
○ open cluster

Watching the Sky

DIARY OF EVENTS

It is a good idea to make a diary of what you see from day to day in the night sky, in that way you have a record of what you can expect to see, and which objects are at their best, at a certain time of year. Below is a guideline of how to lay out your diary, and this diary can be used for any year and in both northern and southern latitudes.

JANUARY

AT THEIR BEST
M42, the Orion Nebula in the sword of Orion the Hunter, is a prominent nebula best seen with the naked eye when it is high above the horizon.
The Hyades and Pleiades (Taurus) can be seen with the naked eye.

ALSO VISIBLE
Aldebaran (Taurus)
Castor and Pollux (Gemini)
Sirius (Canis Major)
Procyon (Canis Minor)
M36, M37 and M38 (Auriga)
M41 (Canis Major)
M44 (Cancer)

METEOR SHOWERS
Viewed from the Northern hemisphere: Quadrantids around January 3 and 4. They radiate from the northern part of the constellation Boötes and is best seen after midnight.

FEBRUARY

AT THEIR BEST
M41 (Canis Major) can be seen with the naked eye in good observing conditions. **NGC2244** is a star cluster seen at the centre of the Rosette Nebula (Monoceros). **Betelgeuse** (Orion), **Procyon** (Canis Minor) and **Sirius** (Canis Major) are three brilliant stars that form the so-called Winter Triangle for Northern hemisphere observers. The same star triangle can also be seen from the Southern hemisphere where it is summer.

ALSO VISIBLE
Aldebaran (Taurus)
Castor and Pollux (Gemini)
Rigel (Orion)
M36, M37 and M38 (Auriga)
M44, the Beehive Cluster (Cancer)
Hyades and Pleiades star clusters (Taurus)
M42, the Orion Nebula (Orion)
NGC3372, the Eta Carinae Nebula (Carina)

MARCH

AT THEIR BEST
M44, the Beehive Cluster (Cancer), can be seen with the naked eye in good observing conditions. Through binoculars a swarm of faint stars becomes visible. **NGC3372**, the Eta Carinae Nebula (Carina), lies along the path of the Milky Way and looks like a bright patch to the naked eye.

Watching the Sky

The Coalsack (Crux) is a dark nebula in the path of the Milky Way and looks like a hole in the sky.

ALSO VISIBLE
Castor and Pollux (Gemini)
Rigel and Betelgeuse (Orion)
Sirius (Canis Major)
Procyon (Canis Minor)
Regulus (Leo)
Spica (Virgo)
M36, M37 and M38 (Auriga)
M41 (Canis Major)
NGC4755 (Crux)
M42, Orion Nebula (Orion)
NGC2244 (Monoceros)

APRIL

AT THEIR BEST
The Jewel Box Cluster, NGC4755 (Crux), is high in the sky in the late evening sky in the Southern hemisphere. It is visible to the naked eye as a fuzzy star, but viewed through a telescope or binoculars its different-coloured stars will shine like gems in the sky.

ALSO VISIBLE
Arcturus (Boötes)
Spica (Virgo)
Regulus (Leo)
Procyon (Canis Minor)
M44 (Cancer)
NGC2244 (Monoceros)
NGC5139 Omega Centauri (Centaurus)
The Coalsack (Crux)

NGC3372, the Eta Carinae Nebula (Carina)

METEOR SHOWER
Observers in the Northern hemisphere will be able to spot the Lyrids around April 21. They radiate from a point near the bright star, Vega, in Lyra.

MAY

AT THEIR BEST
Omega Centauri, NGC5139, is the best globular cluster in the night sky. For southern observers it is clearly visible in the late evening sky with the naked eye, and will appear as a fuzzy star.

ALSO VISIBLE
Arcturus (Boötes)
Spica (Virgo)
Regulus (Leo)
Antares (Scorpius)
Vega (Lyra)
M6 and M7 (Scorpius)
M44 (Cancer)
NGC4755 (Crux)
M13 (Hercules)
NGC3372 the Eta Carinae Nebula (Carina)

METEOR SHOWER
The Eta Aquarids can be seen by observers in the Southern hemisphere. They radiate from the constellation Aquarius at the end of April right through to late May, peaking around May 5.

Watching the Sky

JUNE

AT THEIR BEST

M13 in Hercules is the most spectacular globular cluster in the northern sky, and is positioned high above the horizon in the late evening sky. It can be seen clearly with the naked eye when the sky is clear and dark.

M6 and M7 are two impressive star clusters in Scorpius. Both are visible with the naked eye against the backdrop of the Milky Way, but they are best viewed through binoculars, giving you a clearer view of the stars within the clusters.

ALSO VISIBLE

Arcturus (Boötes)
Spica (Virgo)
Antares (Scorpius)
Vega (Lyra)
M22 (Sagittarius)
NGC5139 Omega Centauri (Centaurus)
M8, the Lagoon Nebula (Sagittarius)
M27, the planetary nebula (Vulpecula)

JULY

AT THEIR BEST

M22 (Sagittarius) is one of the best globular clusters to be seen in the sky. To the naked eye it will appear as a fuzzy star, but the view is much improved through binoculars.

Summer Triangle can be seen by northern observers, and consists of three bright stars positioned in different constellations – **Vega** (Lyra), **Deneb** (Cygnus) and **Altair** (Aquila).

The **Cygnus Rift** (Cygnus), also known as the Northern Coalsack, is a dark nebula positioned across the path of the Milky Way.

ALSO VISIBLE

Arcturus in Boötes
Spica (Virgo)
Antares (Scorpius)
M13 (Hercules)
M6 and M7 (Scorpius)
M27, planetary nebula (Vulpecula)

AUGUST

AT THEIR BEST

M8, the Lagoon Nebula (Sagittarius) can be seen with the naked eye in a dark sky. If viewed through binoculars it is possible to see a swarm of faint stars.

Albireo (Cygnus) is a double star that is easily seen with a small telescope.

ALSO VISIBLE

Vega (Lyra)
Deneb (Cygnus)
Altair (Aquila)
Antares (Scorpius)
Fomalhaut (Piscis Austrinus)
M13 (Hercules)
M22 (Sagittarius)
NGC104 (Tucana)
M27, planetary nebula (Vulpecula)

METEOR SHOWER

The richest meteor shower of all is the

Watching the Sky

Perseids, which is visible the whole month, peaking in the middle of August.

SEPTEMBER

AT THEIR BEST
M27, is a planetary nebula called the Dumbbell Nebula because of its shape. It can be seen through binoculars and its shape becomes clearly defined when seen through a telescope.
Delta Cephei is a variable star that changes regularly in brightness. A faint companion star is also visible through a small telescope.
NGC104 (Tucana) is the second-best globular cluster in the sky. It is also known as 47 Tucanae and appears as a fuzzy star to the naked eye.

ALSO VISIBLE
Vega (Lyra)
Deneb (Cygnus)
Altair (Aquila)
Fomalhaut (Piscis Austrinus)
NGC869 and NGC884, the Double Cluster (Perseus)
M31, the Andromeda Galaxy (Andromeda)
Cygnus Rift (Cygnus)

OCTOBER

AT THEIR BEST
M31, although a long way away the Andromeda Galaxy can still be seen with the naked eye. The Great Square of Pegasus is formed by three stars within Pegasus, and one in Andromeda, and they are in a good position for both northern and southern observers.

ALSO VISIBLE
Fomalhaut (Piscis Austrinus)
Achernar (Eridanus)
NGC104 (Tucana)
Hyades and Pleiades (Taurus)
NGC869 and NGC884 (Perseus)
Cygnus Rift (Cygnus)

METEOR SHOWER
The Orionids can be seen in the second half of the month.

NOVEMBER

AT THEIR BEST
NGC869 and **NGC884** (Perseus). This double cluster lies in the spiral arm of the Milky Way and is visible with the naked eye.

ALSO VISIBLE
Betelgeuse and Rigel (Orion)
Aldebaran (Taurus)
Capella (Auriga)
Achernar (Eridanus)
Hyades and Pleiades (Taurus)
M36, M37 and M38 (Auriga)
M41 (Canis Major)
NGC2070, the Tarantula Nebula (dorado)
M42, the Orion Nebula (Orion)
M31, the Andromeda Galaxy

Watching the Sky

METEOR SHOWERS
The Taurids peak in early November
but can be seen from late October.
The Leonids, radiating from Leo, peak
around November 17.

DECEMBER

AT THEIR BEST
M36, M37 and **M38** (Auriga) are
visible through binoculars. The Large
Magellanic Cloud (Dorado) can be seen
as a fuzzy patch to the naked eye, but is
more clearly defined through
binoculars.

ALSO VISIBLE
Betelgeuse and Rigel (Orion)
Aldebaran (Taurus)
Capella (Auriga)
Achernar (Eridanus)
Procyon (Canis Minor)
Canopus (Carina)
M41 (Canis Major)
M44, the Beehive Cluster (Cancer)
Orion Nebula

METEOR SHOWER
The rich shower of Germinids,
radiating from near the bright star
Castor (Gemini), can be seen at its best
around December 13.

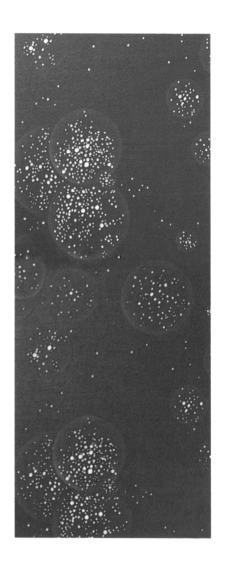

Watching the Sky

PHASES AND ECLIPSES

The Moon is the Earth's nearest neighbour and only natural satellite. If you look at the Moon's position in the sky from night to night, you will see how it moves across different constellations. Travelling at about 1 km per second, it takes the Moon about 27 days 7 hours to orbit the Earth once. Because the Earth moves in its orbit around the Sun at the same time, the Moon's cycle of phases (one New Moon to the next) lasts 29 days 12 hours. The Moon rotates on its axis once every 27 days 7 hours, the same time as it takes to orbit the Earth (which is called synchronous rotation). This explains why we only ever see the same features of the Moon's near side.

The appearance of the bright part of the Moon gradually changes from a thin crescent to a Half Moon to a Full Moon and then back again, and these are known as the phases of the Moon.

Sometimes it is possible to see an eclipse of the Moon or Sun, when the Moon passes between the Earth and Sun. When it is in line, the Moon hides all or part of the Sun's bright surface and we see a solar eclipse. A lunar eclipse occurs when the Earth lies between the Sun and a Full Moon and casts its shadow on the surface of the Moon.

PHASES OF THE MOON

The Moon is almost perfectly spherical in shape. Over a period of one lunar month (29 days 12 hours), however, the Moon's shape appears to change in a regular and predictable way. Like the Earth, the parts of the Moon that face the Sun are lit by it and experience day (a lunar day) while the parts that face away from the Sun remain in darkness and experience night (a lunar night).

The apparent shapes or phases of the Moon are caused by the location of the Moon in its orbit around the Earth and the different amounts of the Moon's sunlit side that we can see from it. The line separating the lit part of the Moon from the dark is known as the terminator. From a New Moon, when the Moon is situated in orbit between the Earth and the Sun with its dark side in shadow facing towards us, the amount of lunar surface visible from the Earth increases through waxing crescent, first quarter and waxing gibbous phases until it becomes full. From Full Moon, when the Moon is situated in orbit on the side of the Earth opposite the Sun with its lit side facing directly towards us, the amount of lunar surface visible from the Earth decreases through waning gibbous, last quarter and waning crescent phases until it disappears from view again.

Watching the Sky

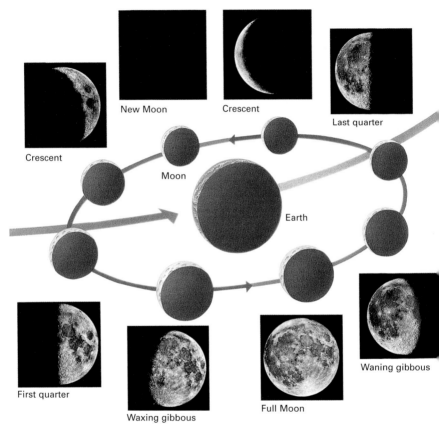

New Moon

Crescent

Last quarter

Crescent

Moon

Earth

First quarter

Waxing gibbous

Full Moon

Waning gibbous

As the Moon travels around Earth, its shape in the sky seems to change. The shape we see is called the Moon's phase. At New Moon, we cannot see the Moon at all. A week later, we see a half Moon, although its phase is called First Quarter because it has gone one quarter of the way around its orbit.

Halfway around its orbit it becomes a full circle called the Full Moon. When more of the Moon is becoming visible each night, we say it is 'waxing'. After Full Moon it starts to 'wane' and we see less and less of it each night. When it is less than a full circle, more than a half circle, it is called a gibbous Moon.

Watching the Sky

ECLIPSES

A total solar eclipse occurs when the Moon is exactly positioned between the Sun and the Earth and the Earth passes through the Moon's shadow. Solar eclipses can only happen during the day and at the time of a New Moon. Total solar eclipses last for only a few minutes. A total lunar eclipse occurs when the Earth is exactly positioned between the Sun and the Moon and the Moon passes through the Earth's shadow. Lunar eclipses can only happen at night and when the Moon is full. Total lunar eclipses last for about two hours. While New Moons and Full Moons occur every 29 days 12 hours, eclipses only happen once or twice a year. This is because the plane of the Moon's orbit around the Earth is tilted at an angle of 5 degrees relative to the plane of the Earth's orbit around the Sun. Partial solar and lunar eclipses can occur too.

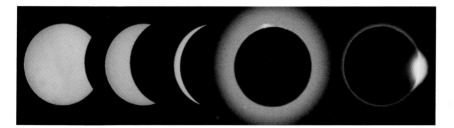

TOTAL ECLIPSE OF THE SUN

In the picture above, starting from the left, the first three photographs show the eclipse when it is still partial. The Moon gradually covers more of the Sun then moves directly in front of it. The eclipse is total and the sky is dark enough for the faint solar corona to be visible. The instant the total eclipse ends, a beam of sunlight bursts through a valley on the edge of the Moon. For a brief moment the effect is like a single sparkling diamond on a ring.

TOTAL ECLIPSE OF THE MOON

Even when the Moon is in the darkest part of Earth's shadow during a total eclipse, it does not disappear from sight in the sky. It turns into a dark orange or copper colour and this is because it is reflecting the faint glow of sunlight scattered in its direction by Earth's atmosphere. In fact, the total phase of a lunar eclipse is so interesting and beautiful precisely because of the filtering and refracting effect of Earth's atmosphere.

SPACE EXPLORATION

For untold thousands of years we have gazed up at the heavens from our small world. Ancient astronomers observed points of light that appeared to move among the stars. They called these objects planets, meaning wanderers, and named them after Roman deities, for example – Jupiter, the king of the gods. What these early stargazers also saw were comets with sparkling tails, and meteors or shooting stars which apparently just fell out of the sky. Science flourished during the European Renaissance, and in the seventeenth century astronomers had the power of a new device called a telescope to view the heavens, and from then on made startling discoveries.

GOING INTO SPACE

In the years since 1959, technology has advanced to such a degree that it has become a golden age of solar system exploration. Advancements in rocketry after World War II enabled our machines to break the grip of Earth's gravity and travel to the Moon and to other planets.

The United States has sent automated spacecraft, then human-crewed expeditions, to explore the Moon. Our automated machines have orbited and landed on Venus and Mars, explored the Sun's environment, observed comets, and asteroids and made close-range surveys while flying past Mercury, Jupiter, Saturn, Uranus and Neptune.

These travellers brought a quantum leap in our knowledge and understanding of the solar system. Through the electronic sight and other 'senses' of our automated spacecraft, colour and complexion have been given to worlds that for centuries appeared to Earth-bound eyes as fuzzy discs or indistinct points of light. And dozens of previously unknown objects have been discovered.

Future historians will likely view these pioneering flights through the solar system as some of the most remarkable achievements of the twentieth century.

HISTORY OF THE ROCKET

The twentieth century marked a turning point for mankind and we went from the industrial age to the space age. Modern rocketry was started by three men – Dr. Robert H. Goddard, Hermann Oberth and Kanstantin Tsiolkovsky.

Kanstantin Tsiolkovsky became known in the USSR as the father of 'cosmonautics', having been inspired by Jules Verne's writings. The brilliance of his work in rocketry and interplanetary travel is clear when it is considered that a large bulk of his theories of space travel

Space Exploration

were produced years before the Wright brothers made the first powered, sustained and controlled flight on December 17, 1903, in an aeroplane that flew just a few yards. There is no question Tsiolkovsky was a true visionary, he theorized many aspects of space travel, and laid out the theoretical foundations for rocket propulsion, including the use of liquid fuel propellant.

In 1903 a Russian schoolteacher, Konstantin Tsiolkovsky, correctly concluded that rockets fuelled with liquid hydrogen and liquid oxygen would be considerably more efficient than the simpler solid-fuelled rockets that were already in use. He also devised a concept for stacking rockets on top of each other to produce the exceptionally high speeds necessary for successful interplanetary travel. To go into space and stay above Earth, a satellite or spacecraft has to reach a speed of about 27,350 km (17,500 miles) per hour. At that speed, the satellite's power is shut off and it coasts on an orbit around Earth. The satellite is still in Earth's gravity, but the pull of gravity back towards Earth is exactly cancelled out by the speed at which the satellite is travelling.

Twenty-three years later Dr. Robert Goddard knelt on the frozen ground in his aunt's cabbage patch at Auburn, Massachusetts, and using a blowtorch, managed to ignite the world's first liquid-fuelled rocket. Although the rocket flew for just 2.5 seconds and rose to a height

Korolev's Zemiorka R7 rocket

Von Braun's V2 rocket

Space Exploration

of only 41 feet, it proved that liquid fuel rockets worked. Four years later, at Roswell, New Mexico, Dr. Goddard fired a rocket that reached an altitude of 2,000 feet and a speed of 500 miles per hour. His experiments led him to develop many of the devices still used in modern rockets including fuel feeding devices, propellant pumps and gyroscopic stabilizers, as well as instruments for monitoring rocket flights.

Hermann Oberth was a German Physicist and Mathematician. By the time he graduated to become a doctor, he had not only decided that spaceships were possible, but had also come to the conclusion that they should be liquid-fuel rockets. Not only did Oberth work out numerous ideas for rockets and even spaceships, but he continued research into propellants and their compositions. Two of his projects were a single-stage, high-altitude sounding rocket and a three-stage rocket.

Wernher Von Braun (*below*) was one of the world's first and foremost rocket

The old Austrian Hermann Oberth is regarded as a father of space travel - in the photograph to the right beside the rocket. First from the right is the young Wernher Von Braun.

engineers and a leading authority on space travel. His will to expand man's knowledge through the exploration of space led to the development of the Explorer satellites, the *Jupiter* and *Jupiter-C* rockets, Pershing, the *Redstone* rocket, *Saturn* rockets and *Skylab*, the world's first space station. Additionally, his determination to 'go where no man has gone before' led to mankind setting foot on the Moon. Dr. Von Braun first directed the technical development of the US Army's ballistic missile programme at Redstone Arsenal, and later served as Director of NASA's Marshall Space Flight Center.

In 1961, when President Kennedy bravely announced that the United States would conquer the Moon, America's rocketeers had not yet orbited a single astronaut. The *Saturn V* Moon rocket later developed for the mission, was the pinnacle of the rocket maker's art.

Space Exploration

THE SPACE SHUTTLE

Unlike most rockets, which can be sent into space only once, the Space Shuttle is a reusable space vehicle. At launch, its three rocket thrusters and two solid fuel boosters provide almost the same lift as a *Saturn V* rocket. They get the shuttle into space in less than five minutes. It takes off vertically like a rocket and glides back to Earth to land like a normal aircraft.

The Space Shuttle will continue to be a vital element in the future of space exploration, and is currently playing a pivotal role in the assembly of the International Space Station and will provide the tools, technology and human ingenuity to operate the Space Station in the challenging environment of Earth's orbit.

The Space Shuttle has given us the opportunity to:

- Learn how to live and work in space
- Perform on-orbit research
- Explore our solar system
- Understand the formation of our Universe and search for Earth-like planets
- Learn more about our own planet.

One of the Shuttle's greatest strengths, in addition to its amazing array of capabilities, is its ability to adapt and evolve to meet new mission requirements. Whether it means installing a spare part or sending astronauts on a spacewalk to retrieve a satellite, the Shuttle is unrivalled in its ability to complete its mission.

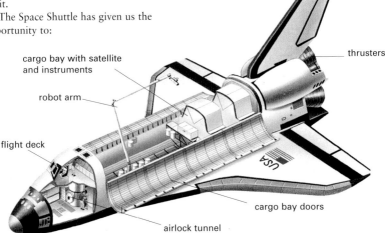

cargo bay with satellite and instruments

robot arm

flight deck

thrusters

cargo bay doors

airlock tunnel

Space Exploration

HUMANS IN SPACE

Mankind has always had a natural curiosity and a need to explore the unknown. Since 1961, more than 400 human beings have ventured into space. Now aboard the International Space Station, astronauts are working to improve life on Earth and extend life beyond our home planet.

Humans in space play a crucial role that cannot be duplicated. Indeed, the more demanding Space Shuttle missions have become, the more they highlight the Shuttle's most flexible and crucial element – the presence of people in space. For example, if it were not for humans in space

the Hubble Space Telescope would be much less capable. Repairs and ongoing maintenance by the Space Shuttle and its crews have enabled the Hubble Telescope to produce the most stunning and vibrant images of our Universe ever seen. In fact, the Hubble was originally launched aboard the Space Shuttle, as were the Venus probe *Magellan,* the Jupiter probe *Galileo* and the solar probe *Ulysses.*

The value of human involvement in space operations has been demonstrated in both routine procedures and the ability to respond to the unexpected. Human roles in space span a broad range of areas and complement the work being done by robotic explorers and probes.

First Man in Space
On April 12, 1961, Russian-born Yuri Gagarin became the first human to orbit Earth. The name of his spacecraft was *Vostok 1. Vostok 1* had two sections. One section was for Yuri. The second section was for supplies needed for Gagarin to live such as oxygen and water. A crater on the far side of the Moon has been named after Yuri.

Space Exploration

SPACE STATIONS

For years man has dreamed of being able to live in space and with the placement of space stations this has become possible. A space station is a complete environment for living and working, where astronauts can spend many months at a time in space. Inside, astronauts are weightless and must use exercise machines to keep their bones and muscles strong.

The Russians were the first to place a space station, called *Salyut 1*, in orbit in 1971. It was about 15 metres (45 feet) long and held three main compartments that housed dining and recreation areas, food and water storage, a toilet (specially adapted to the weightless environment), control stations, exercise equipment and scientific equipment. The *Soyuz 11* crew was the first crew to live on *Salyut 1* for 24 days, but tragically they died upon their return to Earth. Further missions to *Salyut 1* were abandoned, and the spacecraft was redesigned. This programme eventually led to the development of Russia's *Mir* Space Station.

The United States placed its first, and only, space station, called Skylab 1, in orbit in 1973. During the launch the station was damaged, and a crew was launched ten days later to fix the ailing station. With the station repaired, that crew and two subsequent crews spent a

Mir Space Station

The Russian *Mir* Space Station was launched on February 20, 1986, and over the years has been enlarged by the addition of new modules. It was badly damaged in a collision with a supply vehicle in 1997, but still managed to keep going until 1999. In March 2001 the *Mir* Space Station returned to Earth in pieces ending its 15-year, 2.2 billion-mile odyssey with a fiery plunge into the South Pacific.

Space Exploration

total of 112 days in space, conducting scientific and biomedical research.

INTERNATIONAL SPACE STATION

The International Space Station (ISS) is the largest and most complex international scientific project in history. The proposed completion of the ISS is planned in 2008, and when it is finished, will represent a move of unprecedented scale off our home planet.

Led by the United States, the International Space Station draws upon

The state-of-the-art International Space Station

the scientific and technological resources of 16 nations – Canada, Japan, Russia and 11 nations of the European Space Agency and Brazil.

The ISS will be four times as large as the Russian *Mir* space station and will

eventually have a mass of about 471,736 kg (1,040,000 lb.). It will measure 108.5 metres (356 feet) across and 88 metres (290 feet) long, with almost an acre of solar panels to provide electrical power to six revolutionary laboratories.

The station will be in orbit with an altitude of 250 statute miles with an inclination of 51.6 degrees. This orbit will allow the station to be reached by the launch vehicles of all the international parties involved, so they can deliver both crews and supplies. This orbit will also provide excellent Earth observations with coverage of 85 percent of the globe.

The first phase of the ISS, the Shuttle-Mir Programme started in 1995 and involved more than two years of continuous stays by astronauts aboard the Russian *Mir* Space Station and nine Shuttle-Mir docking missions. Seven US astronauts spent a cumulative total of 32 months on board *Mir* with 28 months of continuous occupancy since March 1996.

The ISS will establish an unprecedented laboratory using the latest technology available, which will lead to discoveries in medicine, materials and fundamental science that will benefit people all over the world. Through its research and technology, the station will also serve as an indispensable step in preparation for future human space exploration.

Space Exploration

MISSIONS IN SPACE

Spacecraft have visited the Sun, the Moon, planets, comets and asteroids. They usually carry cameras and other instruments to gather information, which is beamed back to Earth by radio. The spacecraft involved can be used in various ways, for example, in a fly-by a craft passes close to an object in space. An orbiter goes into orbit around a planet or to the surface of a rocky planet or moon, whilst a probe is dropped into an atmosphere to take measurements as it falls.

MILESTONES IN SPACE EXPLORATION

Sputnik-1, Oct 4, 1957
World's first artificial satellite. Launched by Russia.

Sputnik-2, Nov 3, 1957
Satellite takes first animal into orbit, a dog named Laika.

Explorer 1, Feb 1 1958
First successful launch by US.

Luna 1, Jan 2, 1959
First fly-by of the Moon by Russia. Discovered the solar wind.

Luna 2, Sept 12, 1959
First spacecraft to hit the Moon. Russia.

Luna 3, Oct 4, 1959
Returned first pictures of the Moon's far side. Russia.

Venera 1, Feb 12, 1961
First fly-by of Venus. Russia.

Vostok 1, April 12, 1961
First human in space – Russian Yuri Gagarin.

Ranger 7, July 28, 1964
US hard lander crash-landed on the Moon. Sent back first detailed images of the Moon's surface as it approached.

Mariner 4, Nov 28, 1964
First fly-by of Mars – sent back 22 photographs showing cratered surface. US.

Venera 3, Nov 16, 1965
First object launched from Earth to reach another planet. Crash-landed on Venus. Russia.

Luna 9, Jan 31, 1966
First soft lander (using parachutes or air bags to land gently) on the Moon. Sent back first photographs from the Moon's surface. Russia.

Surveyor 1, April 30, 1966
First US soft lander on Moon.

Venera 4, June 12, 1967
First probe to return data on atmosphere and surface temperature of Venus. Russia.

Apollo 8, Dec 21, 1968
First humans go to the Moon and back, without landing on the Moon. US.

Apollo 11, July 16, 1969
First manned landing on Moon, followed by five more. US.

Venera 7, Aug 17, 1970
First successful landing on another planet (Venus). Russia.

Luna 16, Sept 12, 1970
First unmanned mission that returned sample of Moon dust to Earth. Russia.

Luna 17, Nov 10, 1970
First Moon landing with robotic explorer – Lunokhod 1. Russia.

Salyut 1, April 19, 1971
First space station. Russia.

Mariner 9, May 30, 1971
First spacecraft to orbit another planet – returned details of Mar's surface. US.

Space Exploration

MILESTONES IN SPACE EXPLORATION

Pioneer 10, **March 3, 1972**
First spacecraft to fly past Jupiter, returning 500 images. US.

Skylab, **May 26, 1973**
First US space station, manned for 171 days.

Apollo 18 and *Soyuz 19*, **July 15, 1975**
First docking of US and Russian spacecraft in orbit.

Viking 1, **Aug 20, 1975**
First successful lander on Mars. Returned images for six years. US.

Columbia, **April 12, 1981**
First successful use of a reusable space vehicle. US.

Mir, **Feb 20, 1986**
Launch of Russian space station – remained in continuous occupation until 1999.

Magellan, **May 4, 1989**
Carried out the first detailed mapping of the surface of another planet (Venus) by radar. Features only a quarter of a mile in size show up. US.

Hubble Space Telescope, **April 25, 1990**
Regularly returns detailed images of planets, moons and comets. US/Europe.

Mars Pathfinder, **Dec 4, 1996**
First US robotic exploration of the surface of another planet.

Galileo, **Dec 8, 1997**
Mission to Jupiter and its moons and fly-by of Europa.

Delta II, **February 1996**
Near-Earth asteroid rendezvous, a mission to explore asteroid 433 Eros.

Mars Global Surveyor, **November 1996**
Launched on a Delta II rocket, a mission to image and map the Red Planet.

Mars Pathfinder, **4 July, 1997**
Mission included small landers and a Sojourner to regularly explore Mars.

Cassini, **October 1997**
Mission to Saturn carrying the Huygens Probe to bring back details of the planet.

Mars Surveyor, **Dec 1988**
First of NASA's 1998 mission to Mars.

Deep Space 1, **Oct 1998**
NASA comet and asteroid mission.

Mars Surveyor Orbiter, **March 2001**
Mapping the Red Planet.

Mars Express, **Jun 2, 2003**
European Space Agency first mission to Mars.

Pluto/Kuiper Belt, **2004**
Exploration of the region beyond Neptune.

SPACE DEBRIS

An amazing fact is that there are over 8,000 artificial objects orbiting Earth. Over 2,500 are satellites, both operative and inoperative. The remaining objects are orbital debris – parts such as nosecone shrouds, lens, hatch covers, rocket bodies, payloads that have disintegrated or exploded and even objects that 'escape' from manned spacecraft during operations. Thousands of launches have taken place over the last century and as a result, satellites and rockets weighing thousands of tons in total, have been sent into space. At the end of their mission, they are left in orbit, and turn into space debris.

Space Exploration

ULYSSES – THE SUN

The *Ulysses* spacecraft was launched from the Space Shuttle *Discovery* on October 6, 1990 on its mission over the Sun's South and North Poles. It was the first spacecraft to explore these regions and, because it couldn't be put straight into the correct orbit around the Sun, it was first sent on a path that swept past Jupiter. Jupiter's strong gravity boosted it into an orbit that passed over the Sun's South Pole in 1994, and its North Pole in 1995.

The mission was designed to sample the solar wind and the heliosphere at latitudes unexplored by any other spacecraft. It passed over the Sun's South Pole again in the autumn of 2000 and the North Pole in the autumn of 2001. These two orbital passes provided views of the solar wind at times near the minimum of solar activity and the maximum of solar activity.

Instruments carried on board *Ulysses* measure particles, magnetic fields and electromagnetic radiation from radio wavelengths to gamma-rays.

Ulysses Meets a Comet

During an unplanned rendezvous, the Ulysses spacecraft found itself gliding though the immense tail of Comet Hyakutake, revealing that comet tails may be much, much longer than previously believed.

The spacecraft and all scientific instruments remain in good working condition and preparations are underway for the Jupiter Distant Encounter campaign that will take place between the end of January and mid-March 2004. The spacecraft's closest approach to Jupiter occurred on February 4, 2004, at a distance of 120 million km (or 1684 Jupiter radii) from the planet.

Since early 1992 *Ulysses* has been monitoring the stream of stardust flowing through our solar system. The stardust is embedded in the local galactic cloud through which the Sun is moving at a speed of 26 kilometres every second. As a result of this relative motion, a single dust grain takes 20 years to traverse the solar system.

Space Exploration

PIONEER VENUS

The *Pioneer Venus Orbiter* was the first of a two-spacecraft orbiter/probe combination designed to conduct a comprehensive investigation of the atmosphere of Venus. It arrived at its destination on December 4, 1978. The spacecraft was a solar-powered cylinder about 250 cm in diameter, and attached to it was a high-gain antenna that was mechanically despun to remain focused on the Earth. All the instruments were mounted on the forward end of the cylinder, except the magnetometre, which was at the end of a 4.7 m boom.

The *Pioneer Venus Orbiter* carried out 17 separate experiments:
• a cloud photopolarimetre to measure the vertical distribution of the clouds
• a surface radar mapper to determine topography and surface characteristics
• an infrared radiometre to measure infra-red emissions from the Venus atmosphere
• an airglow ultraviolet spectrometre to measure scattered and emitted ultra-violet light
• a neutral mass spectrometre to determine the composition of the upper atmosphere
• a solar wind plasma analyser to measure properties of the solar wind
• a magnetometre to characterize the magnetic field at Venus
• an electric field detector to study the solar wind and its interactions
• an electron temperature probe to study the thermal properties of the ionosphere
• an ion mass spectrometre to characterize the ionospheric ion population
• a charged particle retarding potential analyser to study ionospheric particles
• two radio science experiments to determine the gravity field of Venus
• a radio occultation experiment to characterize the atmosphere
• an atmospheric drag experiment to study the upper atmosphere
• a radio science atmospheric and solar wind turbulence experiment
• a gamma ray burst detector to record gamma ray burst events.

Pioneer Venus consisted of two spacecraft to study Venus: the Orbiter and the Multiprobe. The latter separated into five separate vehicles near Venus.

Space Exploration

GIOTTO SPACECRAFT

The *Giotto* was the European Space Agency's first deep space mission. It was designed to help solve the mysteries surrounding Comet Halley by passing as close as possible to the comet's nucleus, which it achieved on March 13, 1986.

Fourteen seconds before its closest approach, *Giotto* was hit by a large dust particle, and no one expected the spacecraft to survive its battering from the comet dust. However, although *Giotto* was damaged during the fly-by, most of its instruments remained operational.

The major objectives of the *Giotto* mission were to:
• obtain colour photographs of the nucleus
• determine the elemental and isotopic composition of volatile components in the cometary coma, particularly parent molecules
• characterize the physical and chemical processes that occur in the cometary atmosphere and ionosphere
• determine the elemental and isotopic composition of dust particles
• measure the total gas-production rate and dust flux and size/mass distribution and derive the dust-to-gas ratio
• investigate the macroscopic systems of plasma flows resulting from the cometary-solar wind interaction.

All the experiments performed well and returned a wealth of new scientific results, of which perhaps the most important was the clear identification of the cometary nucleus. For the first time images of a comet nucleus could be taken during the encounters with Comet Halley. The nucleus was larger than expected at 16 x 7.5 x 8 km (10 x 4.7 x 5 miles). The discovery of gas and dust jets being emitted from the nucleus suggested that only about 10 percent of the surface was active. The images showed structures such as hills and depressions, which were obviously related to a continuous variation in the surface morphology.

The *Giotto* spacecraft was named after the the medieval Italian artist Giotto di Bondone. After four years in hibernation, *Giotto* was given new instructions and directed towards comet Grigg-Skjellerup. It arrived on July 10, 1992.

Space Exploration

MARINER 10

Mariner 10 was the seventh successful launch in the Mariner series and the very first spacecraft to visit two planets – Mercury and Venus. Launched in November 1973, the mission lasted until March 1975 when the spacecraft was shut down and placed in orbit around the Sun.

The *Mariner 10* mission required more course corrections than any previous mission and was the first spacecraft to use the gravitational pull of one planet to help it reach another planet. This craft was also the first to use the solar wind as a means of locomotion; when the probe's thruster fuel ran low, scientists used the solar panels as sails to make course corrections.

The instruments on board *Mariner 10* measured the atmospheric, surface and physical characteristics of Mercury and Venus. Experiments included television photography, magnetic field, plasma, infrared radiometry, ultraviolet spectroscopy and radio science detectors. An experimental high-frequency transmitter was flown for the first time on this spacecraft.

The *Mariner 10* spacecraft weighed 503 kg (1,108 lb.), including 29 kg (64 lb.) of fuel. Its body was an eight-sided framework with eight electronics compartments. It measured 1.39 metres (4.56 feet) diagonally and 0.457 metres (1.5 feet) in depth, and had two solar

Mariner 10 is still orbiting the Sun, even though its electronic systems have probably been destroyed by solar radiation.

panels attached at the top. The rocket engine was liquid-fuelled, and the interior of the spacecraft was insulated with multilayer thermal blankets at the top and bottom. A sunshade was deployed after launch to protect the spacecraft on the solar-oriented side. *Mariner 10* was the last in a series of Mariner missions designed to survey other planets in the solar system.

Space Exploration

LUNAR PROSPECTOR

Lunar Prospector was one of the NASA Discovery Programme missions designed to perform a low polar orbit study of the Moon. Its mission was to include mapping the surface composition and locating lunar resources, measuring magnetic and gravity fields and studying outgassing events.

The mission began on January 15, 1998, and *Lunar Prospector* spent one year mapping the entire surface of the Moon from a distance of about 100 km (60 miles). The data collected during this phase of the mission was far more detailed and of better quality than any data that had been collected before.

Due to its success, the mission was extended for an additional seven months, starting in January 1999. This time the orbit of the spacecraft was lowered to about 30 km (18 miles) and then even closer to within 10 km (6 miles) of the lunar surface. This allowed the spacecraft to obtain data at much higher resolutions which produced greatly enhanced results.

The mission was to have ended with the spacecraft crashing into the Moon when it ran out of fuel. However, as the mission neared its end, scientists suggested that they use the crash as part of an experiment to confirm the existence of water on the Moon. The spacecraft was successfully directed into a crater near the lunar south pole, but no water was detected.

The spacecraft itself was shaped like a

drum and was made of epoxy graphite material. It was approximately 1.2 metres (4 feet) tall and 1.4 metres (4.5 feet) in diameter. Its total weight, when fully loaded with fuel, was about 295 kg (660 lb.).

The *Lunar Prospector* mission lasted for 19 months and successfully completed all of its objectives. The data collected will be used to construct a detailed map of the surface composition of the Moon. The mission ended on July 31, 1999.

Space Exploration

CASSINI-HUYGENS SPACECRAFT

Cassini-Huygens is one of the most ambitious missions ever launched into space. Roughly two storeys tall and weighing more than six tons, *Cassini* is one of the largest interplanetary spacecraft ever launched. Carrying a wide range of powerful instruments and cameras, the spacecraft is capable of taking accurate measurements and detailed images in a variety of atmospheric conditions.

Two elements comprise the spacecraft: The *Cassini* orbiter and the *Huygens* probe. Launched on October 15, 1997, the *Cassini-Huygens* is scheduled to reach Saturn and its moons in July 2004. There the spacecraft will orbit around the system for four years; beaming home valuable data that will help us understand the vast regions of Saturn. *Huygens* will enter the murky atmosphere of Titan, Saturn's biggest moon, and eventually descend via parachute on to its mysterious surface. The *Huygens* probe will send its measurements and images to *Cassini*, which will then beam them back to Earth.

The *Cassini* orbiter has 12 instruments and the *Huygens* probe has six. The instruments often have multiple functions, equipped to thoroughly investigate all the important elements that the Saturn system may uncover. The spacecraft will communicate through one high-gain and two low-gain antennas. It is only in the event of a power failure or other such emergency situation however, that the spacecraft will communicate through one of its low-gain antennas.

Three Radioisotope Thermoelectric Generators (commonly referred to as RTGs) provide power for the spacecraft, including the instruments, computers and radio transmitters on board, attitude thrusters and reaction wheels.

The remote sensing instruments on the *Cassini* Spacecraft can calculate measurements from a great distance. This set includes both optical and microwave sensing instruments including cameras, spectrometres, radar and radio.

The *Cassini* has already returned its first publicly-released image of Saturn as it heads towards its target.

Space Exploration

THE HIPPARCOS SATELLITE

The part of the Universe that we can see may be about 10 percent bigger than astronomers originally thought, and this is because of the results sent back to Earth from the European Space Agency's *Hipparcos* mission. Originally astronomers relied on the brightness of winking stars called Cepheids, to measure the distances of outer space, but direct measurements from the *Hipparcos* imply that the Cepheids are more luminous and more distant than previously imagined.

The *Hipparcos* satellite was designed by European teams of scientists and engineers and it operated from 1989 to 1993.

Hipparcos was launched by Ariane 4 on August 8, 1989, from the ground base of Kourou in French Guyana. It carried a small 29 cm telescope, with the task of scanning the celestial sphere several times in order to obtain positions, distances and proper motions of about 120,000 stars.

It fixed precise positions in the sky of 120,000 stars (Hipparcos Catalog) and logged a million more. The satellite was designed to spin slowly, completing a full revolution in just over two hours. At the same time, it was controlled so that there was a continuous slow change of direction of the axis of rotation. In this way the telescope was able to scan the complete celestial sphere several times during its planned mission.

The outstanding observational capabilities of the *Hipparcos* satellite could well be the key towards the solution of one of the major problems in contemporary astronomy, namely the understanding of the structure, formation and evolution of the galaxy.

The *Millennium Star Atlas* contains 1,548 sky charts, depicting the heavens with unprecedented information on the nature of our galaxy using the stellar information taken from ESA's Hipparcos and Tycho Catalogues.

Space Exploration

VIKING 1 AND VIKING 2

NASA's Viking Mission to Mars was composed of two spacecraft, *Viking 1* and *Viking 2*. Each spacecraft consisted of an orbiter and a lander, and the primary mission objectives were:

- obtain high-resolution images of the Martian surface
- characterize the structure and composition of the atmosphere and surface
- to search for evidence of life.

Viking 1 was launched on August 20, 1975 and arrived at Mars on June 19, 1976. The first month of orbit was devoted to imaging the surface to find appropriate landing sites for the Viking Landers. On July 20, 1976 *Viking Lander 1* separated from the Orbiter and touched down at Chryse Planitia. *Viking 2* was launched on September 9, 1975 and entered Mars orbit on August 7, 1976. *Viking Lander 2* touched down at Utopia Planitia on September 3, 1976.

The Viking Landers transmitted images of the surface, took surface samples and analysed them for composition and signs of life, studied atmospheric composition and meteorology and deployed seismometeres. *Viking Lander 2* ended communications on April 11, 1980, and *Viking Lander 1* on

November 13, 1982, after transmitting over 1,400 images of the two sites.

The results from the Viking experiments give our most complete view of Mars to date. Volcanoes, lava plains, immense canyons, cratered areas, wind-formed features and evidence of surface water are apparent in the orbiter images. The surface material at both landing sites can best be described as iron-rich clay. Seasonal dust storms, pressure changes and transport of atmospheric gases between the polar caps were observed, but the experiment produced no evidence of life at either of the landing sites.

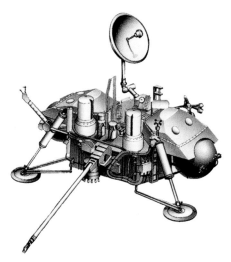

Space Exploration

OBSERVATORIES

Professional astronomers carry out their telescopic observations at observatories, which house a variety of instruments. Most of the leading astronomical observatories are located at high altitude on mountain tops or extinct volcanoes, where the air is clear and dry. This means that they are above the thickest part of the atmosphere, which is laden with dust and water vapour, and prone to distorting air currents.

Kitt Peak is one of the world's finest observatories, located in the Quinlan Mountains on a peak 2,095 metres (6,875 feet) above the Sonora Desert. Other important sites include the Canary Islands, Hawaii, Chile and southern Arizona. Kitt Peak National Observatory is part of the National Optical Astronomy Observatory, and supports the most diverse collection of astronomical observatories on Earth for nighttime optical and infrared astronomy and daytime study of the Sun. Founded in 1958, Kitt Peak operates three major nighttime telescopes, shares site responsibilities with the National Solar Observatory and hosts the facilities of consortia which operate 19 optical telescopes and two radio telescopes. Kitt Peak is located 56 miles southwest of Tucson, Arizona, and has a Visitor Centre open daily to the public.

The Big Bear Solar Observatory is located 160 km east of Pasadena at an elevation of 6,700 feet in the middle of Big Bear Lake, California. The observatory is located in water to avoid the disturbance of images by convection from ground heating. As a result it is the world's premier site for observing the Sun. It carries out one of the most extensive observing programmes of any solar observatory. The observatory operates a series of solar telescopes which image the whole Sun and selected areas which are highly magnified. Other programmes are focused on the extremely high-resolution observations of the time development of solar phenomena, especially sunspots, flares and prominences, which may be observed because of its unique location in the lake.

Mauna Kea is the tallest volcano on the Island of Hawaii. The Mauna Kea Observatory is located on top of Mauna Kea, at a height of 4,200 metres (13,800 feet) above sea level. It first opened in 1970, and it is positioned in one of the best places in the world for optical and infrared astronomy because the air is so clear and dry. The observatory is home to 11 internationally sponsored telescopes, including the two largest telescopes currently in operation, each bearing a 10-metre primary mirror. Astronomers working with one of the 10-metre telescopes helped to discover that the Universe is expanding at an accelerated rate.

Situated on the slope of the Mauna Loa volcano on the Island of Hawaii, the Mauna Loa Observatory has been in existence for over 40 years, accumulating

Space Exploration

the longest continuous measurements of greenhouse gases on the planet. And it is poised to make even greater contributions in the twenty-first century. From a modest beginning as a small, meteorological station, it became the first site to provide conclusive evidence that carbon dioxide was increasing in the atmosphere. The observatory continues to play a central role in studies of climate change and is now prepared to monitor the ozone layer for long-term environmental effects.

The Norikura Observatory is located at Nyukawa-mura, Ohno-gun, Japan, 2,770 metres above sea level. It was founded in 1953 and provides facilities necessary for preparing for and carrying out cosmic ray experiments at a high altitude. Facilities such as accommodations and experimental rooms are made available to all qualified scientists in Japan. Norikura Observatory celebrated its 40th anniversary of its foundation on September 25, 1993.

An observatory for radio astronomy is located at Jodrell Bank, Macclesfield, Cheshire. It was founded in 1945 on the site of a botanical experiment station, and it is administered by the University of Manchester. Originally known as the Jodrell Bank Experimental Station, it was officially the Nuffield Radio Astronomy Laboratories from 1966 to 1999. The principal instrument is one of the world's largest fully steerable radio antennas, the Lovell Telescope, which is 76 metres (250 feet) in diameter. The observatory's research programmes include studies of galactic structure, angular sizes and structure of radio sources, polarization of radio sources, quasars, pulsars, molecules in interstellar space and lunar radar.

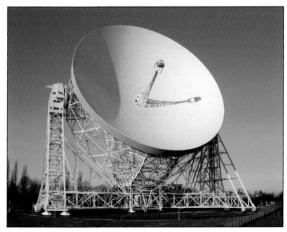

LEFT: For over 40 years the giant Lovell Telescope at Jodrell Bank has been a familiar feature of the Cheshire landscape and an internationally renowned landmark in the world of astronomy.

Space Exploration

ABOVE: Stonehenge on Salisbury Plain, England, probably functioned as an astronomical observatory 4,000 years ago. The experts are now unanimous that the designers of Stonehenge exhibited a remarkable knowledge of astronomy. Nowhere is this more evident than in the rectangle formed by the four Station Stones, which marks an exact alignment to the eight key points of the 18.6-year cycle of the Moon.

Space Exploration

The United States Naval Observatory is one of the oldest scientific agencies in the country. A government observatory, founded in 1844 and originally based at the aptly-named Foggy Bottom on the banks of the Potomac River in Washington, D.C. It was from here, using the 26-inch Clarke refractor – the largest refracting telescope in the world at that time – that Asaph Hall discovered the two tiny moons of Mars, Phobos and Deimos in 1877. The atrocious seeing conditions at the original site led to the observatory being relocated to the northwest of the capital in 1893, at which time it also absorbed the US Navy's office of the Nautical Almanac. Since 1955, the US Naval Observatory has operated an observing station near Flagstaff, Arizona, at an altitude of 2,315 metres.

The observatory's primary mission was to care for the US Navy's chronometres, charts and other navigational equipment. Today, the US Naval Observatory is the leading authority in the areas of Precise Time and Astrometry, and distributes Earth Orientation parametres and other

Astronomical Data required for accurate navigation and fundamental astronomy. The Astrometry Department is responsible for the determination of the positions and motions of stars and solar system objects and the establishment of celestial reference frames.

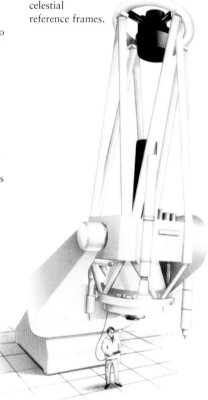

RIGHT: This 61-inch reflecting telescope at the US Naval Observatory is used to measure star positions very precisely. Its length gives a high magnification, making it easier to see small changes in position. It could measure the thickness of a human hair more than half a mile away. This is good enough to measure distances of stars up to 100 light years away.

Space Exploration

ORBITING SPACE OBSERVATORIES

Since the early years of spaceflight, the advantages of astronomical observing above the Earth's atmosphere were recognized, and led to the introduction of astronomical instruments on spacecraft, that is, astronomical observatories in space, and in most cases, in Earth's orbit.

The Hubble Space Telescope (HST) is the largest orbiting public optical telescope in history. Its 2.4 metre diameter reflecting mirror and its perch above Earth's atmosphere allow it to create exceptionally sharp images. Originally launched in 1990, HST optics were repaired to their intended accuracy in 1993 by the first of several regular servicing missions. Astronomers using HST continue to make numerous monumental scientific discoveries, including new estimates of the age of our Universe, previously unknown galaxies, evidence of massive black holes in the centres of galaxies, previously unknown moons and a better understanding of physical processes in our Universe.

The Compton Gamma Ray Observatory (CGRO) was the most massive instrument ever launched by a NASA Space Shuttle in 1991 and continues to revolutionize gamma-ray astronomy. Before Compton loses more stabilizing gyroscopes, NASA is considering firing onboard rockets to bring it on a controlled re-entry into the ocean. This orbiting observatory sees the sky in gamma-ray photons – light so blue

Compton
Gamma-Ray
Observatory

that humans are unable to see it. These photons are blocked by the Earth's atmosphere from reaching the Earth's surface. Results from CGRO have shown the entire Universe to be a violent and rapidly changing place. Astronomers using CGRO data continue to make monumental discoveries, including identifying mysterious gamma-ray bursts that uniquely illuminate the early Universe, discovery of a whole new class of Quasi-Stellar Objects, and discovery of objects so strange that astronomers as yet are unable to figure out what they are.

NASA's Chandra X-ray Observatory, which was launched and deployed by Space Shuttle *Columbia* on July 23, 1999, is the most sophisticated X-ray observatory built to date. Chandra is designed to observe X-rays from high-energy regions of the Universe, such as the remnants of exploded stars.

The Compton Gamma Ray

Space Exploration

International
Ultraviolet
Explorer

Nobel prize for his work in physics.

The International Ultraviolet Explorer satellite (IUE) was a joint project between NASA, ESA and PPARC (formerly SERC). IUE was the longest and most productive astronomical space observatory, the first general user UV space observatory and the first astronomical observatory in High Earth Orbit. It was launched into geo-synchronous orbit on January 26, 1978, from Kennedy Space Center, and was turned off on September 30, 1996.

The Spitzer Space Telescope (formerly the Space Infrared Telescope Facility) was launched into space by a Delta rocket from Cape Canaveral, Florida on 25 August, 2003. During its $2^1/_2$-year mission, Spitzer will obtain images and spectra by detecting the infrared energy, or heat, radiated by objects in space. Most of this infrared radiation is blocked by the Earth's atmosphere and cannot be observed from the ground.

Consisting of a 0.85-metre telescope and three cryogenically-cooled science instruments, Spitzer is the largest infrared telescope ever launched into space. Its highly sensitive instruments give us a unique view of the Universe and allow us to peer into regions of space which are hidden from optical telescopes. Many areas of space are filled with vast, dense clouds of gas and dust which block our view. Infrared light, however can penetrate these clouds, allowing us to peer into regions of star formation, the centres of galaxies and into newly forming planetary systems.

Observatory was the second of NASA's Great Observatories. Compton, at 17 tons, was the heaviest astrophysical payload ever flown at the time of its launch on April 5, 1991, aboard the space shuttle *Atlantis*. Compton was safely deorbited and re-entered the Earth's atmosphere on June 4, 2000.

Compton had four instruments that covered an unprecedented six decades of the electromagnetic spectrum. In order of increasing spectral energy coverage, these instruments were the Burst And Transient Source Experiment (BATSE), the Oriented Scintillation Spectrometre Experiment (OSSE), the Imaging Compton Telescope (COMPTEL) and the Energetic Gamma Ray Experiment Telescope (EGRET). For each of the instruments, an improvement in sensitivity of better than a factor of ten was realized over previous missions. The observatory was named in honour of Dr. Arthur Holly Compton, who won the

Space Exploration

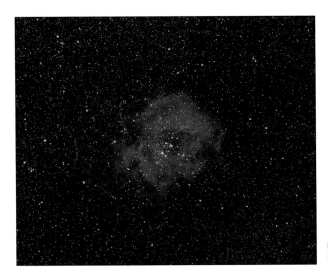

LEFT: Rosette Nebula

ASTROPHOTOGRAPHY

If you have a camera, you can photograph the night sky and begin astrophotography. Even with the simplest equipment, you can take pictures of the Moon, stars, planets, meteors, asteroids, comets and eclipses.

Astrophotography combines what are almost certainly the two most widely practiced hobbies in the world – astronomy and photography. The simplest form of astrophotography is done with a camera and tripod and preferably a collection of quality widefield lenses available for the camera. The camera must have the capability of locking the shutter open for a few seconds so that the very low levels of light have time to build up on the film. Most 35mm cameras have a setting which allows you to do this (often called a 'B' setting). If the shutter on your camera is completely automatic, then it won't be suitable for long-exposure astrophotography but will suffice for exposures of a few seconds or less. A photographer's eye for composition is an advantage when shooting the sky, using terrestrial objects like trees, mountains and man made structures, in the foreground.

A sturdy tripod is essential, as this is needed to hold the camera absolutely rigid during the time exposure. If the

Space Exploration

camera wobbles, you will get a blurred image. Hanging extra weights on the tripod is also a good idea.

Commercially available film emulsions available today do a fantastic job on the purpose for which they were intended and that is to produce high quality photographs in daylight conditions or in low light conditions when used with a flash. Astrophotography, however, is an entirely different ballgame. Here we are usually dealing with very low levels of light that these emulsions were never intended to work with. The exceptions to this would include lunar photography and photography of the brighter planets. The Moon, for example, receives virtually the same illumination from the Sun as the Earth does during daylight. Exposure times and film selection are nearly the same as those you would make photographing terrestrial subjects but can vary somewhat according to the phase the Moon is in when the shot is made. The question of colour balance can come into play since some film types seem to colour the Moon in an unnatural way and cause the sky to take on a 'muddy' appearance in the photo. Good results can be obtained using fast film with an ISO (ASA) rating of 400, especially when it is developed as if it were a much faster film. Very fast films are available today, of 1600 or more, but they tend to produce 'grainy' pictures.

RIGHT: Star trails

Glossary

asteroid A rocky object orbiting the Sun. Asteroids are similar to planets but much smaller. They are also called minor planets.

astronaut A person who travels in space. Russian astronauts are called cosmonauts.

astronomer A person who studies astronomy.

astronomy The study of the Universe and all things in it beyond Earth.

atmosphere Gases that surround a planet, held there by the pull of the planet's gravity.

atom A tiny particle that makes up all materials. Atoms are made of even smaller particles called protons, neutrons and electrons. Each type of atom has a particular number of these particles. The protons and neutrons are found at the centre of the atom, in its nucleus, while the electrons move around outside the nucleus.

axis The imaginary line around which a spinning object (such as a planet) rotates.

billion One thousand million.

black hole A tiny volume of space into which a huge amount of material is packed. Its gravity is so strong that nothing escapes from it – not even light.

carbon An element, which is found in all forms of life on Earth.

celestial To do with the sky.

cluster A family of stars or galaxies, held together in space because the gravity of each member of the cluster pulls on all the others.

comet A frozen chunk of ice and dust that orbits the Sun and releases a cloud of gas and dust when it travels near enough to the Sun to be warmed by the Sun's heat. The gas and dust streams out into space to form tails.

constellation One of 88 recognized star patterns that together cover every part of the sky.

core A region in the very middle of something. It is often of a different material from the material that surrounds it.

crater A bowl-shaped hollow on the surface of a planet or moon. Craters are formed when rocks from space crash onto a planet or when material collapses down inside the top part of a volcano.

crust The thin outside layer of something.

diameter The largest distance from one side to the other of a circle or sphere.

electron (*see* atom)

elements (chemical) The basic materials that make up all matter in the Universe. Hydrogen, carbon and oxygen are examples of elements. Chemical elements combine together to form other materials.

ellipse A shape that looks like a squashed circle. Ellipses range in shape from extremely long and thin to very nearly circular.

elliptical Having the shape of an ellipse.

energy The ability of something to do work, such as cause movement or increase temperature. Heat and light are forms of energy.

galaxy A collection of hundreds of billions of stars and other materials such as gas and dust, all held together by gravity.

gas Material in which particles are widely separated and move around freely at high speeds.

geyser A jet of hot gas or water that shoots out of a crack, usually in rock.

gravity A force that pulls every object in the Universe

owards every other object. The more massive an object is, the stronger is the pull of its gravity.

greenhouse effect The effect created in the atmosphere of a planet by some gases that trap the Sun's heat and warm up the planet. Some gases, such as carbon dioxide, create an especially strong greenhouse effect.

helium The second simplest atom after hydrogen, with two protons, two neutrons and two electrons. It is rare on Earth, but is very common in the rest of the Universe.

hemisphere Half of a sphere. On a planet, the Northern hemisphere lies to the north of the equator and the Southern hemisphere lies to the south.

hydrogen The simplest atom of matter, containing one proton and one electron. Hydrogen is the most common element in the Universe.

infared light A type of light that is invisible to human eyes. All warm things give out infared rays and we feel them as warmth on our skin.

interstellar material Gas and dust between stars.

latitude A measurement that shows how far north or south of the equator a place is. It is measured in degrees.

lava Liquid rock from a volcano, which turns solid when it cools.

lens A piece of shaped glass, or other transparent material, used to collect light and direct it in a particular way. Binoculars and refracting telescopes use lenses to collect light and bring it to a focus.

light year The distance light travels in one year.

liquid Material in which particles are close together, but can move around slowly.

lunar On the Moon or to do with the Moon.

magnetic field The area around a magnet where the pull of the magnet is felt.

magnetic pole One of two areas of a magnet where its effect is strongest.

magnetism A force that acts around magnetised materials (such as a solid piece of iron) and around materials in which electric currents are flowing (such as a wire or the metal core inside a planet). Magnetic forces can be attractive (pulling towards) or repulsive (pushing away).

magnification The increase in size of an object as it appears when seen through a telescope or binoculars.

mantle The main layer of rock that lies under the crust of a planet and above the core.

mare (pronounced mah-ray. Plural is maria, pronounced mah-rear.) The Latin word for 'sea', which is given to the dark areas on the Moon, once thought to be seas.

mass The amount of material in an object.

matter All material. Matter makes up all things in the Universe, whether gas, liquid or solid.

meteor A bright streak visible for a few seconds in the night sky. It is caused by a piece of space dust or rock speeding into Earth's atmosphere, where it burns up.

meteorite A chunk of rock from space that lands on the surface of a planet or moon.

meteoroid A small piece of rock in space.

microscopic Describing something that is so small you need a microscope to see it.

Milky Way A faint hazy band across the night sky where we see the light of huge numbers of stars in the galaxy to which our Sun belongs. We call our galaxy the Milky Way Galaxy.

molten In the form of a liquid. It is used particularly to describe something that is normally solid, but has become a liquid because it has been heated.

moon A natural body orbiting a planet. Moons are also called natural satellites. The Moon (with a capital 'M') is Earth's natural satellite.

naked eye Observing with just the eyes and without the help of a telescope or binoculars.

nebula (plural nebulae, pronounced neb-you-lee) A cloud

of gas or dust in space. *Nebula* is the Latin word for cloud. Bright nebulae are growing gas. Dark nebulae are clouds of fine dust.

nitrogen A fairly common element in the solar system. It is the main gas in Earth's atmosphere.

nuclear energy Energy produced when the nucleus of a hydrogen atom collides with another at high speed.

nucleus The central part of an object, such as the central group of particles in an atom.

observatory A place where astronomers use telescopes or have their offices.

optical To do with light that we can see.

orbit The path of an object around another larger object in space. The smaller object is held in its orbit by the pull of the larger object's gravity.

oxygen An element, which is the gas we need to breathe on Earth.

particle A very small piece of matter.

phase The change in the shape of the sunlit part of a planet or moon.

planet A large body that orbits a star. A planet does not shine by producing its own light, but reflects the light of the star. The Earth is a planet which orbits the Sun.

pole The poles of a planet or moon are the places where the axis on which it spins meets the surface. There is a North Pole and a South Pole. The celestial poles are the points in the sky directly above the North and South Poles of the planet's or moon's surface.

pressure The strength of the force with which something presses.

quasar A very distant galaxy with a centre that shines much more brightly than the rest of the galaxy.

radiation The energy sent out by an object, such as beams of light or X-rays from the Sun.

radio waves A type of radiation, similar to light, although invisible and less powerful.

satellite A small object that orbits something larger. It can be a natural satellite, such as a moon, or an artificial object, such as a spacecraft.

solar To do with the Sun.

solar system The Sun and everything that orbits around it. The solar system includes the nine major planets and their moons, asteroids, comets, meteoroids and dust – all held in their orbits by the pull of the Sun's gravity.

solid Material in which particles are locked together in a fixed shape.

space Everywhere beyond Earth's atmosphere.

spacecraft A vehicle that travels through space.

space probe An unmanned spacecraft carrying equipment to find out about space and objects within it.

star An immense ball of gas, which produces vast amounts of heat and light.

stellar To do with the stars.

sulphur An element often produced by volcanoes. It is used in making gunpowder.

sunspot An area on the Sun's surface that is darker and cooler than normal.

supernova The explosion of a large star at the end of its life.

terminator The boundary between the sunlit and dark halves of the Moon or a planet.

ultraviolet light A type of light that is given off by very hot objects and is invisible to human eyes.

universe Everything that exists.

volume The amount of space that something takes up.

x-rays A form of energy that travels on its own through space.

zenith The point on the celestial sphere directly above an observer.

Index

Index

Index

Index

Credits

Star maps by Richard Monkhouse and John Cox.